CRIMINAL MIND

TIME
LIFE
BOOKS

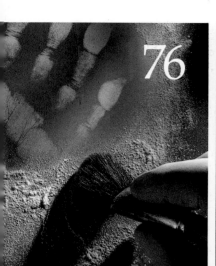

76

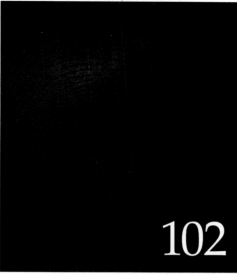

102

CONTENTS

174

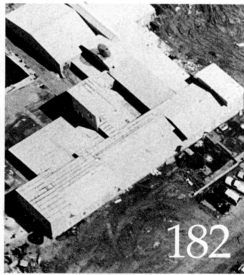

182

250

NOT CROSS

DO NOT CROS

NOT CROSS

NOT CROSS

DO NOT CROSS

NOT CROSS

INTRODUCTION

When someone commits a heinous crime, we often turn to the same question: What made them do it? Sometimes the answer is predictable: It was greed. It was lust. It was envy. It was revenge. But often, it is impossible to imagine a motivation. A violent impulse to destroy defies the social contract. Can we truly untangle the dark forces that would cause a mother to take the life of her child, a serial killer to slaughter strangers, a cannibal to consume his victim? What is inside the mind of a delusional murderer?

In *Mysteries of the Criminal Mind*, Time-Life editors tackle lawlessness and the law from multiple angles. Here, we trace the origins of criminology and the ongoing efforts to grasp the causes of violence. We go inside law enforcement to see the tools used to track down offenders and bring them to justice. We look at instances of justice gone awry, when innocent people are falsely tarred and prosecuted. We present heartbreaking accounts from victims and their families.

It is a sobering catalogue. But it has also inspired fascinating research into criminal behavior. Some of the earliest theories on the roots of crime now seem bizarre. In the 16th century, Italian scientist Giambattista della Porta concluded from autopsies that felons shared certain facial features: small ears and noses, large lips, and shaggy eyebrows. In the centuries to follow, physicians would study the shape of people's heads and other physical traits to determine their criminal potential. More recently, sociologists, scientists, and criminologists have looked to internal forces, such as the role of brain chemistry.

While cutting-edge technology has not yet been able to identify a universal "crime gene," many researchers now believe that a variant of the monoamine oxidase A, or MAOA gene could be linked to aggressive behavior. One Danish study showed a stronger correlation in the rate of criminal conviction between male adoptees and their biological fathers than between the adoptees and their adoptive fathers. A professor of criminology at the University of Pennsylvania who has studied the brains of violent convicts has discovered that a large percentage of so-called hot-blooded murderers have decreased function in the part of the brain that determines whether an action is good or bad.

These findings are then considered in the context of external forces, such as poverty and unemployment, teen pregnancy, and racism. It is believed that early life experiences have an especially strong influence on the development of criminality and that childhood trauma can lead to violent behavior later in life.

Yet understanding a criminal's past does not always help us reconcile the brutal reality of the violence that follows. John Wayne Gacy, molested at nine by a family friend, went on to torture and murder over 30 boys, stashing many of their bodies in the crawl space under his home. Abandoned by her mother, Aileen Wuornos began prostituting herself at 12 for beer and cigarettes, and then became a serial killer. George Emil Banks, a Pennsylvania man, slaughtered 13 people, including five of his own children.

What do these shocking cases say about the society where they unfold? Is evil a constant that must be dealt with as best possible? What is the nature of responsibility? These are the questions explored in cases and examples in *Mysteries of the Criminal Mind*. There are no fast and easy answers. Not all people exposed to the same circumstances react in the same way. Genetics cannot always explain why some people with certain traits become productive citizens while others end up behind bars. Many high school students are alienated and ridiculed by their classmates, but only a few become deadly shooters.

Greed, lust, rage, or just pure evil? Here are the stories. Decide for yourself.

MYSTERIES OF THE CRIMINAL MIND

GY CRIMINOL

GY CRIMINOL

Over the past 200 years, advances in forensic science, such as fingerprinting, ballistics, lab analysis of evidence, and surveillance, have become an increasingly crucial part of criminal investigation. But, while TV shows tend to make technology seem infallible, sometimes the facts are ambiguous or the science is dead wrong.

Gathering evidence and finding patterns are still at the heart of solving crimes, and criminologists continue to theorize about what makes the criminal mind tick. Nineteenth-century scientists tried predicting criminal potential based on physical characteristics, while recent advances in DNA testing suggest that genetics may play a role. Today, brain scans reveal clues to traits including aggression and impulsivity, while other studies consider environmental influences such as poverty, neglect, and abuse.

Is the criminal mind different from yours or mine? And if so, how can we better understand it and prevent crimes from happening? These questions are at the core of modern criminology. Despite varying religious beliefs or shifting social mores, the definition of criminal appears to have changed little since ancient times, though methods of detection, prosecution, and punishment certainly have.

Computer-generated graphics help researchers envision the structure, function, and dynamics of human DNA at the atomic level.

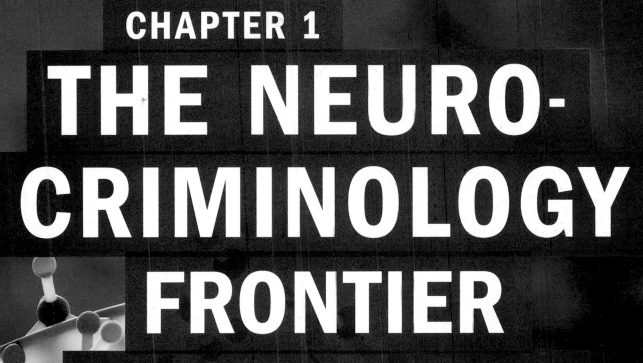

CHAPTER 1

THE NEURO-CRIMINOLOGY FRONTIER

BREAKTHROUGHS IN MOLECULAR BIOLOGY ARE MAKING IT POSSIBLE FOR RESEARCHERS TO EXAMINE DNA AND EXPLORE HOW GENETICS MAY AFFECT THE BRAINS OF CRIMINALS.

BAD TO THE BONE

THE FATHER OF MODERN CRIMINOLOGY, CESARE LOMBROSO, BELIEVED THAT LAWBREAKERS SHARED PHYSICAL TRAITS. HIS WORK HAS SINCE BEEN DEBUNKED.

Cesare Lombroso (1835–1909)

FACIAL RECOGNITION

According to Cesare Lombroso, the following physical traits were a sign someone was likely a lawbreaker:

➔ Large jaw

➔ Forward projection of jaw

➔ Low sloping forehead

➔ High cheekbones

➔ Flattened or upturned nose

➔ Handle-shaped ears

➔ Large chin

➔ Hawk-like nose

➔ Fleshy lips

➔ Hard, shifty eyes

➔ Scanty beard

➔ Bald head

➔ Insensitivity to pain

➔ Long arms

The phrase "born criminal" was first used by Cesare Lombroso, a 19th-century Italian physician who spent decades dissecting the corpses of lawbreakers, the mentally ill, and "normal" individuals. Villains possessed similar inherited physical characteristics, according to Lombroso, which in turn provided evidence of a genetic and physiological basis for criminal behavior. Under this theory, a miscreant could be identified from the shape of his jaw, forehead, and even his lips. Lawbreakers were not only born bad, they looked it, Lombroso said. The ideas, as outrageous as they seem today, caught on at the time and quickly spread throughout Europe and to the United States.

Lombroso based his research almost solely on anthropometry, the measurement of anatomical characteristics. From precise skull dimensions and other details recorded during postmortem exams, Lombroso concluded that the physical characteristics of criminals were similar to those of "pre-human" life forms such as apes. He made the case that specific kinds of criminals, such as thieves and murderers, share distinct physical characteristics.

In 1876, Lombroso published a book detailing his claims, titled *L'uomo delinquente* (*Criminal Man*). In it, Lombroso wrote that tattoos were an indicator of criminality, that criminals had a higher threshold for physical pain, that they

possessed keener senses of sight and smell, and that they were stronger on the left side of their body. He also identified "insane criminals," which included alcoholics and kleptomaniacs, who he said were born without a moral sense, and criminaloids, or individuals who he said were more likely to commit crimes of opportunity for financial gain or impulsive crimes of passion.

Although most of Lombroso's findings were eventually discredited, he continued to experiment with scientific measurement throughout his life. In 1895, he created and used a device to record the bodily changes that result from telling a lie—the prototype for our present-day lie detector.

Criminal skulls in the Cesare Lombroso Museum in Turin, Italy. The Museum of Criminal Anthropology was created by Lombroso in 1876 and opened to the public in 2009.

Alphonse Bertillon in a 1913 mug shot.

IN ALL SHAPES AND SIZES

The inventor of the mug shot took the measure of criminals large and small.

French police officer Alphonse Bertillon (1853–1914) developed a system of detailed physiological measurements that he claimed typified the "criminal type" and identified those who matched it. *Bertillonnage* detailed the dimensions of 12 bodily characteristics, from height and bust to length of the right ear.

Starting in the 1880s, the Paris police department took these measurements of all arrestees, prisoners, and ex-convicts. The method actually proved useful in identifying a number of criminals. Bertillon later added the *portrait parlé* ("spoken portrait"), a written description of the body, face, ethnicity, and skin color of a suspect, to his system. This was highly detailed: The nose alone was assigned six key features.

Bertillon also invented the standardized mug shot, used universally today, which includes full-face and profile views. Together, the anthropometric measurements, *portrait parlé*, and mug shot became the most effective tools ever for disseminating criminal descriptions.

Bertillon's system was adopted throughout the French Empire and in many other countries, but was abandoned in the early 20th century as discriminatory and inefficient. Nevertheless, some of his forensic innovations are still in use, and Sir Arthur Conan Doyle credited Bertillon as one of the inspirations for the character of Sherlock Holmes.

SINISTER DOINGS

Left-handedness has been suspect since Roman times.

Italian physician Cesare Lombroso wasn't the first person to peg lefties as bad guys: The word *sinister* comes from the Latin word for *left*. While there is no evidence that southpaws are disproportionately violent, some famous criminals, including serial killers Jack the Ripper and the Boston Strangler, were left-handed. Here are a few others.

Billy the Kid
(1859–1881)
Legend has it that this famous gunslinger, whose real name was William H. Bonney, killed 21 men. The number has been disputed by historians.

John Wesley Hardin
(1853–1895)
An Old West outlaw who spent most of his life on the run. He was rumored to have killed a man for snoring.

John Dillinger
(1903–1934)
This Depression-era thug ruled a violent gang that robbed two dozen banks, but Dillinger was only charged with one homicide.

13

THE SHAPE OF THINGS

EARLY CRIMINOLOGISTS TRIED TO UNDERSTAND LAWBREAKERS' PERSONALITIES BY STUDYING THEIR FACIAL FEATURES.

Physiognomist Johann Kaspar Lavater provided this sketch of a person with the facial traits of a cheater. Lavater's work became an inspiration for writer Victor Hugo.

CLASSIC LOOKS

In his 1862 novel *Les Misérables*, Victor Hugo used the principles of physiognomy to describe the despicable character Monsieur Thénardier. A blackmailer with a brutal streak, Thénardier lived in the sewers of Paris, making a living as a petty thief and beggar. Hugo described him as "a skinny little runt, pale, angular, bony, rickety."

The author even imagined what leading physiognomist Johann Kaspar Lavater would have to say about Thénardier: "If Lavater had studied this visage, he would have found the vulture mingled with the attorney there, the bird of prey and the pettifogger…"

Pioneering criminologists in the 19th century theorized that certain physical features were associated with—or even caused—wicked behavior. Physiognomists, who studied faces, and phrenologists, who studied head shapes, worked to identify and measure so-called criminal characteristics such as big noses and weak chins.

Large Lips, Shaggy Eyebrows

Physiognomy, the interpretation of facial features as clues to criminal tendencies, dates to ancient Greece, but it wasn't studied methodically until the Renaissance. One pioneer of the era was Giambattista della Porta, a 16th-century Italian scientist who examined the cadavers of prisoners and concluded that many felons had small ears and noses, large lips, and shaggy eyebrows. In the 18th century, Swiss pastor, poet, and physiognomist Johann Kaspar Lavater identified different troublesome traits. According to Lavater, shifty eyes, receding chins, and prominent noses were a cause for concern. Beauty, he said, went hand in hand with morality. "The morally best, the most beautiful. The morally worst, the most deformed," he wrote.

In 1820, a criminal anthropology handbook published by German philosopher Jacob Fries reinforced physical profiling with the introduction of a new concept: that details of a crime could provide insight into the perpetrator's personality. Over time, physiognomy as a practice was debunked.

But Fries's style of psychological profiling was embraced by law enforcement and is still commonly used today.

A Bump on the Head

Phrenology, the study of the head as the key to personality and character, was a widespread practice among criminologists, anthropologists, and scientists in the first half of the 1800s. The field's most influential experts were German physicians Franz Joseph Gall and Johann Spurzheim, who published their theories of phrenology around the turn of the 19th century. According to Gall, the brain was organized into 27 separate organs, each of which controlled a particular emotion or trait. Spurzheim expanded the number to 35. The relative sizes of these brain organs, they said, affected the shape of the surrounding skull. A badly shaped head,

A phrenologist demonstrated techniques used to "read" the bumps on a person's head to determine their character.

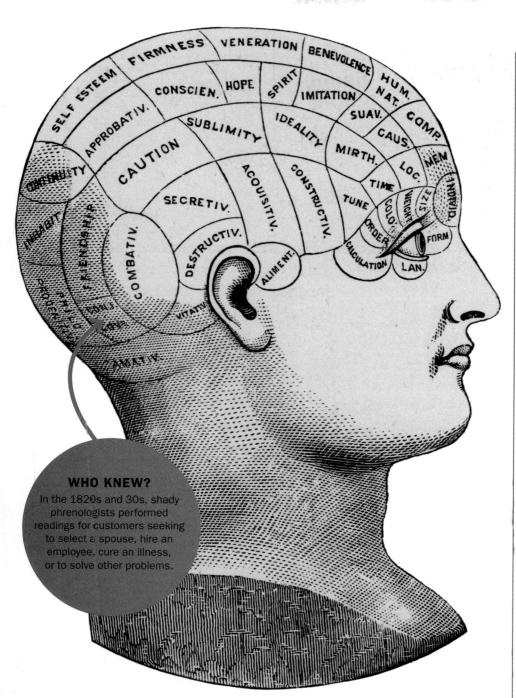

WHO KNEW?
In the 1820s and 30s, shady phrenologists performed readings for customers seeking to select a spouse, hire an employee, cure an illness, or to solve other problems.

An engraving from *Hill's Album of Biography and Art*, published in 1884, illustrated the supposed locations of the mind organs.

they reasoned, was a sign of "a defective or ill-balanced brain." Similarly, a person with a head with bumps over areas associated with criminal characteristics was thought to be predisposed to illegal behavior.

By the mid-1800s, phrenology had been discredited, but the hypothesis that specific areas of the brain were linked to distinct psychological traits would prefigure modern-day neuroscience. Today, lying, depression, criminal behavior, compassion, empathy, and other psychological processes have all been tied to identifiable regions of the brain.

CRIME IN YOUR DNA?

CARRIERS OF THE SO-CALLED WARRIOR GENE MAY BE PRONE TO OVERREACTION—OR MUCH WORSE.

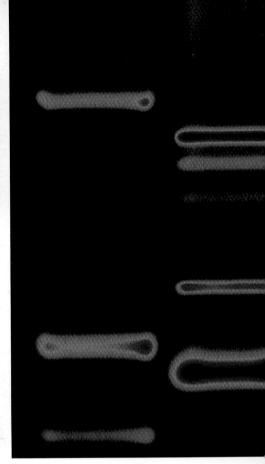

So far, no one has been able to identify a single "crime gene," but researchers believe that a variant of the monoamine oxidase A, or MAOA gene, could be linked to aggression. This so-called warrior gene, sometimes called the "psychopath gene," has been found in a third of men in Western populations. It appears to be inherited through the maternal line.

The MAOA gene is responsible for regulating brain enzymes that control responses to aggression and situations that inspire fear, anger, or frustration. A damaged, malformed, or dysfunctional MAOA gene could block the calming effects of certain brain chemicals and cause a person to overreact. When someone responds inappropriately or excessively to conflict, whether real or imagined, the MAOA gene could be to blame.

A DNA autoradiogram traces the presence of small amounts of radioactive materials.

Pioneering Study

H. G. Brunner, a Dutch geneticist, was among the first to note the importance of the MAOA gene in regulating anger. In 1993, Brunner and his team were studying a Dutch family, most of whose male members were mildly mentally impaired and extremely violent. Brunner discovered that the family's men all had one thing in common: Their MAOA genes were nonfunctional. Unlike previous studies linking genetic abnormality and behavior, Brunner's work held up to subsequent scientific scrutiny.

Of course, just because someone has the warrior gene doesn't mean he will become a killer. The link between genetics and neurochemistry is a complex one and difficult to study in isolation from environmental and other factors, scientists say.

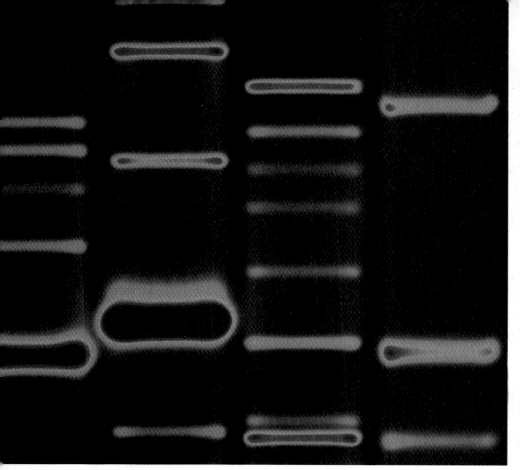

DNA fragments allow researchers to quickly scan for mutations, which may be related to certain behaviors or types of brain activity.

"The Sins of the Fathers"

In 1984, *Science* magazine published an important article, based on a Danish study of adoptees, suggesting a genetic component to criminality. The research compared the rate of convictions for adoptees, relative to their adoptive and biological parents. While results for women adoptees were inconclusive, there was a stronger correlation in the rate of criminal conviction between male adoptees and their biological fathers than between the adoptees and their adoptive fathers.

Thirteen percent of sons of biological fathers with no offenses had been convicted of a crime. Twenty-five percent of sons of biological fathers with three or more offenses had been convicted of a crime.

The study found no genetic link between the types of crimes committed by biological parents and children.

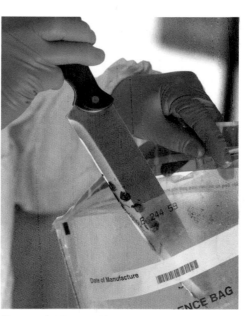

Damaged genes could cause a person to overreact.

GENETICS AS A CRIMINAL DEFENSE

Although some judges have acknowledged that genetics may have played a role in a criminal defendant's behavior, they have been reluctant to admit such evidence in court.

PROS

→ Could offer science over speculation.

→ Could suggest a defendant's behavior is the result of a genetic problem that he cannot control.

→ May help validate psychiatric or behavioral disorders otherwise difficult to prove.

→ Applies to a range of conditions, including alcoholism.

CONS

→ Testing is expensive.

→ Throws into question the notion of free will.

→ Could lead to the targeting of individuals for preventive detention.

→ Could negatively affect efforts to improve social and economic factors that can lead to crime.

WHO KNEW?

By some estimates, the rate of alcohol abuse among serial killers' families-of-origin may be as high as 70 percent.

MY BRAIN
MADE ME DO IT

RESEARCHERS FOR CENTURIES HAVE EXPLORED CONNECTIONS BETWEEN BIOLOGY AND CRIMINALITY. TODAY, MANY SEE A VITAL LINK.

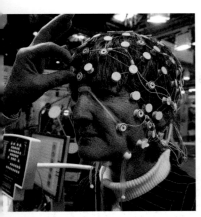

A woman wears an electroencephalogram (EEG) sensor net, which measures brain waves.

Is there a biological basis for criminality? The concept was first advanced in the 19th century by Italian scientist Cesare Lombroso, who theorized that bad behavior was passed down genetically through degenerate family lines. While some of Lombroso's ideas were eventually debunked, his research helped spur today's interest in the connection between the living brain and violent behavior.

Seeing Inside the Brain

If you are a fan of the Fox medical drama *House, M.D.*, watch the CBS hit *Criminal Minds*, or even have had a medical misfortune in your family, you're probably familiar with some of today's advanced neuroimaging tools. These range from the MRI, which allows doctors to observe the brain in real time, to the PET scan, which measures metabolism.

In recent years, researchers have used these machines to explore differences in the brains of violent criminals and have discovered some interesting, albeit inconclusive, patterns. Those who kill on the spur of the moment tend to have a poorly functioning prefrontal cortex, the area that regulates emotion and impulsive behavior. In contrast, serial killers and others who carefully plan their crimes exhibit good

prefrontal functioning. These findings are by no means universal: Not everyone with good prefrontal cortex function behaves rationally, and only a low percentage of those with poor prefrontal cortex function become violent.

Neuroscience and the Law

Recent breakthroughs in molecular biology have made it possible for researchers to examine DNA itself and how genetics may affect the brains of criminals. But there are thousands of genes to consider, and even if some show promise, no single gene is likely to hold the key to criminal behavior.

The legal implications of neurocriminality research are immense. If murderers are biologically different from the rest of us, are they less responsible for their crimes? Increasingly, defense attorneys are using neuroscientific evidence in murder cases to explain their clients' behavior, and judges cite such material in their opinions.

Neurolaw experts are troubled by the potential human-rights issues presented here. Should those with brains predisposed to violence be given lighter sentences—or conversely, be locked away to prevent them from causing further harm? Should an accused killer be forced to have a brain scan? And if a child or young adult's brain

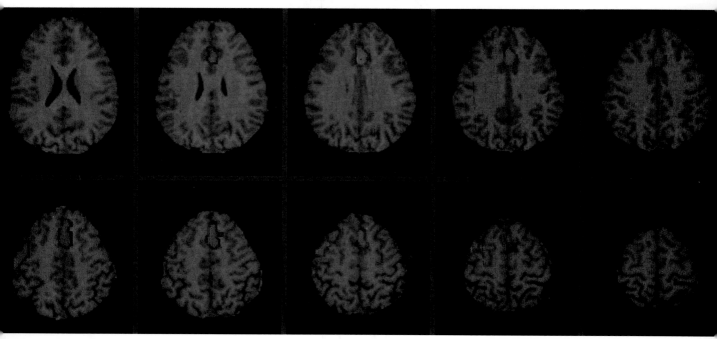

Two areas of the brain exhibit increased neuron activity when a person tells even the simplest of lies. When viewing the brain with an MRI scanner, the increased activity appears as bright spots.

scan indicates a violent predisposition, should he be relegated to a detention or prevention program?

Stephen J. Morse, professor of law and psychiatry at the University of Pennsylvania, has warned of "brain overclaim syndrome." He believes that brain scans give an inaccurate impression of scientific validity and worries that certain brain findings could lead to the wrong moral or legal conclusions. Neuroscientific theories, as intriguing and promising as they are, must be proven beyond reasonable doubt.

THE CEREBRAL WORLD OF ADRIAN RAINE

A groundbreaking researcher offers a literal portrait of criminality.

Adrian Raine's world is the criminal brain. A former prison psychiatrist, Raine is now a professor of criminology, psychiatry, and psychology at the University of Pennsylvania. He and his team are looking for irregularities buried within the gray matter of violent criminals.

Raine's research relies heavily on neuroimaging, a technique that allows him to view brains functioning in real time while the subject is exposed to various stimuli, such as fearful or threatening scenes.

Among other things, Raine has discovered that a large percentage of so-called hot-blooded murderers exhibit decreased function in the prefrontal cerebral cortex, the part of the brain that determines whether an action is good or bad. He also believes that abnormalities in the amygdala—which controls emotions such as fear—may likewise indicate a violent predisposition. If a person's amygdala is underdeveloped or damaged, his "fear switch" might be impaired and possibly lead to reckless behavior or violence.

If these theories are correct and psychopathy is biologically based, the criminal justice system should consider whether psychopaths are fully responsible for their actions, says Raine.

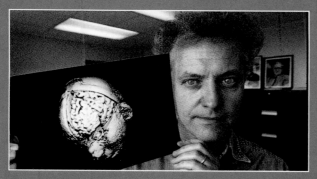

Dr. Adrian Raine holding a 3-D MRI scan of a murderer's brain.

IT'S THE ENVIRONMENT

TODAY, EXTERNAL INFLUENCES LIKE COMMUNITY AND FAMILY ARE OFTEN BLAMED FOR CREATING VIOLENT CRIMINALS.

The evolution of man

EVOLUTIONARY THEORY

When men commit violence, it may be to win a woman's favor.

Sometimes a minor altercation between two men about a trivial matter of honor, status, and reputation spins out of control and turns fatal when neither party is willing to back down.

The phenomenon makes sense from an evolutionary perspective, according to Martin Daly and Margo Wilson, two evolutionary psychologists who have studied violence.

Females are hardwired to be attracted to men of high status and reputation, which directly correlates with expectations of a male's reproductive success, say the psychologists. Males therefore are instinctively motivated to go to extremes to protect their honor.

What causes unlawful behavior? Over the last three centuries, societies have struggled to identify and address the root causes, with varying degrees of success. In the 18th century, as the concept of free will gained in popularity, blame was placed squarely on individuals, who were held responsible for their violent acts. A century later, Italian criminologists championed an opposite point of view, theorizing that genetics were at least partly responsible and that lawbreakers often shared certain physical traits. Starting in the early 1900s, researchers shifted gears again and explored the role of external influences like family and community.

"When you understand where the individual came from, what they were exposed to, and the environment in which they grew up," says Dr. Michael Fogel, associate professor of forensic psychology at the Chicago School of Professional Psychology, "you can understand why they engaged in the behavior that they did."

Are criminals born predisposed to a life of aggression and antisocial behavior, or are they products of their environment? Or is criminality a result of both nature and nurture?

Nurturing Criminal Development

Today, a variety of factors are considered to be contributing to criminal behavior, ranging from poverty and unemployment to teen pregnancy and racism.

Based on studies of crime in the U.S. and throughout the world, criminologist Elliot Currie summarizes the research in his book *Crime and Punishment in America*: "The links between extreme deprivation, delinquency, and violence . . . are strong, consistent, and compelling. There is little question that growing up in extreme poverty exerts powerful pressures toward crime."

Trauma Keeps on Giving

Early life experiences seem to have an especially strong influence on the development of criminality, with childhood trauma sometimes leading to violent behavior later in life. "It's because they start to see the world as a hostile place," says Dr. Kendell Coker, assistant professor of forensic psychology at the Chicago School of Professional Psychology.

While serial killers tend to come from poor backgrounds, the strongest contributing factor appears to be severe childhood abuse or neglect, according to research. It appears that many serial killers were physically, emotionally, or verbally abused and that their parents were often untreated alcoholics or mentally ill. Such circumstances tremendously impact childhood development, and can even damage the brain itself.

Detroit's Frederick Douglass Homes was the nation's first public housing project.

IS LEAD THE BULLET?

Environmental campaigns against leaded gas and lead paint may have reduced crime rates.

Studies have long suggested a link between childhood lead exposure and juvenile delinquency. But has lead poisoning also contributed to fluctuations in the overall crime rate? Researcher Rick Nevin believes it has. Nevin is an economist and consultant to the National Center for Healthy Housing, a charitable organization dedicated to minimizing the impact of environmental hazards. In one of his studies, Nevin examined lead poisoning and crime rates in nine countries over multiple decades. He found that as lead in the environment increased, there was a corresponding rise in violent crime two decades later. In his opinion, toddlers who ingested high levels of lead in the 1940s–50s were more likely to become violent criminals during the 1960s–80s.

Similarly, the economist attributed the decreases in violent crime in the 1990s to the phasing out of leaded gasoline starting in the 1970s. While the economist acknowledges that lead is not the only factor in the crime equation, he argues that it is a significant one.

Blood being tested for lead toxicity

BOY MEETS WORLD

Delinquent friends can trigger genes for aggression.

For boys, having delinquent friends or living in a disadvantaged neighborhood is more likely to trigger genes related to aggression, while being raised in a positive environment is less likely to trigger those genes, according to research conducted by Kevin Beaver, associate professor of criminology and criminal justice at Florida State University.

TEST CASE

TO GET INTO THE HEADS OF CRIMINALS, RESEARCHERS USE SOME TOOLS THAT ARE SOPHISTICATED, AND OTHERS QUITE SIMPLE.

It sounds like a plotline from the science fiction thriller *Minority Report*: A child is born and put through a battery of mandatory brain scans and blood work to determine whether he or she might grow up to be a murderer or a thief. If results come back positive, an arrest is made. The idea is not as far-fetched as it might seem. With the science of neurocriminology growing more sophisticated, one day it could be tempting to detain people for crimes they might commit in the future. Already,

WINDOW ONTO THE MIND

State-of-the-art brain scans and other tests can provide insight into the way offenders think.

THE TEST		WHAT IT MEASURES	HOW IT WORKS	WHAT IT CAN FIND
EEG (Electro-encephalo-gram)		Electrical activity in the brain.	Electrodes are attached temporarily to the scalp; the subject sits still while the electrodes transmit a recording of his brain waves to a computer. The results look a little like a seismograph.	Some studies have shown a link between certain brain-wave patterns and antisocial behavior.
PET (Positron Emission Tomography)		Activity in different parts of the brain.	A radioactive substance is injected into the bloodstream; a computer creates a three-dimensional picture of how the material is absorbed into various areas of the brain. Areas that are working harder show more absorption.	PET scans of the brains of convicted killers reveal abnormally low activity in the area associated with the control of rage.
EMG (Electro-myography)		The physical response to emotions.	Electrodes are attached to the subject's skin; a computer records muscle twitches as he is exposed to various stimuli, such as photographs.	In a study in which researchers attached electrodes to criminals' facial muscles, those that had been diagnosed as psychopaths showed less emotion than others.

Electroencaephalography records electrical activity of the brain.

certain tests can provide insight into bad guys' brains, from high-tech diagnostic tools such as EEGs and PET scans to far more basic assessment procedures.

Intelligence Quotient vs. Criminality Quotient

Standard IQ tests, for example, have unearthed an intriguing connection between intelligence and criminal behavior: Offenders tend to score eight to ten points lower than average. In particular, their verbal skills are poor, possibly indicating trouble with the left side of the brain, which also controls reasoning and problem-solving. Researchers theorize that language helps us define the long-term consequences of our actions. If people don't have an "internal monologue" to temper their behavior, they may act more impulsively, one study suggested.

Psychological tests for a type of thinking called "executive function" also reveal differences between criminals and non-criminals. People with poor executive function have trouble planning ahead, organizing their time, and resisting temptation. In one assessment called the Wisconsin Card-Sorting Test, four cards from a deck are laid on a table. Each depicts one or more simple shapes, such as three yellow stars or two black dots. The subject is asked to match the next card in the deck to one of the four cards but isn't told whether to make the match based on shape, color, or number. The subject makes a choice and is told whether he is correct or incorrect.

Once he figures out the rule ("I'm supposed to match by color") the administrator abruptly changes it. The subject must then determine the new correct way to match the cards. The test is often used to diagnose executive-function disorders in children with learning disabilities. But a study of prisoners who took it revealed that offenders had more trouble than most people changing or relearning behavior for which they'd been rewarded in the past.

As with all studies of the criminal brain, it's dangerous to jump to too many conclusions. Just because two things are linked does not necessarily mean that one causes the other. And most people with executive function disorders or lower-than-average intelligence are not lawbreakers.

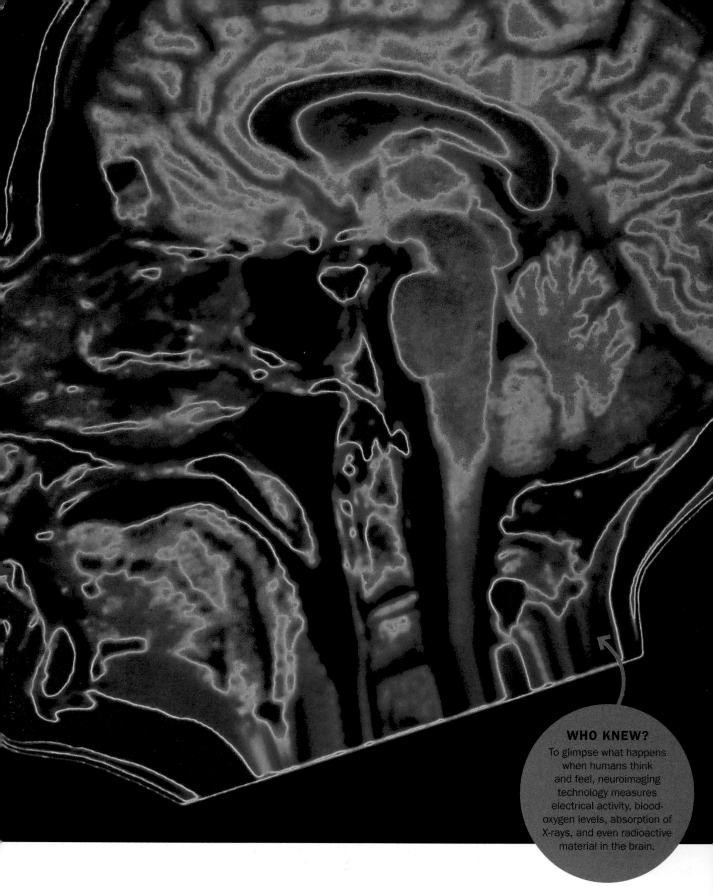

KILLERS AMONG US

SOMETIMES, YOU CAN SPOT A PSYCHOPATH FROM HIS INTENSE, BONE-CHILLING STARE. SOMETIMES, YOU CAN'T.

Studies show that an estimated 1 percent of all adult males have psychopathic tendencies, so everyone has likely had contact with a psychopath, possibly without knowing it.

Scanning for Control

Kent Kiehl, a professor of psychology and neuroscience at the University of New Mexico, says he can see it in their eyes: the intense, calculating, bone-chilling stare of the psychopath. This is psychopathy: the antisocial personality disorder characterized by a complete lack of empathy and remorse.

In recent years, Kiehl has been studying the inmates of the American prison system, where up to a quarter of all prisoners are psychopaths. He has worked in New Mexico and elsewhere, using a mobile magnetic resonance imaging (MRI) scanner to examine the brains of thousands of prison inmates. In a study published in 2013, Kiehl showed that men with lower than normal impulse control were more than twice as likely as others to be rearrested. For nonviolent crimes, that population was more than four times as likely to be arrested again.

James Fallon's Legacy

University of California at Irvine neuroscientist James Fallon has studied thousands of "killer brains" over the past 25 years, but one of the most interesting scans he encountered was his own.

After Fallon's mother told him there had been several criminals in the family tree, he researched the matter and discovered no fewer than seven murderers, including a several times great-grandfather executed in 1667 for matricide. He was also directly related to the legendary ax murderess Lizzie Borden.

Fallon examined his own brain and those of his immediate family and found his was the only abnormal one. Why didn't Fallon follow his forebears down the path of criminality? He credits his upbringing. Unlike many criminal psychopaths whose childhoods are marked by severe, brain-altering abuse, Fallon's family life was stable. While his brain may have conspired to make him a criminal, surrounding circumstances intervened.

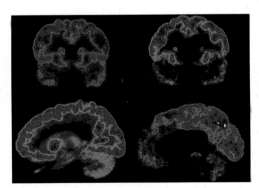

Positive emission tomography reveals that James Fallon's brain activity resembles a general psychopathy pattern. The control reveals normal brain activity. Red and yellow show high glucose metabolism activity; blue and dark blue or black areas indicate very low activity.

PSYCHOPATH VS. SOCIOPATH

TWO CONDITIONS WITH VERY DIFFERENT CAUSES CAN PRODUCE EQUALLY LETHAL PERSONALITIES.

When describing violent criminals who have no sense of remorse, a lot of people, including many doctors and law-enforcement professionals, use the words *psychopath* and *sociopath* interchangeably. Scientists tend to agree that both terms describe the victims of a mental disease called Antisocial Personality Disorder (ASPD), and that each group is the product of both genetic and social factors. Indeed, psychopaths and sociopaths have a lot in common, but psychopaths are controlled more by their genes, and so-

ciopaths more by their life circumstances. When they tip over into criminal insanity, they use different methods to gratify their brutal madness.

According to the *Diagnostic and Statistical Manual of Mental Disorders* used by psychiatrists, psychopaths and sociopaths share "a pervasive pattern of disregard for and violation of the rights of others." Although alienated from the mainstream, many, if not most, appear normal. They know how to act around other people and can even be well-liked, generally by

WHO KNEW?
Experts estimate that between 0.5 and 5 percent of Americans are psychopaths or sociopaths. That's 1.5 to 15 million people.

Mass murderer Ed Gein stored severed body parts in his Wisconsin kitchen.

THE SAME...BUT DIFFERENT

**A psychopath has no sense of right and wrong,
while a sociopath feels unconstrained by morality.**

Psychopathic criminals are especially formidable predators because of their ability to manipulate people and circumstances coldheartedly and to their own advantage. Their sociopathic counterparts, meanwhile, tend to lash out with raw, sudden ferocity.

	PSYCHOPATHS	SOCIOPATHS
Moral Awareness	No sense of right and wrong, lack of conscience, lack of moral insight	Sense of right and wrong, but feels unconstrained by morality
Emotions	Incapable of emotion or empathy for others.	Capable of emotion, limited capacity for empathy
Relationships	Unable to form emotional bonds with others	Able to form emotional bonds with certain individuals under certain circumstances
Outward Appearance	Successful, intelligent, charming, composed, sincere, trustworthy	Irritable, restless, impatient, hot-tempered, disorganized
Social Skills	Manipulative, deceitful, narcissistic, predatory; skilled at playing roles	Antisocial, unsophisticated, heedless; get what they want by taking it
Violence	Cold-blooded, premeditated, controlled, symbolic, deliberately cruel, furtive	Spontaneous, uncontrolled, reactive, explosive, flagrant
Criminal Methods	Detailed planning, secrecy, risk management, prolonged torture	Lack of planning, knee-jerk reaction, confrontation, speed, savagery
Motivation	Power, control, exploitation, greed, revenge	Entitlement, anger, revenge, recreation
Examples	Ted Bundy, Jeffrey Dahmer, John Wayne Gacy	Jack the Ripper, Lizzie Borden

Anthony Hopkins as Hannibal Lecter in the film *Silence of the Lambs*.

SICKNESS ON STAGE AND SCREEN

Psychopaths and sociopaths have always been favorite characters in popular entertainment. They've been portrayed as sadists, sexual deviants, and all manner of dark villains.

→ **Iago.** The classic psychopath in Shakespeare's play *Othello*, Iago is a master manipulator who smoothly—and with no particular motive—steers the title character into self-destruction and suicide. The play has been reimagined in genres from opera to film, and Iago has been played by many famous actors.

→ **Hannibal Lecter.** The blockbuster movie *The Silence of the Lambs*, released in 1991, features Anthony Hopkins as one of the greatest Hollywood psychopaths of all time: psychiatrist Hannibal Lecter, a criminally insane cannibal. First seen in two bestsellers by novelist Thomas Harris, the film won five Oscars and grossed $273 million at the box office.

→ **Dexter Morgan.** More of a sociopath than a psychopath, the protagonist of the television drama *Dexter* (2006–13) lives an outwardly normal life as a blood-spatter expert for the Miami Police Department and attempts to channel his murderous cravings by targeting evildoers.

faking normal behavior. These "wolves in sheep's clothing" are especially dangerous because they are harder to discern than those who are noticeably "off."

Recognizable or not, members of both groups can be selfish, impulsive, or reckless. They may be liars, con artists, or bullies. Some, though not all, are prone to violence. Psychopaths and sociopaths often ignore the rules and don't care whether they hurt other people. If they do inflict pain or break the law, they have no qualms and feel no remorse. Vicious criminals might be—but aren't necessarily—psychopaths or sociopaths.

Caution: Psychopaths at Work

In his 2012 book *The Wisdom of Psychopaths: What Saints, Spies, and Serial Killers Can Teach Us About Success,* psychologist Kevin Dutton posits that psychopaths have the kind of personality required to reach the top echelons of many demanding professions. They are bold, self-assured, charismatic, ruthless, single-minded, and driven to win at all costs. The ten careers most likely attract confident, extroverted psychopaths are: CEO, lawyer, television executive, salesperson, surgeon, journalist, police officer, clergy person, chef, and civil servant.

The same extroverted traits steer psychopaths away from idealistic or creative work, making them least likely to choose these ten occupations: health aide, nurse, therapist, craftsperson, beautician/stylist, charity worker, teacher, artist, doctor, and accountant.

WHY I DID IT

GUILTY BY REASON OF... WHAT? SOME LEGAL STRATEGIES CAN SURPRISE OR EVEN OUTRAGE.

Stephen Reitz claimed he was dreaming when he killed his girlfriend.

NO GUARANTEES

Do unusual defense strategies work? It depends on the judges and juries.

→ **Sleepwalking.** In 2004, Stephen Reitz, 28, who suffered from bipolar disorder, claimed he was dreaming when he threw a flowerpot at his girlfriend's head, beat her repeatedly, and stabbed her in the neck. The verdict: first-degree murder; the sentence: 26 years in prison.

→ **Caffeine intoxication.** In 2010, Woody Will Smith, 33, claimed that too many sodas, diet pills, and energy drinks, plus too little sleep, had led him to falsely confess to strangling his wife. The jury didn't buy it. He's now serving a life sentence for murder.

The accused accidentally committed the murder while sleepwalking. The accused suffered from "affluenza"—too much money. The accused was crazed with PMS. Each of these legal pleas sounds like a punch line in a courtroom comedy, but all have been offered as justifications in real criminal cases. A few even paid off.

For cynics, such tactics are examples of "creative lawyering," even as defense attorneys argue they are representing their clients to the best of their abilities. Either way, legal practitioners have been coming up with novel ways to absolve their clients of responsibility for a very long time. One early

---

DECODING THE "TWINKIE DEFENSE"

Dan White may have murdered two California politicians after bingeing on junk food, but his lawyers never blamed the cream-filled snack cake.

In 1978, former San Francisco supervisor Dan White crawled through a window of City Hall and assassinated a political rival, Harvey Milk, and the city's mayor, George Moscone. During White's trial for first-degree murder, his lawyers argued that their client was suffering from clinical depression. As evidence, they offered testimony from a psychiatrist who pointed to recent changes in White's behavior: A former health enthusiast and tidy dresser, White had been bingeing on junk food and had let his appearance go. The statements were simply meant to illustrate that White was not himself.

Twinkies never even came up during the testimony. But the media coined "Twinkie Defense" and reported that White's lawyers claimed he'd committed the murders under the influence of a sugar rush. Though White was found guilty of the lesser charge of manslaughter, Twinkies weren't the point; his mental illness was. White spent five years in prison, was released, and in 1985 committed suicide.

San Francisco Supervisor Harvey Milk, left, and Mayor George Moscone in 1977 in the mayor's office during the signing of the city's gay rights bill.

Jared Loughner was originally found incompetent to stand trial for murdering six people and wounding others, including Rep. Gabrielle Giffords.

Not many accused criminals meet this definition, and the insanity defense is fairly rare. According to mental-health advocates, fewer than 1 percent of defendants enter a plea of not guilty by reason of insanity, and only a small fraction of those are successful. A handful of states don't allow the insanity defense at all.

Curing "Insanity"

When an accused killer invokes the insanity defense, it can infuriate justice-hungry families of the victims, as well as the general public.

In 2011, at a political event in a supermarket parking lot near Tucson, Arizona, former community-college student Jared Loughner killed six people and wounded many others, including U.S. Representative Gabrielle Giffords.

During pretrial proceedings, Loughner's attorneys argued that he was not mentally competent, a claim that touched off a firestorm in the press. Dr. Christina Pietz, a forensic psychologist, diagnosed Loughner with schizophrenia, and an evaluation at a federal mental hospital deemed him incompetent to stand trial, but that didn't save Loughner from prison.

After being administered antipsychotic medication for several months while in federal custody, Loughner was examined again and found competent. He pleaded guilty to killing six and wounding 13 and is now serving multiple life sentences.

example: In 1859, Congressman Daniel Sickles became the first person in the United States to use a "temporary insanity" defense. Sickles had discovered that his wife, Theresa, had been unfaithful. In retaliation, Sickles shot and killed Theresa's lover in a park directly across the street from the White House. In the ensuing trial, Sickles's lawyer argued that his client had been driven mad by his wife's affair. The court bought the defense, and Sickles was acquitted.

Necessary Compassion

Today, mental health advocates consider the insanity defense a necessary and compassionate way of handling defendants with diminished mental capacity. And the plea doesn't mean that the defendant will simply go free. "Most [people] acquitted by reason of insanity will spend more time locked up than a defendant who is found guilty," one forensic psychiatrist told the *Chicago Tribune* in 2013.

One of the earliest measures of an accused wrong-doer's mental state was called the M'Naghten Rules, after the English case that inspired it. In 1843, while in the throes of a delusional episode, a Scottish man named Daniel M'Naghten attempted to assassinate the British Prime Minister. In the process, M'Naghten killed a bystander and the case led to the development of formal criteria for criminal insanity: Did the defendant know what he was doing? If so, did he understand that what he was doing was wrong?

29

THIS IS YOUR BRAIN ON DRUGS

SUBSTANCE AND ALCOHOL ABUSE ARE MAJOR FACTORS IN A SIGNIFICANT NUMBER OF SAVAGE CRIMES.

WHO KNEW?
One out of every 100 U.S. citizens is currently in jail or prison.

Travis Felder allegedly was high on methamphetamine and wearing nothing but a woman's bra and a pair of capris when he entered the Alaska home of a couple babysitting their granddaughter. It was June 2014 and Felder was at the end of a meth-fueled crime spree in which he had allegedly assaulted a former girlfriend and broken into another home. After punching the grandmother, Felder went upstairs to take a shower. When the police arrived, the 40-year-old was wearing a pair of the homeowner's pajamas. "I was out of my mind by then," Felder told the *Anchorage Press* a few days later from jail.

The methamphetamine scourge is unfortunately familiar to communities across the country. The powerful illegal stimulant has been a factor in numerous brutal crimes, including shootings, stabbings, and severe child abuse. Repeated use of the narcotic, experts say, can alter the brain and central nervous system so that users become psychotic and paranoid. They hear voices and hallucinate. They become desensitized to cruelty. Law-enforcement officials consider meth to be the neurotoxin that most often contributes to violent crimes and thefts, even though it is less commonly used than other illegal substances.

Danger in a Glass

But the mind-altering drug that most often incites mayhem is available legally everywhere. Alcohol is a factor in 40 percent of all violent crimes in the United States.

About three million acts of violence are committed each year by a person or persons who have been drinking, according to the National Council on Alcoholism and Drug Dependence. More than a third of rapes and sexual assaults and a quarter of simple assaults are committed by someone under the influence.

Among the most brutal lawbreakers, especially those who are repeat offenders, drug and/or alcohol abuse is pervasive. For someone with a criminal history, drug dependency can exacerbate existing psychological tendencies. In a study published in 2011, researchers compared brain scans of addicts and nonaddicts who had com-

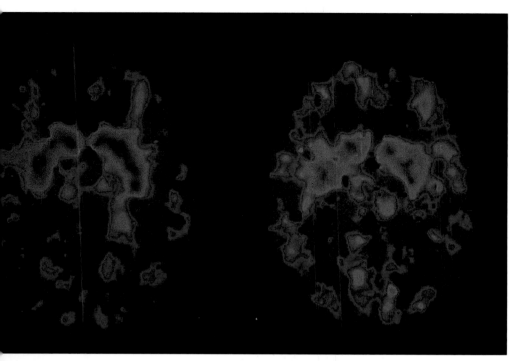

Scans of dopamine receptors in normal and methamphetamine-abuser brains

Sometimes intoxication leads to violence. Other times, it just leads to foolish criminal behavior.

mitted similar crimes. In all of the addicts' brains, the area governing self-control was less robust. In the violent offenders' brains, whether addict or nonaddict, the area that controls pleasure and craving was more robust. The suggestion: A thirst for excitement paired with a lack of self-control can have devastating results.

Violent offenses aren't a joke, but criminals often bumble laughably while under the influence.

→ **The Troublemaker.** In 2013, a 23-year-old got booted from a Florida bar for fighting with his mother. He next broke into a department store by slipping though an air-conditioning conduit on the roof. After falling through the store's ceiling, the man was arrested.

→ **The Streaker.** In 2013, a 39-year-old Ohio man was charged with disorderly conduct for running naked through his neighborhood while intoxicated—after unsuccessfully trying to hide from the police in a neighbor's dryer. He pleaded no contest and was sentenced to five days in jail.

JAILHOUSE SMUGGLERS

Illegal drugs, alcohol, cigars, and cigarettes are just some of the prohibited items that end up in the possession of prisoners.

Who dares smuggle illegal items to the incarcerated? In an infamous case involving the Baltimore City Detention Center, a state prison for men and women, some of the culprits turned out to be female guards who had been romanced by an inmate gang leader.

Working with a ring of collaborators, the security officers slipped marijuana, cell phones, and prescription drugs into the prison by concealing the items in their clothes and hair. In all, 13 women guards as well as a dozen inmates and suppliers were arrested in a 2013 bust. As the FBI special agent in charge of the investigation put it, "The inmates literally took over the asylum."

A cell at Sheridan Correctional Center, Illinois. The center is dedicated to treating inmates with drug and alcohol abuse problems.

U.S. CRIMINAL ARREST DATA

Television drama and news programs often portray the police pursuing and arresting armed robbers, killers, and other violent offenders, and for good reason: There are more than 3.7 million arrests each year for robbery and other property crimes, murder and manslaughter, assault, and rape, according to the U.S. government. Another 3.5 million arrests are made annually for nonviolent crimes such as public-drunkenness, disorderly conduct, and liquor-law offenses. Nearly a quarter of a million of those individuals are arrested for being runaways, vagrants, curfew breakers, or because they are deemed suspicious by police.

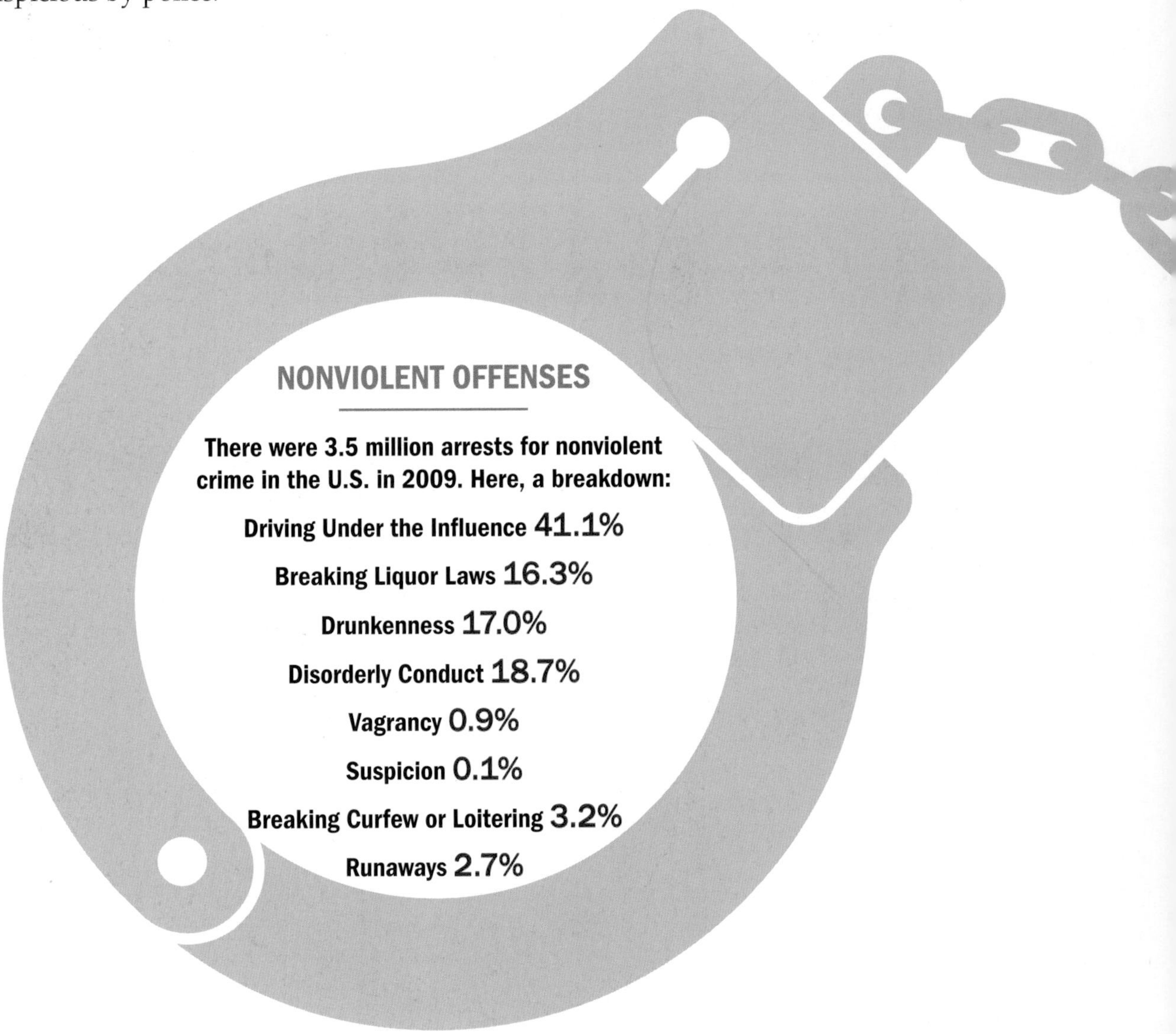

NONVIOLENT OFFENSES

There were 3.5 million arrests for nonviolent crime in the U.S. in 2009. Here, a breakdown:

Driving Under the Influence 41.1%

Breaking Liquor Laws 16.3%

Drunkenness 17.0%

Disorderly Conduct 18.7%

Vagrancy 0.9%

Suspicion 0.1%

Breaking Curfew or Loitering 3.2%

Runaways 2.7%

PUNISHING VIOLENT CRIME IN AMERICA

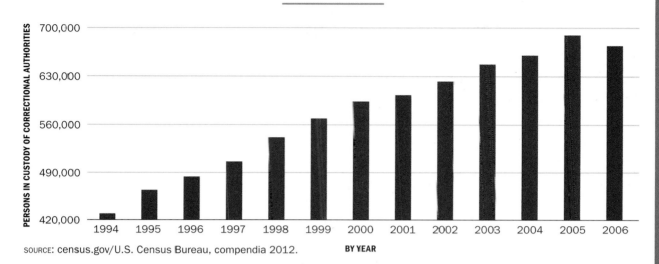

PERSONS IN CUSTODY OF CORRECTIONAL AUTHORITIES

700,000 — 630,000 — 560,000 — 490,000 — 420,000

1994 1995 1996 1997 1998 1999 2000 2001 2002 2003 2004 2005 2006

BY YEAR

SOURCE: census.gov/U.S. Census Bureau, compendia 2012.

VIOLENT CRIMES

There were approximately 3.7 million
arrests for violent offenses in 2009.

Murder **24.3%**

Rape **8.9%**

Other Sexual Assault **15.1%**

Robbery **25.8%**

Assault **18.8%**

Manslaughter and Other Violent Crime **7.1%**

SOURCE: Bureau of Justice Statistics. bjs.gov/2009.

MEDIA AND MURDER

RESEARCH SUGGESTS THAT SOME VIDEO GAMES AND MUSIC CAN INSPIRE VIOLENCE. THE QUESTION IS, TO WHAT DEGREE?

An Alabama college student steals a truck and deliberately crashes into other cars in a reenactment of the video game *Grand Theft Auto*. Two Nevada men shoot themselves in a suicide pact after listening to the heavy-metal band Judas Priest. An Oklahoma couple goes on a murder spree after watching the movie *Natural Born Killers*.

These are just a few of the crimes that have been linked to popular media and helped spark a national debate over the causes of—and solutions to—violent behavior.

Even some books have been pulled into the fray. John Fowles's 1963 debut, *The Collector*, about a lonely man who abducts and imprisons a woman, is said to have inspired several different serial killers to do the same in the decades after its publication. Oklahoma City bomber Timothy McVeigh kept a copy of the 1978 right-wing novel *The Turner Diaries* in his car. After shooting John Lennon, gunman Mark David Chapman stayed at the crime scene reading *The Catcher in the Rye*, J.D. Salinger's classic novel about an alienated teenager.

Killer Skills

These days, video games are considered a prime culprit. Some politicians and parental groups are especially concerned about so-called first-person shooter games, in which the action is viewed from the point of view of the player. The maneuvers can be ruthlessly bloody and numbingly realistic, and it is feared the games may help some would-be murderers hone their marksmanship.

Washington Navy Yard gunman Aaron Alexis, who killed 12 and injured several others in 2013, was enthralled with the games in the *Call of Duty* series. Norwegian Anders Breivik is said to have played the similarly graphic *World of Warcraft* for seven hours a day before taking 77 lives in a 2011 shooting and bombing rampage.

But members of the entertainment and gaming industries as well as others question the validity of linking criminal behavior to pop culture pastimes. They point out that hundreds of millions of people play brutal video games, watch gory movies and TV shows, and listen to explicit music without going on to hurt anyone. A person's mental health, his upbringing, his access to guns, and many other factors affect his chances of becoming a killer. There's no one simple cause of violent crime, or

Aaron Alexis carrying a shotgun at the Washington Navy Yard on September 16, 2013. He acted under the delusion that he was being controlled by extremely low-frequency electromagnetic waves, the FBI said.

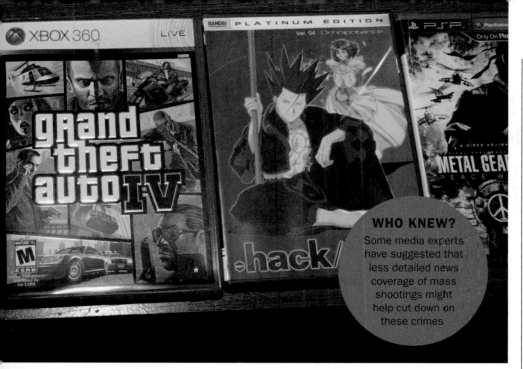

These video games were found in the house of Adam Lanza, the 20-year-old responsible for the massacre at Sandy Hook Elementary School in Newtown, Connecticut.

The Matrix DVD

even one prevalent one that we have discovered.

Still, the American Psychological Association, American Medical Association, American Academy of Pediatrics, American Academy of Child and Adolescent Psychiatry, National Institute of Mental Health, and the FBI all say unequivocally that media violence can lead to real-life aggression.

"You're never sure what caused an individual to commit a specific act," Brad Bushman, an Ohio State University professor of communications and psychology told the *Washington Post* after the Sandy Hook Elementary School massacre in 2012. Violent media is "not the only factor that leads to violence," he said, "but it's one of them."

MULTIPLE COUNTS

Certain songs, movies, and television shows have been cited as the inspiration for some criminal acts.

MUSIC
"*Bodies*," by Drowning Pool. Before mass shooter Jared Loughner killed six people and injured 13 in Tucson, Arizona, in 2011, he posted a video with a soundtrack from this 2001 heavy metal song, which includes the lyrics, "Something's got to give now/ Let the bodies hit the floor."

MOVIES
The Matrix. The Columbine High School shooters, the Beltway Sniper Lee Boyd Malvo, and at least four other killers are said to have been obsessed with this 1999 science-fiction film.

TELEVISION
Dexter. The 2006–2013 Showtime series revolved around a police analyst who led a double life as a serial killer. Prosecutors or criminals referenced it in at least five different murder cases, including a 2009 case in which an Indiana teenager strangled his ten-year-old brother, according to media accounts.

BLAME BUGS BUNNY

Does comic-book gore make good kids do bad things? There was a time when people thought so.

Before there were violent video games, slasher movies, or gangsta rap, parents worried that America's impressionable youth would fall prey to the pernicious influence of…comic books. It seems almost quaint now, but in 1954 the U.S. Senate held hearings on whether the funnies contributed to juvenile delinquency. To avoid government regulations, publishers adopted a code of ethics the same year. Among the rules:

- The words "terror" and "horror" could not be used in a title.

- Crime could only be depicted as 'a sordid and unpleasant activity."

- Cops, judges, and other officials could not be portrayed disrespectfully.

Publishers adhered to the code until it was abandoned in the early 2000s.

There were more than 3.7 million arrests for nonviolent crime in the U.S. in 2009.

CHAPTER 2
LAW ENFORCEMENT

CATCHING KILLERS IS BUILT ON OLD-FASHIONED DETECTIVE WORK, BUT TODAY, OFFICERS ALSO HAVE GADGETS WORTHY OF JAMES BOND TO HELP THEM TRACK DOWN THE BAD GUYS.

THE DETECTIVE'S PLAYBOOK

HOW DO YOU SOLVE A CRIME? PHYSICAL EVIDENCE, OLD-FASHIONED INTERVIEWS, AND COOPERATIVE WITNESSES.

There were 506 murders in Chicago in 2012, the most of any metropolis in the United States. The same year, the Windy City recorded about seven murders per 100,000, more than the national average of five per 100,000. Local police also solved a dismal 25 percent of homicides, the department's worst performance in more than two decades and well below the national clearance rate of 60 percent.

Faced with these statistics, the Chicago Police Department decided to try something new in 2013. It added 70 new detectives to the force and put them to work on homicide cases in teams of eight or 10 instead of one or two. The restructuring allowed for ongoing investigations even during individual vacations or absences. With expanded staff and new avenues for teamwork, the department improved its clearance rate by 5 percent in a single year.

There were unexpected consequences as well. Ordinary citizens, noting how the police were committing more resources to their neighborhoods, became more willing to step forward and identify perpetrators, the department said. Cooperation seemed to increase from the moment a homicide was suspected.

Group Effort

Such collaboration is key to the success of any law enforcement team. It starts the mo-

A display of some of the 3,400 illegal firearms seized by the Chicago police in the first six months of 2014

Chicago police investigate the scene of a shooting.

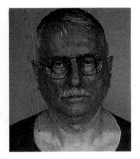

A deathbed confession eventually led to the arrest of Jack Daniel McCullough, formerly known as John Tessier.

WHO KNEW?
The violent crime rate in the U.S. peaked in 1993 and has been falling ever since, according to the FBI.

ment personnel arrive at the murder site, as crews secure the crime scene, collect physical evidence, take meticulous photographs, and send evidence to a crime lab for analysis. While the crime scene investigators are doing their jobs, detectives are identifying and interviewing any witnesses that might have valuable information to contribute about what happened. These are the steps every department relies on for leads to solve crimes.

Friends and Family

If no obvious suspect emerges quickly, police begin interviewing people within the victim's circle. All but about 20 percent of murder victims are killed by someone they know—an acquaintance, spouse, romantic partner, or family member—so investigators start there. If these interviews aren't fruitful, authorities may solicit tips from the public and follow up on them selectively.

Once a suspect is arrested, the easiest and fastest way to close a case is by obtaining a confession. In fact, crime experts estimate that 80 percent of cases end with a suspect admitting he or she did it. At that point, law enforcement usually considers the case cleared, and it's on to the next one.

CRIME SCENE
INVESTIGATION

FINGERPRINTS AND FIBER ANALYSIS CAN MAKE A COURT CASE. BUT SUCH FORENSIC SCIENCE CAN BE LESS RELIABLE THAN YOU THINK.

Crime fighters have used lab tests as evidence for hundreds of years. A postmortem exam to detect arsenic poisoning was first developed in 18th-century Sweden. Scotland Yard began studying the characteristics of bullets in the early 19th century. Fingerprinting came into vogue in the late 1800s in Europe, and by the early 1900s was imported to the United States by the New York City Police Department. These days, forensic science is widely relied on—but it is hardly foolproof.

In 2009, the National Academy of Sciences even published a study, "Strengthen-

NO LIE

The controversial "lie-detector test" is relatively easy to skew in your favor.

Chances are, you'll never have to take a polygraph or lie-detector test. It is illegal to force anybody—even someone under arrest—to submit to one, and it is generally forbidden for an employer to require one. In many states, even voluntary polygraphs are inadmissible in court.

Should you ever be subjected to one, these counter-strategies are said to be fairly effective.

1. Recognize the "control questions." Polygraph tests work by measuring your physical responses when you lie. To get a baseline sense of how much you sweat and how dramatically your pulse and breathing increase, the interviewer first asks questions you will answer truthfully, such as your name and whether you are wearing a gray suit.

He then asks a few questions that you might be inclined to fib about such as, "Have you ever stolen anything?" or "Have you ever been fired from a job?" These questions are broad on purpose—you've probably stolen something in your life, even if it's just a paper clip. When you say no, you've never stolen anything, the machine registers a little jump in your vital signs and your physical parameters are established.

2. Punch up your physical symptoms. Before you answer these kinds of control questions, think of something scary, try to solve a complex math problem in your head, or bite down on your tongue so that your physical response is exaggerated.

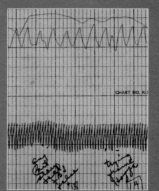

CHART NO. K-

3. Calm yourself down. During the relevant questions —the ones you want to seem to be answering truthfully, even if you aren't—keep your breathing controlled and think of something nice.

Lie-detector test given to Teamster Ed Partin after he claimed that union leader Jimmy Hoffa had threatened to kill Robert F. Kennedy.

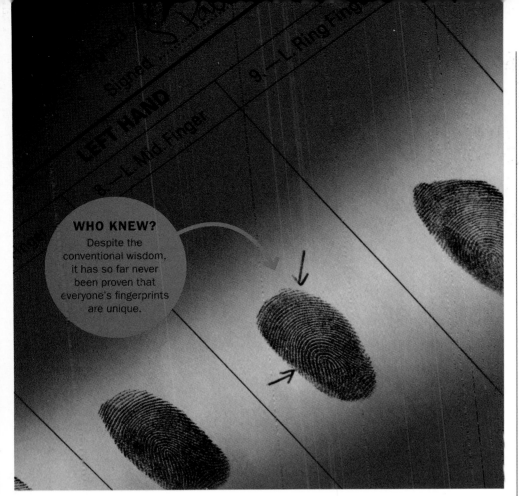

WHO KNEW?
Despite the conventional wisdom, it has so far never been proven that everyone's fingerprints are unique.

Fingerprints are records of the friction ridges found on the skin. Traditional fingerprinting relies on ink and paper to record the individual whorls and loops.

Casey Anthony before the start of her sentencing hearing in Orlando, Florida.

To the dismay of prosecutors, juries who watch popular television shows such as *CSI: Crime Scene Investigation* want iron-clad proof of guilt.

Television dramas in which the leads rely on forensic evidence to solve crimes are wildly popular, endlessly fascinating, and—according to some prosecutors—seriously interfering with their ability to convict bad guys. Thanks to a phenomenon they call "the *CSI* effect," lawyers say more juries now demand absolute proof to render a guilty verdict. They want the kind of evidence they see on TV: high-tech and 100 percent accurate. The trouble is, it's not always possible to obtain definitive forensic evidence, and some of the techniques shown on these shows don't even exist.

Some believe the *CSI* effect played a role in the 2011 acquittal of Casey Anthony, the Florida mother accused of killing her two-year-old daughter, Caylee. Media outlets observed that the prosecution presented significant circumstantial evidence but was unable to provide the kind of conclusive forensics seen on CSI. The jury found Anthony not guilty.

ing Forensic Science in the United States: A Path Forward," that revealed which crime-lab techniques are scientifically sound and which ones aren't. Surprisingly, the "unreliable" category included a number of long-used crime-solving techniques, from hair analysis to lie-detector tests.

Inexact Science

Shoe prints, for example, are a favorite in detective stories, but they are not considered scientifically rigorous evidence. There is no official number of criteria a shoe print must meet before it is determined to be a match to one specific shoe, and drawing conclusions based on such prints can be risky. Similarly, bite marks on a victim's body can be unreliable; the same goes for fingerprints. The alignment of a person's teeth can shift over time, for example, and

police aren't always able to obtain a full fingerprint from a crime scene. Sometimes even the best fingerprint analysts make mistakes.

Then there's hair analysis, identifying a strand of hair or fiber based on characteristics such as texture, diameter, and distribution of pigment. Even highly competent analysts can have trouble distinguishing between human and animal hair, let alone reliably connecting the strand to a particular human.

The one forensic test that is quite reliable in proving a suspect's guilt or innocence is DNA. Developed in the early 1980s by a British geneticist, this procedure has been refined in the ensuing decades and has even been used to exonerate a number of innocent people who had been convicted on the basis of other forensic evidence.

INSPECTORS WITH GADGETS

CUTTING-EDGE TECHNOLOGY IS HELPING LAW ENFORCEMENT PREVENT CRIME AND CATCH CRIMINALS.

In July 2013, after a number of auto burglaries were reported in a parking garage in Fort Lauderdale, Florida, the local police set up a sting operation. They parked a "bait car" in the garage, with unlocked doors and a purse inside. When the thief showed up, opened the car door, and began to search through the purse, he got a surprise: The bag had been rigged to spray him with Smart-

A special flashlight reveals yellow markings to show where SmartWater was sprayed.

Water CSI—a long-lasting high-tech liquid (not to be confused with the similarly named brand of bottled water) that goes on clear but is visible under a special light. When detectives caught up with the 21-year-old suspect several hours later, the proof of his misdeed was all over his face.

Crime-fighting tools are getting positively James Bond–like; they include a wide array of gadgets and software to help nab bad guys and even stop crime before it starts. In Memphis, Tennessee, for example, a database called Blue CRUSH, which identifies crime patterns by neighborhood, helped reduce murders and robberies by more than a

third and car thefts by more than half in the six years following its 2006 inception.

Electronic Eyes

Some police departments are enlisting the public in high-tech crime prevention. In Akron, Ohio, police ask local businesses and homeowners with security cameras to register with a program called DIVRT. The DIVRT software can connect to participating surveillance cameras and grab footage of holdups or other crimes captured on a particular camera. Then cops can quickly broadcast the footage on social media and send it to local news outlets, netting them valuable tips from eyewitnesses

and the general public.

In some cases, technology can be better than humans. In East Chicago, Indiana, police use a device called ShotSpotter, which can detect the sound of gunfire via special sensors posted around the city. The technology pinpoints the exact location of a shooting within about a minute, allowing police to rush to the scene more quickly than they could by relying on phoned-in tips.

These futuristic methods and gadgets are not mistake-proof, and could lead criminals to become more tech-savvy themselves. But law enforcement is working to stay a step ahead of them.

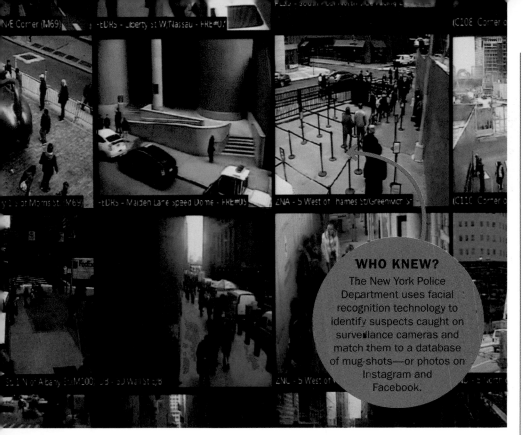

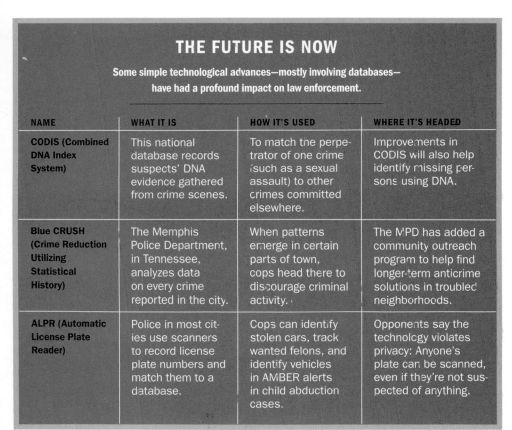

WHO KNEW?

The New York Police Department uses facial recognition technology to identify suspects caught on surveillance cameras and match them to a database of mug-shots—or photos on Instagram and Facebook.

Monitors from security cameras at the Lower Manhattan Security Initiative in New York City, 2013

A street surveillance camera on a light pole in Chicago

WE'RE WATCHING YOU

Is the huge increase in the number of private and public surveillance cameras a boon to crime-fighters, or an invasion of your privacy?

If it seems as if there are video cameras everywhere, it's because there are. In the decade after the September 11, 2001, terrorist attacks, American businesses, governments, and private citizens bought an estimated 30 million video cameras in an effort to boost security. In Chicago alone, there are an estimated 24,000 cameras posted around the city.

In numerous instances nationwide, recordings from security cameras have helped prevent and solve crimes, including acts of terrorism. After the Boston Marathon attacks in April 2013, footage from the area's hundreds of private and public cameras helped the FBI identify alleged bombers Dzhokhar and Tamerlan Tsarnaev. But at what price? Critics of the security-camera boom say it's an invasion of citizens' privacy to constantly monitor us wherever we go. That debate is likely to continue, as is the escalation of video security measures in urban centers and high-risk areas.

THE FUTURE IS NOW

Some simple technological advances—mostly involving databases— have had a profound impact on law enforcement.

NAME	WHAT IT IS	HOW IT'S USED	WHERE IT'S HEADED
CODIS (Combined DNA Index System)	This national database records suspects' DNA evidence gathered from crime scenes.	To match the perpetrator of one crime (such as a sexual assault) to other crimes committed elsewhere.	Improvements in CODIS will also help identify missing persons using DNA.
Blue CRUSH (Crime Reduction Utilizing Statistical History)	The Memphis Police Department, in Tennessee, analyzes data on every crime reported in the city.	When patterns emerge in certain parts of town, cops head there to discourage criminal activity.	The MPD has added a community outreach program to help find longer-term anticrime solutions in troubled neighborhoods.
ALPR (Automatic License Plate Reader)	Police in most cities use scanners to record license plate numbers and match them to a database.	Cops can identify stolen cars, track wanted felons, and identify vehicles in AMBER alerts in child abduction cases.	Opponents say the technology violates privacy: Anyone's plate can be scanned, even if they're not suspected of anything.

TO CATCH A KILLER

A SPECIAL FBI DATABASE HELPS LAW ENFORCEMENT AGENCIES ACROSS THE NATION CONNECT THE DOTS IN UNSOLVED VIOLENT CRIMES.

A police officer looks at a photo of Rafael Resendez-Ramirez, wanted by the FBI.

Catching killers has always revolved around quality detective work, from composing detailed crime scene reports to scrutinizing autopsy results. Today, it may also depend on a search of a special FBI database, the Violent Criminal Apprehension Program (ViCAP), which collects information from police departments around the country about homicides, sexual assaults, and missing persons.

Finding Patterns

Created in 1985 and headquartered in Quantico, Virginia, the Violent Criminal Apprehension Program is a unit of the FBI that assimilates and analyzes information about serial crimes and seeks to identify the perpetrators. ViCAP agents look for patterns that might reveal the "signature" of a criminal, drawing parallels among widespread or seemingly disparate cases. The database they use includes contributions from more than 4,000 law enforcement agencies covering as many as 90,000 cases. In 2008, this data was made available for the first time to local law enforcement agencies around the country via a secure internet link.

How It Works

Here is a hypothetical example that illustrates how ViCAP can help find a suspect.

A young jogger in Texas disappears while out on a run in her local park. Her body, showing signs of sexual assault, is found a week later, and it is determined that she has died from a blow to the head. Investigators clear all of the woman's known associates, then turn to ViCAP.

Texas police discover in the database information about another jogger who was sexually assaulted five months earlier in Alabama. They contact authorities in Alabama to compare notes. Meanwhile, a ViCAP analyst in Virginia is reviewing a similar case involving a Georgia jogger. That victim, who escaped, has described her attacker as a tall, thin, redheaded man with glasses, wielding a lead pipe.

While researching the Georgia incident, the ViCAP analyst finds the Texas and Ala-

WHO KNEW?
Rafael Resendez-Ramirez, known as the "Railroad Killer," was caught after ViCAP tied him to murders by searching for cases of vagrants murdered in railroad yards.

Rafael Resendez-Ramirez, who is suspected of killing at least eight people, is driven to jail in Houston, Texas, after surrendering to officials, 1999.

bama cases in the database. The analyst and the Texas, Alabama, and Georgia investigators pool what they know about the cases, and a suspect is identified and arrested: He is a high school track coach who had visited Texas, Alabama, and Georgia for track meets around the times of the corresponding murders. His DNA is tested and found to match that retrieved from the various victims.

ViCAP's Critics

The FBI does not release information on how many criminals are apprehended because of ViCAP, so it is difficult to judge its effectiveness. Critics point to various shortcomings, such as the wording of questions on the ViCAP form. They also complain that the links between the various crimes in the database can be tenuous. Crimi-nologist Jack Levin worries that the data is incomplete since most states do not require their police to register reports with ViCAP. Only a third of the nation's homicide cases are reported to ViCAP, says Levin, who adds that serial killers don't always stick to a pattern. "Their methods often change from victim to victim," which makes their crimes more difficult to link, Levin told the *Oakland Press.*

Nevertheless, ViCAP serves a valuable purpose for law enforcement, says former detective Robert Keppel. "What these critics don't realize is that ViCAP was not intended to provide any sort of expert linkage or sophisticated statistical analysis. Its main function is that of a pointer system to help detectives find similar cases so they can communicate with each other one-on-one about the possibility that cases are linked."

CRIME IN AMERICA

According to the U.S. government statistics, there were 440 violent crimes for every 100,000 people in the United States in 2009, the most recent year such national data is available. But violent crimes per capita vary greatly from state to state and there is not always a correlation between a state's violent crime rate and the size of local law enforcement. The three states with the lowest violent crime rates have among the smallest police forces per capita in the country. New Hampshire, with the lowest murder rate, hasn't had the death penalty for more than 130 years.

THE MOST DANGEROUS STATES

NEVADA

654.7 violent crimes per 100,000 people—highest in the country

13th in number of police officers

LOUISIANA

628.4 violent crimes per 100,000 people

11.2 murders per 100,000 people

542.8 police officers per 100,000 residents

Has **8th** highest violent crime rate in the U.S.

TENNESSEE

607.7 violent crimes for every 100,000 people

Ranks **22nd** of 50 in incarceration rates

Spends an average of **$11.67** billion annually to combat violent crime

The crime rate has gotten steadily worse each year since 1991.

THE SAFEST STATES

MAINE

120.2 violent crimes for every 100,000 people

Lowest incarceration rate— **148** per 100,000 people

Smallest police force of all states

VERMONT

135.1 violent crimes per 100,000 people

1.1 murders per 100,000 people— the second lowest in the United States

4th lowest in number of police officers

Spends an average of **$447** million to combat violent crime

NEW HAMPSHIRE

169.5 violent crimes per 100,000 people

1 murder per 100,000 people—the lowest in the United States

WHAT'S THE MOST COMMON WEAPON USED IN ROBBERIES?

In 2009, more than a third of robberies were committed without a weapon, according to the U.S. Census.

gun 131,000

physical intimidation 126,000

knife 24,000

other weapon 27,000

WHEN DO MOST BURGLARIES OCCUR?

The common assumption is that most burglaries occur at night, but government statistics show otherwise.

daytime: 910,000

nighttime: 625,000

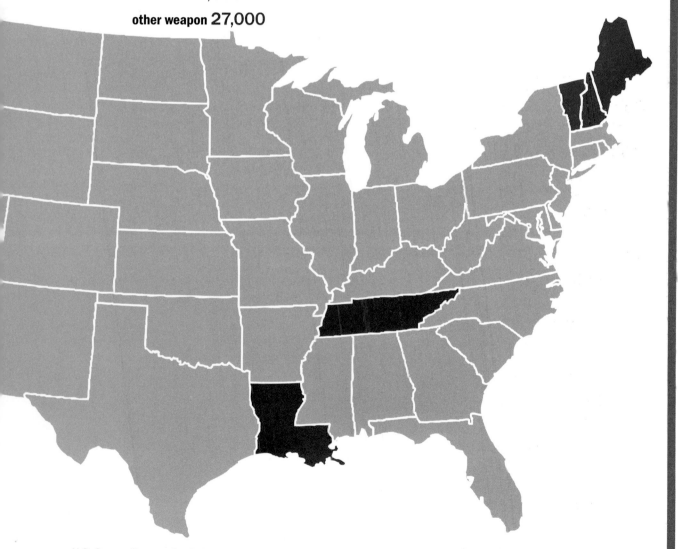

SOURCES: U.S. Census Bureau, Statistical Abstract of the United States, 2012; census.gov. FBI Crime Clock Statistics; fbi.gov.

ADMITTING IT

A SURPRISING NUMBER OF PEOPLE CONFESS TO HORRIBLE CRIMES THEY DID NOT COMMIT.

O n March 30, 1934, a white planter, Raymond Stuart, was brutally murdered in Kempner, Mississippi. The three suspects, Ed Brown, Arthur Ellington, and Henry Shields, were black tenant farmers who were initially denied an attorney and were tortured by police until they confessed. Though their statements were the only evidence linking the sharecroppers to the crime, they were convicted and sentenced to be hanged within a week. A series of appeals took the case, *Brown v. Mississippi*, all the way to the Supreme Court. In 1936, the justices unanimously reversed the convictions and outlawed coerced confessions.

It is not unusual for plaintiffs to admit to crimes they have not committed. According to the Innocence Project, roughly 27 percent of those who have been convicted of a crime and later exonerated by DNA evidence confessed to something they didn't actually do.

Forced to Lie

Psychologists divide false confessions into three categories.

COERCED-COMPLIANT CONFESSIONS. These are instances where the innocent person is compelled to confess by outside pressures, such as police interrogation.

WHO KNEW?

In the early 1980s, Henry Lee Lucas was convicted of 11 murders, but he officially confessed to 600 more.

Fleeing the Great Fire of London, illustration, published in 1815

THE GREAT LONDON SCAPEGOAT

Watchmaker Robert Hubert claimed to have started this notorious and devastating fire. But did he really do it?

The Great Fire of London in 1666 destroyed about 80 percent of the city, left 100,000 homeless, and is thought to have killed thousands.

Robert Hubert, a mentally ill French watchmaker, came forward to take responsibility for the crime. Claiming to be an agent of the Pope, Hubert said he set the conflagration by throwing a bomb through a bakery window. Predominantly Protestant London was quick to turn the Catholic foreigner into a scapegoat, even though it became clear during the trial that his confession was suspect. It was established that he had never been near the bakery; that the bakery had no windows; and that he was physically incapable of throwing a bomb. Hubert hadn't even arrived in England until two days after the fire started.

But the Frenchman stuck to his story, and an eager jury found him guilty. After he was hanged, the Earl of Clarendon, Lord Chancellor of England, who was responsible for the court system, noted that "neither the judges, nor any present at the trial did believe him guilty; but that he was a poor distracted wretch, weary of his life, and chose to part with it."

Interrogation tactics such as intimidation can produce false confessions.

The coerced-compliant confession is the most common type of false admission, though reasons for cooperation vary. Sometimes, the accused doesn't have legal representation. Subjected to rigorous questioning, discomfort, or psychological abuse for hours without a break, he may confess just to put an end to the agony, or out of stress or confusion.

This confessor might be falling for a bluff—a claim that someone has implicated him in the crime, that evidence has been found in his home, or that other incriminating facts have come to light. Similarly, this kind of suspect might react to interrogators who threaten a harsh sentence; or might confess to win leniency for another, more serious crime that they actually have committed.

The inexperienced, the young, the mentally disabled, and the mentally ill may confess simply in an effort to live up to the expectations of police officers and other authority figures. Similarly, adults who are ill-informed, poorly educated, or even intoxicated often can be easily manipulated into making false, self-implicating statements that they don't fully understand.

VOLUNTARY CONFESSIONS. Here, the suspect might be motivated by allegiance to a loved one or an organization, or might have been paid to take the blame.

The voluntary confessor doesn't need to be persuaded. Typically, he cooperates enthusiastically, without pressure from law enforcement. Voluntary confessions are sometimes meant to draw attention away from an actual criminal—perhaps to protect a guilty loved one. Other voluntary confessions have unconscious psychological roots: On rare occasions, an innocent person confesses falsely in an attempt to atone for some other perceived or real wrongdoing.

Some false confessors pretend to have committed a crime, often a high-profile, unsolved murder, in a bid for notoriety. Forensic psychologists attribute this behavior to a pathological craving for attention so strong that it transcends fear of punishment. These impostors are usually quickly unmasked.

COERCED-INTERNALIZED CONFESSIONS. In such cases, an innocent person persuades himself that he is guilty of the crime, sometimes even falsely "remembering" it. Confessions of this type are relatively rare and are extremely difficult to disprove in court.

AND JUSTICE FOR ALL?

WHEN A COUSIN OF THE KENNEDYS IN JAIL FOR MURDER WAS FREED FOR A POSSIBLE RETRIAL, SOME CRITICS CALLED FOUL.

WHO KNEW?

In 2013, teen Ethan Couch was tried for causing a drunken crash that killed four. An expert witness testified that Couch was a victim of "affluenza," or living a privileged life. He pleaded guilty to intoxication manslaughter.

Advocates for social justice have long complained that America has a two-tiered legal system: one for the elite who can afford the best defense lawyers money can buy, and another for everyone else. In this view, criminals from powerful or well-to-do backgrounds lead such privileged lives that they feel the rules don't apply to them. In addition to acting as if they were born with a get-out-of-jail-free card, these lawbreakers are often treated that way.

A Question of Privilege

Michael Skakel today is the middle-aged nephew of Ethel Skakel Kennedy and Sen. Robert F. Kennedy. Growing up in the wealthy town of Greenwich, Connecticut, Skakel led a cosseted life, but struggled in the shadow of his abusive and alcoholic father, according to media accounts. He allegedly began using alcohol and drugs as a teen and soon landed in serious trouble.

In 1975, when Skakel was 15 years old, his next-door neighbor and friend Martha Moxley, also 15, was found dead. An autopsy indicated that Moxley had been bludgeoned with a golf club that was traced to the Skakel home.

Michael Skakel allegedly confessed to two friends that he was the killer and bragged, "I'm going to get away with murder. I'm a Kennedy." At different times, the teen was investigated as a suspect, and so was his brother Thomas, the last person to be seen with Moxley. But neither young man was arrested, and many complained that the Skakels, with their link to America's most famous family, had been afforded special treatment.

A New Investigation

A number of books published on the crime as well as media attention prompted a new investigation, launched in 1991. This time, Michael Skakel was arrested, charged, and convicted of Moxley's murder. Again, claims surfaced suggesting that Skakel received special treatment at the hands of the criminal justice system.

In one instance, the *Hartford Courant* ran a story while Skakel was in prison awaiting sentencing. According to the account, Skakel, in violation of prison policy, was admitted into treatment programs without waiting time and was allowed direct contact with visitors. Michael Sherman, Skakel's lawyer at the time, denied the claims. "Sometimes the system has to be a little flexible, but it isn't bending over to accommodate him," he said. Some months later, in January 2003, Skakel's cousin Robert F. Kennedy Jr. wrote his own article, for the *Atlantic Monthly,* claiming that Skakel had been railroaded by the media and wrongly convicted.

Michael Skakel stands outside a courthouse in Stamford, Connecticut, on November 21, 2013, after being released following a hearing.

Throughout his time in prison, Skakel maintained his innocence but lost a series of attempts to gain new hearings and parole. In October 2013, he finally convinced a Connecticut court to grant him a new trial on grounds that his representation in 2002 was inadequate. He was released on bond of $1.2 million.

RICH MAN, POOR MAN

Do the wealthy kill differently?

Killers of different social classes tend to murder in recognizable patterns, according to a 1979 study by researchers Edward Green and Russell P. Wakefield published in the *Journal of Criminal Law and Criminology*.

PATTERN ONE	PATTERN TWO
Killer most often white male over 30	Killer most often black male under 30
Crime usually premeditated	Crime often spontaneous
73% are intrafamilial homicides	24.7% are intrafamilial homicides
27% are followed by suicide of perpetrator	0.8% to 9% are followed by suicide of perpetrator
Method mainly shooting; rarely stabbing	Method may be shooting or stabbing
Alcohol rarely a factor	Over half are alcohol related
Usually takes place between 8 PM and 2 AM	Usually takes place between 8 PM and 2 AM
Most likely to occur at the victim's home	May occur at the victim's home or elsewhere

WHAT HAPPENED?

THE ANGUISH OF THE COLD CASE HAUNTS FAMILIES AND LAW ENFORCEMENT ALIKE.

The lack of closure in unsolved cases can be devastating to those left behind, but about 6,000 murders remain unsolved in the United States and there are about 87,000 missing persons. Here are some haunting examples.

Family and friends of slain NBA basketball player Lorenzen Wright grieve during a memorial service at the FedExForum in Memphis, Tennessee, 2010.

A Fallen Star

The words in the 911 recording are difficult to make out, but the danger is unmistakable. On July 19, 2010, emergency operators near Memphis, Tennessee, got a disturbing call: A barely audible shout from an unidentified man, a volley of gunfire, and then nothing. Nine days later, a bullet-riddled body was found in a wooded area in Memphis—the location from which the call was placed. The victim was Lorenzen Wright, a 13-year NBA veteran who had most recently played with the Cleveland Cavaliers. He had been missing, but his disappearance had not been connected to the 911 call made from his cell phone.

Talented, handsome, and active in his community, Wright was last seen visiting his ex-wife and their six children; he often took a shortcut from their house through the area in which his remains were found. Early on, there were rumors that Wright was somehow connected to a dangerous drug kingpin. But as of 2013, the Memphis Police Department had hit a dead end, and to this day his murder remains a mystery.

The Washington, D.C., townhouse where lawyer Robert Wone was killed

Conspiracy Theory

Who killed Robert Wone? On August 2, 2006, the 32-year-old lawyer from suburban Virginia was staying overnight at a townhouse near his office in Washington, D.C. It belonged to Joseph Price, a friend of Wone's from college, who lived there with two other men. Wone had worked late and arranged to stay with Price instead of returning to his home about 20 miles away.

A little before midnight, one of the housemates, Victor Zaborsky, called 911. Responders arrived to find Wone, whom they later determined had been restrained, drugged, sexually assaulted, and stabbed to death. Price, Zaborsky, and the third housemate, Dylan Ward, maintained that Wone must have been killed by an intruder.

Police determined there was no evidence of a break in. The housemates seemed obvious suspects. But in the end, Price, Zaborsky, and Ward were tried for obstruction of justice and conspiracy—and found not guilty.

The Teens Who Disappeared

Bonnie Bickwit and Mitchel Weiser were young and in love when they vanished in July 1974. Bonnie, 15, was working at a summer camp in Narrowsburg, New York, a few hours from her Brooklyn home. Mitchel, 16, her boyfriend and a fellow student at a Brooklyn high school for gifted students, was home for the summer. Unbeknownst to their parents, the two had made plans to meet up in Narrowsburg and hitchhike 75 miles to the town of Watkins Glen for a concert featuring the Grateful Dead and the Allman Brothers. Mitchel picked up Bonnie at camp, and the two set off for the concert. It is not known if they made it to their destination, but they never came back.

Did they meet with foul play? Did they have an accident? Did they vanish deliberately? The teens came from stable, middle-class backgrounds and were bright and relatively happy. Authorities assumed they ran away together, but in 2000 a man came forward to say that he had seen the teens get swept away down a river as they splashed around for fun. More than 25 years after the incident, though, the witness could not remember which river, and the lead went cold.

The couple's families still hold out hope for their return. Mitchel's family maintains a listing in the Brooklyn phone book in case Mitchel should ever want to call them. A website, MitchelandBonnie.com, keeps their story alive.

A police detective in front of cold case files in a police department basement

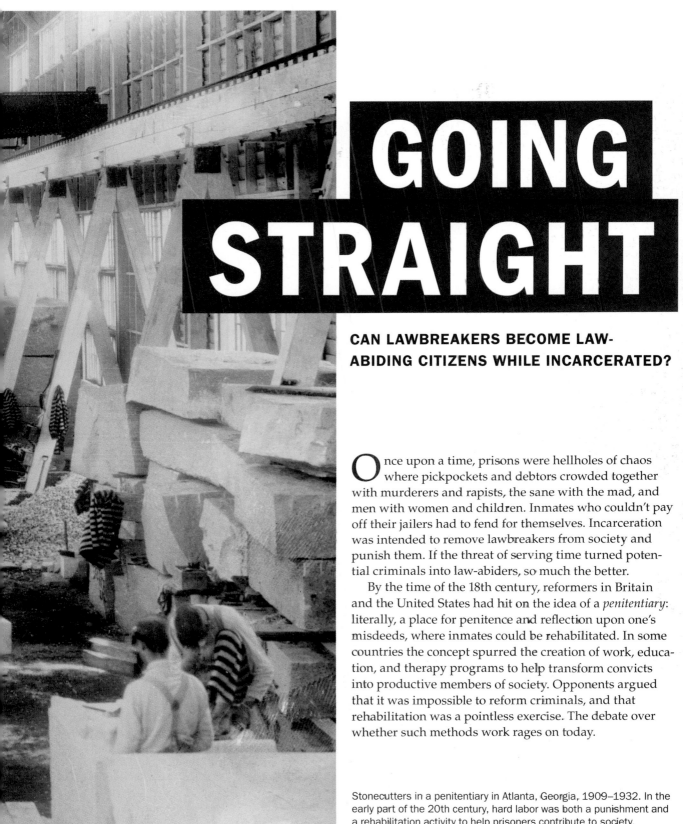

GOING STRAIGHT

CAN LAWBREAKERS BECOME LAW-ABIDING CITIZENS WHILE INCARCERATED?

Once upon a time, prisons were hellholes of chaos where pickpockets and debtors crowded together with murderers and rapists, the sane with the mad, and men with women and children. Inmates who couldn't pay off their jailers had to fend for themselves. Incarceration was intended to remove lawbreakers from society and punish them. If the threat of serving time turned potential criminals into law-abiders, so much the better.

By the time of the 18th century, reformers in Britain and the United States had hit on the idea of a *penitentiary*: literally, a place for penitence and reflection upon one's misdeeds, where inmates could be rehabilitated. In some countries the concept spurred the creation of work, education, and therapy programs to help transform convicts into productive members of society. Opponents argued that it was impossible to reform criminals, and that rehabilitation was a pointless exercise. The debate over whether such methods work rages on today.

Stonecutters in a penitentiary in Atlanta, Georgia, 1909–1932. In the early part of the 20th century, hard labor was both a punishment and a rehabilitation activity to help prisoners contribute to society.

As part of the rehabilitation program at a prison near Pisa, Italy, the inmates operate Fortezza Medicea, an exclusive restaurant for the public. Workers include a sommelier and a pianist in for murder.

Lifestyle of Crime

Hard-line law-and-order proponents contend that recidivism—an offender's relapse into crime—is evidence that criminals are incapable of changing their ways. In the United States, research studies show that up to 53 percent of arrested males and 39 percent of arrested females end up re-incarcerated.

In contrast, advocates of rehabilitation maintain that correctional systems themselves are the problem. Life on the inside is violent and corrupt, and crime prolifer-ates. Many inmates are forced to hone a range of unsavory skills, and return to society more dangerous than ever. Ex-cons face steep challenges in employment, housing, and family life, and must rely on criminal knowledge and contacts to get by. Many end up back in prison.

Getting to the Root of Relapse

Despite fundamentally different ideas between hardliners and progressives on the goals of the penal system in general, the reduction of repeat offenses is an objective that both sides can agree on. To this end, recent research emphasizes the need to distinguish among the kinds of approaches that have been used, in order to more effectively evaluate what really works.

Punitive measures, like electronic monitoring of ex-cons, strict probation, and "scared straight" programs for juvenile offenders, wield the threat of punishment in an attempt to deter individuals from turning to crime. However, studies have concluded that these methods have generally not had any significant impact on the rate of recidivism.

Proactive efforts, like in-prison GED and education programs, vocational training, and life-skill training, seek to instill inmates with a basic understanding of how to function effectively in society, manage money, and be a good parent, among other skills. They have shown a modest amount of success overall, resulting in a decrease in the recidivism rate of 10 percent, as compared to offenders who have received no rehabilitation.

So what does work? The most effective strategies so far have focused on finding accurate predictors of the problem—such as antisocial values, associating exclusively with people who view crime as an acceptable or admirable way of life, and psychological issues such as lack of impulse control. With an eye toward correcting these specific indicators, research suggests that tailoring rehabilitative efforts to offenders based on their skills, IQ, and other particular needs is the way

to go. Treatment includes cognitive-behavioral therapy to train them in more positive ways of thinking and acting, as an alternative to the antisocial behaviors and criminal values. This approach demands more experienced staff and specialized training, as well as follow-up care after the offender has finished the program, and is expensive. However, studies have shown this type of targeted solution to decrease rates of repeat offenses by around 25 percent.

Prison records for Robert Stroud, who became known as the Bird Man of Alcatraz.

BIRDMAN BEHIND BARS

Violent psychopath Robert Stroud died in Alcatraz, but his story flew free in a popular novel and movie

One famous, semi-rehabilitated convict was Robert Stroud, also known as the Birdman of Alcatraz. Diagnosed as an incurable and violent psychopath, Stroud began serving a life sentence for multiple murders in 1909 and spent most of his sentence in solitary confinement. After rescuing three abandoned sparrow chicks and fostering them to adulthood in his cell, Stroud's curiosity was sparked. He went on to raise and care for almost 300 canaries and to teach himself ornithology.

From prison, Stroud published two well-regarded books about bird diseases, discovered a cure for a fatal avian infection, and ran a successful business selling birds and bird medicines. His story fascinated the outside world and Stroud became a celebrity. But he never was truly rehabilitated, and remained aggressive, defiant, and detested by his fellow convicts and prison staff until his death in 1963. The movie *The Birdman of Alcatraz*, starring Burt Lancaster, offered a fictionalized account of Stroud's life. Although it came out a year before Stroud died, he was never allowed to see it or to read the novel upon which it was based.

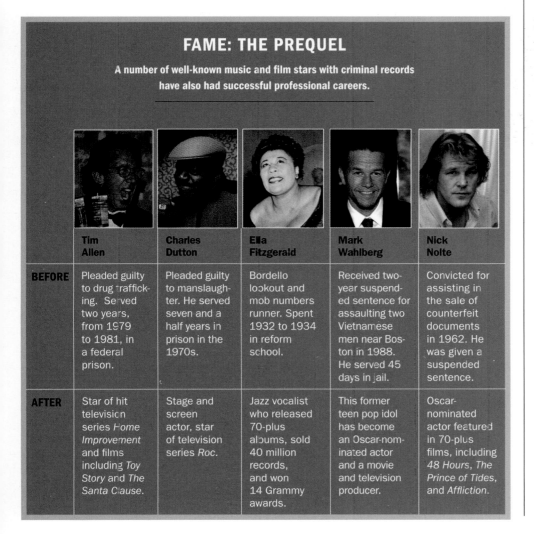

FAME: THE PREQUEL

A number of well-known music and film stars with criminal records have also had successful professional careers.

	Tim Allen	Charles Dutton	Ella Fitzgerald	Mark Wahlberg	Nick Nolte
BEFORE	Pleaded guilty to drug trafficking. Served two years, from 1979 to 1981, in a federal prison.	Pleaded guilty to manslaughter. He served seven and a half years in prison in the 1970s.	Bordello lookout and mob numbers runner. Spent 1932 to 1934 in reform school.	Received two-year suspended sentence for assaulting two Vietnamese men near Boston in 1988. He served 45 days in jail.	Convicted for assisting in the sale of counterfeit documents in 1962. He was given a suspended sentence.
AFTER	Star of hit television series *Home Improvement* and films including *Toy Story* and *The Santa Clause*.	Stage and screen actor, star of television series *Roc*.	Jazz vocalist who released 70-plus albums, sold 40 million records, and won 14 Grammy awards.	This former teen pop idol has become an Oscar-nominated actor and a movie and television producer.	Oscar-nominated actor featured in 70-plus films, including *48 Hours*, *The Prince of Tides*, and *Affliction*.

BAD GUYS GONE GOOD

REFORMED CRIMINALS CAN BE THE MOST EFFECTIVE CHAMPIONS OF JUSTICE— PERHAPS BECAUSE THEY UNDERSTAND THE IMPULSE AS WELL AS THE TECHNIQUES.

In the 2002 movie *Catch Me If You Can*, Leonardo DiCaprio stars as a con artist who poses as an airline pilot, a doctor, and a criminal prosecutor to make millions of dollars, all before he's old enough to vote. It's not just the work of some screenwriter's imagination: The story is based on the experiences of real-life grifter-turned-crimestopper Frank William Abagnale Jr.

One of the most notorious impostors ever, Abagnale pulled off his first identity switch in 1964, at age 16, posing as a first officer for Pan American airlines. Over the course of two years, Abagnale backed up the captains on more than 250 flights and logged one million flight miles, even though by his own admission he "couldn't fly a kite." He next signed on as a pediatrician at a hospital in Atlanta, Georgia, for a year, relying on interns to do most of his work. Then he put together a counterfeit transcript from Harvard Law School, passed the

Louisiana Bar exam, legitimately, and went to work for the state's attorney general.

Abagnale eventually served time in France, Sweden, and the United States before agreeing to help the FBI catch check forgers in exchange for early parole. He now runs a financial-fraud consultancy firm and works with the FBI. He is just one in a long line of felons who've turned their bad-guy ways into lucrative careers on the other side of the law.

A Very Expert Witness

Who knows better than a felon how a felon's mind works? Forensic psychologist Paul Fauteck's public

Frank Abagnale's life inspired the movie *Catch Me If You Can*.

school education ended at 15 when he was caught stealing from classmates. Charges on weapons, auto theft, burglary, smuggling, and counterfeiting followed, until Fauteck decided to reinvent himself at 24, while serving time in a federal prison.

Upon his release, Fauteck worked at a number of jobs before returning to school and eventually earned his master's degree, in 1976. He practiced psychotherapy in Chicago and over time gravitated to work as a forensic psychologist and expert witness. In 1992, Fauteck was granted a presidential pardon from George H. W. Bush. He has since become a self-help guru to ex-convicts and a prominent advocate of prisoner rehabilitation programs.

Conquering Son of Kings

Before he was out of his teens, Frizzell Gray (b. 1948) had fathered five children and landed in jail in Baltimore more than a few

times. At 23, Gray decided to make something of his life and returned to school. He eventually graduated from Morgan State University with high honors and earned a master's degree from Johns Hopkins. In the early 1970s, Frizzell Gray changed his name to Kweisi Mfume, which translates as "Conquering Son of Kings." Mfume went on to serve on the Baltimore City Council, win election to Congress for five terms, and serve as president of the NAACP. In 2013, he was named the new chair of the Board of Regents of his alma mater, Morgan State University.

Father of Criminology

From the cast of *CSI* to police around the world, the modern-day detective owes a debt to a 19th-century hoodlum, Eugène François Vidocq.

Born in France in 1775, Vidocq fell in with a rough crowd as a teen and became a petty thief. He enlisted in the army, then deserted it, returning to a life of crime

Frenchman Eugène François Vidocq founded what is considered the first private detective agency.

as a swindler, forger, and duelist. Vidocq spent time in prison and on the lam, but when he was arrested at age 34, he offered the police his services as an undercover informant. Within a few years, Vidocq had set up a plainclothes brigade that helped reduce the Parisian crime rate. The model was soon adopted in cities all over France, and in 1833 he founded what is now considered the world's first private detective agency.

Vidocq often hired ex-convicts who knew their way around the criminal underworld, and introduced tactics such as criminal profiling, ballistics, and crime scene investigation. He was among the first crime fighters to set up a forensics laboratory.

Vidocq's exploits inspired Victor Hugo's Jean Valjean and Inspector Javert in *Les Misérables* (1862), as well as the detective in Edgar Allan Poe's *The Murders in the Rue Morgue* (1841), thought to be the first detective story ever written.

AMERICAN INJUSTICE

WHAT HAPPENS WHEN THE LEGAL SYSTEM GETS A VERDICT WRONG?

Family members greet James Bain, center, outside the Polk County Courthouse in Florida after his release, 2009.

James Bain was sentenced to life in prison for the 1974 kidnapping and rape of a little boy in Florida. It was a horrible, dehumanizing crime, and the sentence appeared appropriate—except for one thing: Bain didn't do it. He had an alibi and no criminal record. Police began questioning Bain, then 19, after the victim's uncle implicated him.

Human beings are fallible, the scales of justice aren't always balanced, and in spite of the sophistication of the U.S. justice system, innocent men and women end up in prison. Studies estimate that between 40,000 and 100,000 innocent people are currently behind bars, some of them on death row.

One organization working to change that is the Innocence Project, a New York nonprofit that uses DNA profiling to exonerate the wrongly convicted. Founded by two defense lawyers in 1992, the group and its spinoffs have helped to free more than 300 innocent prisoners nationwide. In 40 percent of those cases, the DNA profile used to help overturn the wrongful conviction also led to the discovery of the true perpetrator.

Genetic "Fingerprint"

In DNA profiling, a sample of an individual's cells is collected via a swab of the inside of his or her cheek, or from other bodily fluids or tissue samples. The genetic material within the cells is then analyzed and compared with DNA evidence found at a crime scene. Because everyone's DNA is different (except in the case of identical twins), DNA profiling, though not foolproof, is considered the most reliable way to identify or rule out the perpetrator of the crime.

The Innocence Project's work with DNA takes aim at a flawed legal system, one that they point out is stacked against certain races and socioeconomic groups. More than 60 percent of the Innocence Project's exonerees are black; most are also poor. The organization has issued recommendations to help make the system more foolproof, including the videotaping of interrogation sessions and the revamping of police lineup procedures so that they are conducted more fairly.

Justice (Re)done

James Bain was one of the Innocence Project's success stories. Bain had unsuccessfully requested to have his case reopened five times when the Innocence Project of Florida stepped in to help him get the DNA testing he had asked for. (The perpetrator's bodily fluids had been found

WHO KNEW?
Only 5 to 10 percent of criminal cases include physical evidence that can be used for DNA testing.

Huy Dao of the Innocence Project stands among files of prisoners hoping to be exonerated.

MISTAKES WERE MADE

The most common reasons for wrongful convictions

Witness errors play a part in almost three-quarters of wrongful convictions, according to the Innocence Project. Witnesses generally don't make these mistakes on purpose; it's just that memories can be faulty. Here are other common causes for faulty convictions:

→ **Unreliable or phony forensic evidence**

→ **False confessions**

→ **Negligence, fraud, or misconduct by the police or prosecutors**

→ **Bad information from informants**

→ **Ineffective, overburdened, or incompetent defense lawyers**

on the victim's clothing in 1974, but DNA technology did not exist back then.) The DNA profile showed that Bain could not have committed the crime, and in 2009 a Florida judge signed an order to set Bain free.

In all, Bain had spent 35 years in prison, but he told a college audience in 2011 that he was moving forward. "What can I do about yesterday?" said Bain, who had recently married and, at 57, become a father. "I can only live for tomorrow."

WRONGED MAN

**He spent 16 years doing time for a murder he didn't commit.
Now free, Jeffrey Deskovic is trying to change the system.**

Jeffrey Deskovic

Jeffrey Deskovic was only 17 in 1990, when he was sent to maximum-security prison for raping and killing a 15-year-old girl. DNA evidence found at the scene wasn't a match to Deskovic. But the jury convicted him of killing Angela Correa, who had been a high school classmate at Peekskill High School in New York, based on a false confession.

Deskovic said the police coerced him into admitting to the crime. "I made up a story based on information they had given me during the course of the interrogation," Deskovic said in a 2013 interview. "By the police officer's own testimony, by the end of the interrogation I was on the floor crying uncontrollably in what they described as a fetal position." Deskovic filed seven appeals but wasn't freed until 2006, after the Innocence Project got involved. The DNA at the crime scene was retested and found to match a man named Steven Cunningham, who confessed. Since Deskovic's release, he has earned a master's degree in criminal justice and established the Jeffrey Deskovic Foundation for Justice. He has partially funded the group with some of the settlement he received for the wrongful conviction.

CRIME AND PRISONS IN AMERICA

The United States has one of the largest prison populations in the world, but the majority of the states have reduced their incarceration rates in recent years. Thirty-one states recorded overall declines in imprisonment rates between 2007 and 2012, with 15 of those states reporting drops of 10 percent or more, according to a 2013 Pew Charitable Trusts report.

The decline in incarceration rates fits into a broader decrease in crime rates across the United States. Between 1991 and 2012, the crime rate in the U.S. has fallen 45 percent, according to a 2014 Pew Charitable Trust report. But trends in incarceration rates and crime rates do not always dovetail. For example, crime rates in both Arizona and Maryland fell 21 percent from 2007 to 2012. But over the same period, Arizona's imprisonment rate grew 4 percent while Maryland's declined 11 percent.

STATES WHERE RATE OF IMPRISONMENT DROPPED 2007–2012*

Hawaii –20%

Massachusetts –20%

Connecticut –19%

Rhode Island –19%

New Jersey –16%

New York –14%

South Carolina –13%

Nevada –12%

Michigan –12%

Alaska –11%

Maryland –11%

Texas –11%

Wisconsin –10%

STATES WHERE RATE OF IMPRISONMENT INCREASED 2007–2012*

West Virginia +12%

Pennsylvania +10%

Illinois +8 %

Alabama +5%

Louisiana +5%

South Dakota +5%

BEHIND BARS

Some statistics about the U.S. prison population in 2008–09, according to the U.S. Department of Justice.

There were nearly 2.3 million inmates. The U.S. housed a quarter of the world's prison population. Approximately 3,250 U.S. inmates were on death row. More than 140,000 U.S. inmates were serving life sentences.

The average U.S. prison sentence was 5 years. 1 in 104 Americans were behind bars, but rates varied by racial background:
1 in 106 were white men
1 in 36 were Hispanic men
1 in 15 were African-American men

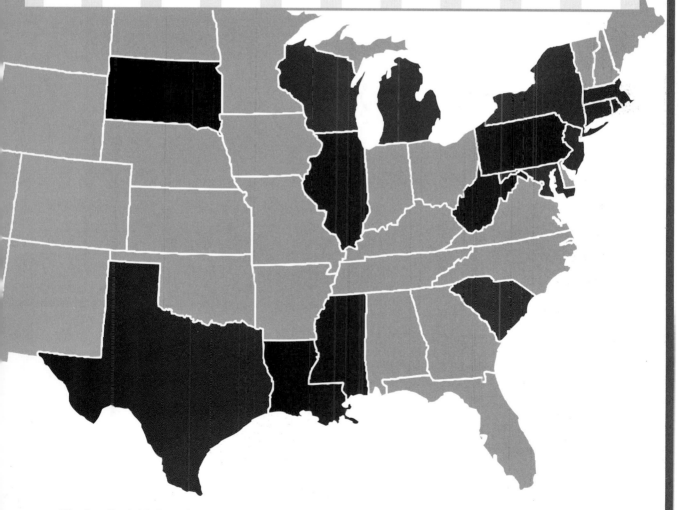

SOURCES: *The Pew Charitable Trusts reports, 2014, 2013. The United States Department of Justice; bjs.gov.

CLEANING UP THE SCENE

THE GRISLY TASK OF DECONTAMINATING A CRIME SCENE OFTEN FALLS TO WORKERS WITH HAZMAT GEAR AND STRONG STOMACHS.

A decontamination crew dressed in hazmat suits stands outside a crime scene.

THE WOMEN IN THE TYVEK SUITS

Who are the real people who do this kind of work?

The 2008 movie *Sunshine Cleaning* took a fictional look at a pair of sisters who start a crime-scene decontamination business. The film was inspired by a 2001 National Public Radio profile of Theresa Borst and Stacy Haney, owners of Bio Clean near Seattle, Washington. The two met in the 1990s. Both were married moms; Borst had been a house cleaner, while Haney was a Boeing engineer who'd been laid off. Both were volunteers for Shonomish County Search and Rescue, an emergency service that helps find lost hikers. After hearing in a lecture that crime scene cleanup most often fell to family members, the two got hazardous-waste certified and launched their company.

"From taking something that looks so horrific and putting it back like it once was, plus cleaner, you know, we feel good about that," Borst told *All Things Considered*.

The emotional aftermath of a crime lasts a lifetime, but in the hours immediately following the collection of evidence and questioning of witnesses, someone has to clean up. That responsibility may fall to the victim's landlord or bereaved friends and family. Or, relatives may call one of the private companies that specialize in Crime and Trauma Scene Decontamination—*CTS decon* for short.

CTS decon is a unique type of cleaning that involves handling hazardous waste as well as dealing compassionately with distraught clients. The job is not for everyone. Often, decon technicians have had experience as nurses or emergency medical technicians or have served in the military. They've developed coping tools and are able to detach emotionally from what they're seeing and doing.

Much of it is quite gruesome. A CTS decon crew might be called in to restore a home, office, or car after a homicide or assault. More commonly, they are scrubbing up after someone died alone at home and was not discovered for days or weeks. Technicians contain, remove, and properly dispose of blood and other bodily fluids. They may have to remove bone fragments from walls or collect body parts left behind by the medical examiner. And all of it must be done with the utmost discretion and care, to protect the health and safety of the living.

Germs and Poisons

The job can be dangerous. Blood, officially classified as a biohazard, can carry pathogens such as HIV and hepatitis. The chemicals used by investigators to detect fingerprints or tiny amounts of blood can leave a toxic residue. If the crew happens to be decontaminating a methamphetamine lab, they're exposed to extremely poisonous chemicals that can be absorbed through the skin.

To protect themselves, technicians routinely wear full-body coveralls, gloves, boots, and respirators; use hospital-grade disinfectants; and sometimes clean with hands-free equipment such as power sprayers.

Why would anyone go into this line of work? For starters, the pay is good, especially for a job that does not require a college education. CTS decon companies may charge $250 or more an hour, plus additional fees. Individual technicians can make as much as $80,000 a year. But there's an emotional component, too. Most CTS decon workers view themselves as "second responders" who continue the work the police began while helping bereaved families begin to heal.

Officers carry the remains of a victim who had been aboard the Malaysia Airlines flight shot down over Ukraine in 2014.

NO SUCH PLACE

Sometimes the only way to rid a property of its horrible past is to destroy it.

Certain killings are so upsetting and so widely publicized that the site where they took place becomes tainted. These crime scenes have been razed.

THE SHARON TATE HOUSE

The French Country-style home at 10050 Cielo Drive in Benedict Canyon, Los Angeles, was the site of the chilling Manson Family murder of actress Sharon Tate and four others in 1969. The house remained standing for a while after the murders and Trent Reznor from the band Nine Inch Nails rented it in the early 1990s. It was demolished in 1994 and replaced with a new home and a new address: 10066 Cielo Drive.

THE HEAVEN'S GATE HOUSE

In 1997, the leader and 38 members of the Heaven's Gate cult attempted to reach an alien spacecraft by committing mass suicide. They were found in a 9,200-square-foot mansion at 18241 Colina Norte, Rancho Santa Fe, California. Afterward, the neighbors in this wealthy area bought the home for pennies on the dollar, had it razed, and changed the name of the street to Paseo Victoria.

JOHN WAYNE GACY'S HOUSE

The 1970s rapist and serial killer tortured and murdered more than 30 victims at his modest ranch-style home at 8213 West Summerdale Avenue in Des Plaines, Illinois, and stored 29 of the bodies in the house's crawl space. The property was demolished in 1979 and the lot remained vacant until the late 1980s. Now, there's a new house there with the address 8215 West Summerdale.

Citizens found guilty of treason in ancient Rome were often beheaded.

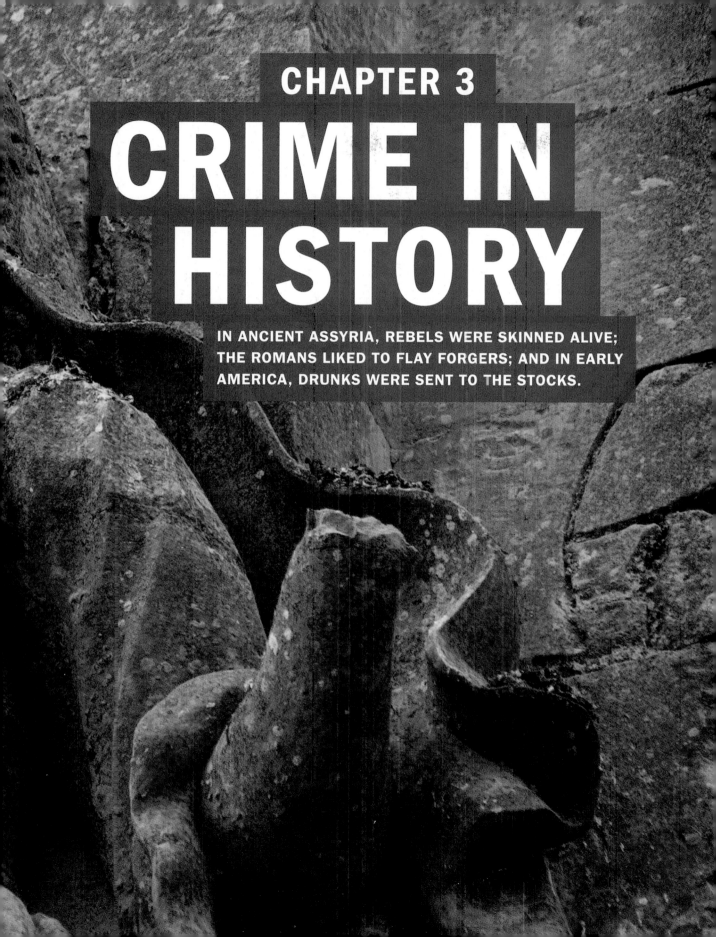

CHAPTER 3
CRIME IN HISTORY

IN ANCIENT ASSYRIA, REBELS WERE SKINNED ALIVE; THE ROMANS LIKED TO FLAY FORGERS; AND IN EARLY AMERICA, DRUNKS WERE SENT TO THE STOCKS.

THE ANCIENT ART OF MURDER

SERIAL KILLERS HAVE EXISTED FOR THOUSANDS OF YEARS.

Although the concept of serial killing is a relatively recent phenomenon, mass slaughter has been a fixture throughout human history. In Biblical times, there were bloodthirsty rulers like King Herod of Judea, who ordered the massacre of all male children under age two in the kingdom, fearing the birth of a usurper. The Greeks, Romans, and Mayans sacrificed men, women, and children to deities, usually for the purpose of nourishing or appeasing them. During the Iron Age, the Celts are thought to have sacrificed prisoners, sometimes for divination purposes: The victim would be stabbed and his death throes scrutinized for clues to the future, according to one account.

Rome's Serial Murderess

In a culture that openly celebrated violence—gladiators fought to the death and Christians were fed to ravenous dogs—it was difficult to achieve fame for murder in ancient Rome. But herbalist and professional poisoner Locusta of Gaul attained that notoriety, going down in history as one of the first recorded serial killers.

Locusta is thought to have murdered for personal pleasure and profit, helping clients eliminate rivals and family members. One well-known patron was Agrippina the Younger, the fourth wife of Emperor Claudius. Evidence suggests that Agrippina, who wanted her son Nero to replace Claudius as ruler, hired Locusta in 54 AD to kill her husband. Locusta fed Claudius poisonous mushrooms, killing him and propelling young Nero to the throne. Nero himself is believed to have had Locusta murder his stepbrother Britannicus. Her payment? Full pardon for previous offenses, among other gifts.

The Blueblood

Gilles de Rais was a nobleman and warrior who fought alongside Joan of Arc in the 1400s, and even served in her special guard. He also lived lavishly and was a patron of the arts. But Rais also may have been the most notorious serial killer of the medieval era. An alleged Satanist who engaged in sorcery and wild orgies, Rais was accused of abduct-

Gilles de Rais may have been the medieval era's most notorious serial killer.

ing, sexually abusing, and murdering more than 140 children. When he was arrested in 1440, Rais was tortured until he confessed to the crimes of sodomy, homicide, and heresy. He was executed by hanging and burning.

The Bandit Killer

In 1557, Peter Niers, a roving bandit and reputed practitioner of the black arts, was arrested in Gersbach, Germany. After being tortured, he confessed to 75 murders, only to escape in 1577. When he was recognized at an inn a few years later, Niers was arrested again and charged with 544 murders, including those of 24 pregnant women whose fetuses he is said to have ripped from the womb to invoke evil spirits. His execution included being burned with hot oil, tied to a wagon wheel, bludgeoned, and being drawn and quartered.

Emperor Nero with the body of his mother, Agrippina, who was assassinated on Nero's orders. Painting by Antonio Rizzi, c. late 1800s.

MUSICAL NUMBERS

Peter Niers and other killers have inspired everything from folk ballads to rock tunes.

Musician/Band	Song	Inspiration
Elliott Smith Indie singer-songwriter	*Son of Sam*, 2000	**David Berkowitz**, aka Son of Sam, who shot 13 people, killing six, in New York City in 1976 and 1977
Pearl Jam Rock band	*Dirty Frank*, 1992	**Jeffrey Dahmer**, who murdered and dismembered 17 males in Ohio and Wisconsin from 1978 to 1991
Sufjan Stevens Indie singer-songwriter	*John Wayne Gacy Jr.*, 2005	**John Wayne Gacy**, who tortured and murdered more than 30 males between 1972 and 1978
Nick Cave and the Bad Seeds Post-punk band	*Jack the Ripper*, 1992	**Jack the Ripper**, the still-unidentified serial murderer who killed at least 12 women in London in 1888
Jane's Addiction Rock band	*Ted, Just Admit It*, 1988	**Ted Bundy**, who tortured and murdered at least 36 young women in several states in the 1970s

Priest offering the heart taken from a living human victim to the Aztec sun god and god of war, Huitzilopochtli.

RITES AND WRONGS

Most human sacrifices were offered to the gods in exchange for some form of divine intervention, such as a fertile growing season.

→ **The Egyptians.** The First Dynasty pharaohs (c. 2950–2775 BC) were buried in tombs, surrounded by servants, artisans, and other courtiers whose lives were sacrificed to ensure that the rulers would have company and help in the afterlife.

→ **The Aztecs.** Aztec priests (c. 1345–1521 AD) offered up thousands of human sacrifices each year for the purpose of pleasing the sun god Huitzilopochtli. Their rituals included cutting out their sacrificial victims' still-beating hearts.

→ **The Maya.** These ancients (500 BC–900 AD) forced captive foes to play a symbolic ball game. At its conclusion, the captain or entire team was sometimes sacrificed, often by decapitation or disembowelment.

→ **The Carthaginians.** Some archaeologists have long suspected that Carthaginians (c. 800–146 BC) sacrificed their own infants as an offering to the gods, then buried them in special cemeteries known as *tophets*.

A CRUEL WORLD

ANCIENT ROME VALUED FAMILY, HONOR, RESPECT— AND BRUTAL PENALTIES FOR LAWBREAKERS.

Ancient Roman rulers were deadly serious when it came to punishing transgressors. Depending on their social status, thieves and forgers might be banished or lashed—no more than 40 times so as not to cause accidental death. Citizens found guilty of treason were summarily beheaded. Soldiers convicted of desertion and slaves who attempted to escape their owners were often whipped, then crucified. Anyone found guilty of parricide, or the killing of a family member, received the most gruesome punishment of all: They were blindfolded and beaten, then bound around the arms and feet. The convicts were then sewn into a sack with a viper, and thrown into the river. Later variations added a dog, a monkey, and a rooster for good measure.

Nero's Excesses

As time passed, emperors relied on ever crueler punishments, including torture for enemies of the state. When the first-century Emperor Nero suspected that Epicharis, a woman of ill repute, knew of an assassination conspiracy against him, he sent her repeatedly to the rack—a device that gradually pulled the limbs from its subject. He also began to use gruesome punishments and executions and as entertainment for the masses.

Nero is credited with popularizing the practice of *damnatio ad bestias*: tossing humans into an arena to fight bears, lions, or other wild animals. To punish Christians, whom he blamed for causing the Great Fire of 64 AD, Nero developed an even more heinous spectacle: He forced the faithful to don a *tunica molesta*, a garment covered in a flammable material such as pitch, wax, or naphtha. A soldier would ignite the tunic, turning the victim into a human fireball, while the public watched. In some cases, Nero used the practice to light parties he hosted.

Crime and Persecution

After an era of disorder, the military leader Diocletian took power in the third century, stabilized the empire, and introduced some of the most severe punishments in all of Rome for dissenting religious beliefs. In 296, Diocletian ordered Manicheans, who worshiped non-Roman deities, to be burned alive with their scriptures. Seven years later, he imposed edicts calling for the persecution of Christians. Thousands were eventually killed, including Diocletian's Christian butler, who was stripped, whipped, then had salt and vinegar poured in his wounds before he was boiled alive.

Diocletian's successor, Constantine, the first Christian emperor of Rome, had some strict ideas of his own. Tax evaders were beaten and tortured, while other small crimes were punished by maiming or eye gouging. Rapists were burned at the stake. Girls who ran away were also burned alive, and anyone who helped them could expect a mouthful of molten lead. Adultery was punishable by death, and Constantine even had his own son killed—allegedly for adultery and treason.

One way a criminal couldn't die under the Christian Constantine, however, was by crucifixion: he banned the practice in 337.

WHO KNEW?
Since slaves were considered property in ancient Rome, the laws dictating their punishment prevented inflicting any permanent damage on them. They were usually let off with a beating or branding for crimes.

Nero overseeing the torture of Christians by burning at the stake in ancient Rome

Execution using a Brazen Bull, a torture traced to 6th-century Sicily.

BRUTAL REALITY

Ancient cultures were savage in meting out punishment for lawbreakers.

→ **The Elephant.** A symbol of royal power in ancient Asia, the animal was trained to place a foot on the offender's head and slowly bear down, in order to inflict maximum suffering.

→ **The Brazen Bull.** First used in Sicily in the 6th century BC, a hollow bronze statue of a bull was constructed with a door in its abdomen. Victims were locked inside and a fire was set underneath, roasting them alive. Their screams were meant to replicate the sound of a bellowing bull.

→ **Flaying.** This practice dates to the 9th century BC, when the Assyrians used it on rebels to discourage uprisings. The object was to remove the victim's skin while he was still alive. Techniques varied: Hypatia of Alexandria, a female philosopher, was flayed by a mob with sharpened oyster shells in 415 AD.

→ **Impalement.** The Babylonian Code of Hammurabi from the 18th century BC specifies impalement for murderous adulteresses. This grisly method also found favor with the Romans, Chinese, Greeks, and Turks. It involved inserting a wooden stake into the nether regions, up through the victim's body, and out the mouth.

KINDER AND GENTLER GREEKS?

For Athenians, capital punishment could involve the cross, or a poisoned drink.

When the philosopher Socrates was sentenced to death for impiety and corrupting the young, the court allowed him to die by drinking a potion containing the poison hemlock.

It's not that the Greeks were skittish about using violence to punish wrongdoers. A Greek crucifixion involved clamping the offender to a board and tightening a collar around his neck until he strangled.

But in general, the rulers stuck to bloodless methods, to distinguish the acts of a civilized society from the savagery of war. Most capital convicts, like Socrates, were offered the option of drinking hemlock if they paid for the dose themselves. Those who refused sometimes escaped into exile. Socrates himself had an opportunity to do so, but accepted his punishment as part of a social contract. Ethical until the end, his last words were to a dear friend: "Crito, we owe a rooster to Asclepius. Please don't forget to pay the debt."

The Death of Socrates by Jacques-Louis David, c. 1787. He rejected the options of paying a fine or escaping from prison, and instead submitted to his sentence of death by drinking hemlock.

71

SINS OF OUR FOREFATHERS

LAWS IN COLONIAL AMERICA WERE HEAVILY INFLUENCED BY THE BIBLE. THAT MADE FOR SOME HARSH SENTENCES.

END OF LIFE

These crimes brought the death penalty in Plymouth Colony:

➜ Treason

➜ Willful murder

➜ Conversing with the Devil by way of witchcraft, conjuration, or the like

➜ Willful or purposeful burning of ships or houses

➜ Rape and other "crimes against nature," including bestiality, incest, sodomy, and adultery

WHO KNEW?

The Massachusetts Bay Colony enacted a law in 1646 stating that "a stubborn or rebellious son, of sufficient years and understanding" could be put to death.

To the earliest American settlers, there was little difference between crime and sin. Both Plymouth Colony, founded in 1620, and Massachusetts Bay Colony, established in 1630, modeled their criminal laws on Biblical tenets rather than English common law. Those rules, in turn, served as guidelines for later colonists who adapted them to suit their own settlements. Transgressions, no matter how small, were typically treated as crimes against society and God, and therefore deserving of the harshest penalties.

No Smiling During Church

Following the Ten Commandments, murder and theft were classified as punishable offenses. But so were such activities as lying, lewdness, and idleness. Some of the more obviously religious offenses included blasphemy, idolatry, and missing church services. Sabbath Day behavior even had its own set of laws: A couple in Connecticut was once fined for smiling during services; Plymouth children were penalized for playing with chalk at church. Sexual crimes such as adultery, bastardy, masturbation, and sodomy were particularly disturbing to church leadership.

While fines were imposed often, many sanctions were physical and public, intended to shame offenders and make examples of them so they would repent. Flogging was common, as was time in the stocks or pillory for infractions such as drunkenness, forgery, wife-beating, and fortune-telling. Branding was sometimes inflicted for the crimes of adultery or theft.

Murder was a capital crime. When Alice Bishop killed her 4-year-old daughter in 1648, she was sentenced to hanging. Barnett Davenport, who committed the first mass murder in the United States, in Washington, Connecticut, was lashed 40 times then hanged in nearby Litchfield.

As today, punishment was not always meted out uniformly or fairly. Although colonists of all ages and backgrounds—including magistrates and ministers—were known to engage in criminal activity, it was women, children, slaves, and the poor who were punished most often and most harshly. The abuses were legend, but none so much as the Salem Witch Trials of 1692.

The Landing of the Pilgrim Fathers (Charles Lucy, c. 1868) depicts the arrival of the *Mayflower* passengers in New England on November 19, 1620.

That Old Black Magic

When Reverend Samuel Parris moved to Salem in 1690, he brought with him his wife, daughters, niece, and a West Indian slave named Tituba. Two years later, after Parris's niece and one of his daughters started having spontaneous fits, they were taken to the village doctor, who concluded all three had been bewitched. Under pressure from the local magistrates, the girls, along with a friend who exhibited similar symptoms, accused Tituba of witchcraft. They also claimed that a poor, elderly neighbor and a local beggar had cast spells, thus setting off a wave of hysteria that spread from Salem to its surrounding villages. As accusations flew, authorities extracted false confessions through torture, and by the end of 1692, 150 men, women, and children had been charged with practicing witchcraft.

Of these, 28 were convicted and 19 were hanged. One man, Giles Corey, was pressed to death beneath a pile of rocks.

An artist's rendering of Tituba telling witchcraft tales to children in Salem, Massachusetts, 1690s

Stocks and pillories, which were often erected in a public square and locked a person's head, hands, and/or feet in place in a wooden frame, were common punitive devices.

TIME AND PUNISHMENT

Colonial-era lawbreakers paid a heavy price for their crimes, no matter how small.

Here are some ordinary citizens and their punishments.

→ **1638, Samuel Powell, Northampton, Virginia**

Crime: Stole a pair of breeches
Punishment: Forced to sit in the stocks for a day with a pair of pants around his neck

→ **1648, John Goneere, Maryland**

Crime: Perjury
Punishment: Nailed by the ears to a pillory, plus 20 lashes

→ **1656, Captain Kemble, Boston**

Crime: Kissing his wife on the Sabbath
Punishment: Two hours in the stocks

→ **1661, Anna, Mary, and Dorcas Bessey, Plymouth**

Crime: Disrespectful to a male relative
Punishment: Anna sentenced to pay a fine or be publicly whipped; Mary and Dorcas sent to the stocks

THE MOST DE

ADLY KILLERS

Kidnappings. Brainwashing. Torture. Cannibalism. From the unseemly to the unfathomable, acts such as these have defined the world's most notorious crimes. Society at large is both disturbed and fascinated by these cases. Perhaps it's the vicarious thrill of a shocking story that draws us in, or maybe we feel a strange empathy for the perpetrators as well as their victims.

Stories of scandalous love triangles, mysterious getaways, and satanic cults seem almost scripted to make enthralling news. And while some of the characters involved are just plain repugnant, others have an undeniable charisma and charm, even drawing fans and admirers. It's no surprise that some of history's most infamous killers have reveled in their celebrity, interacting with the press, taunting authorities, and heightening the drama.

No matter how lurid the details of the crimes may be, the question remains: What made them do it?

Dusting for prints involves coating a surface with a powder that adheres to the oils secreted by skin, then carefully brushing away the loose powder to reveal a pattern.

CHAPTER 4
GREED.
LUST.
RAGE.

WHETHER THEY ARE COMMITTED IN THE HEAT OF THE MOMENT, SPONTANEOUSLY, OR JUST FOR THE MONEY, CERTAIN CRIMES SEEM TO PERSONIFY THE BASEST HUMAN INSTINCTS.

THE MILLIONAIRE AND THE SHOWGIRL

A GILDED-AGE LOVE TRIANGLE ENDS IN ONE OF THE MOST SALACIOUS SOCIETY MURDERS IN NEW YORK CITY HISTORY.

American architect Stanford White (1853–1906) designed everything from the Boston Public Library to lavish mansions in Newport, Rhode Island.

In the early 1900s, Evelyn Nesbit was the most beautiful girl in America, a turn-of-the-century teenage celebrity as sexy as Marilyn Monroe and as famous as Kim Kardashian. Her husband was Harry Thaw, a millionaire with a mean streak. The man who came between them was Stanford White, a celebrated New York architect whom Shaw would murder in cold blood, in front of the crème de la crème of Manhattan, on the rooftop of a building White had designed.

Considering the cast and storyline, it's no surprise that White's killing was called the Crime of the Century, though the century was but a few years old.

Young and Desirable

Nesbit was born in Pennsylvania and moved to New York City in 1900 when she was 14. She lived with her struggling, widowed mother and younger brother and, because of her fresh good looks, soon became a favorite model of the city's artists and photographers. Over the next two years Nesbit appeared in numerous advertisements, graced magazine covers, and landed roles in Broadway shows. She also caught the eye of White, a notorious womanizer 30 years her senior. White seduced the virginal Nesbit, and at age 16 she became his mistress, a relationship that lasted a year.

Meanwhile, Thaw, the spoiled, mentally unbalanced son of a Pittsburgh railroad and coal mogul, became obsessed with Nesbit, stalking her and showering her with gifts and money. Eventually he persuaded Nesbit's mother to let him take Nesbit to Europe, where, in a bizarre and violent episode, he held the teenager prisoner in an Austrian castle for two weeks, repeatedly beating and sexually assaulting her. Afterward, he begged her forgiveness and in 1905 convinced her to marry him.

Jealousy and Madness Made Him Do It

Thaw could never forget that it was White who'd stolen his young bride's virginity, and he hated White for it. His resentment came to a head on the sweltering night of June 25, 1906, at the opening of a new musical called *Mam'zelle Champagne*.

An audience of wealthy New Yorkers had gathered to watch the open-air, rooftop production. Thaw and Nesbit were there, as was White. During the final number, a song called "I Could Love a Million Girls," Thaw stood, produced a pistol, and shot White point blank. As he hovered over White's body, he reportedly said to the horrified crowd, "He had it coming to him."

Thaw's twisted chivalry did not ultimately pay off, nor did his money buy him lasting happiness. Though he managed to avoid jail, Nesbit divorced him in 1915.

Harry Thaw in the Poughkeepsie jail shortly after he killed Stanford White.

THE GIRL IN THE RED VELVET SWING

Stanford White's 24th Street architecture included some racy aspects.

Evelyn Nesbit will forever be remembered as "the girl in the red velvet swing," thanks to a novel feature of architect Stanford White's West 24th Street apartment in New York City. In a softly illuminated, forest-green room up two flights of stairs, White installed what Nesbit described in her memoirs as "a gorgeous swing with red velvet ropes around which trailed green smilax [vines], set high in the ceiling at one end of the studio."

At White's urging, Nesbit would ride the swing for his enjoyment, often in the nude, once flying so high that she kicked a hole in a paper parasol he'd installed near the ceiling.

The scene was recreated in the 1981 film *Ragtime*, featuring Elizabeth McGovern as Nesbit.

Evelyn Nesbit

THE DEADLIEST EMOTION?

Sexual jealousy can have deadly consequences.

According to a study of 5,000 people in six cultures, more than 90 percent of men and nearly 85 percent of women have fantasized at least once about murder, almost always of a romantic rival.

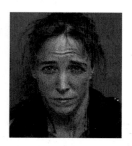

→ **Lisa Nowak.** In 2007, the 44-year-old Nowak, a former naval flight officer and NASA astronaut, was charged with the attempted kidnapping of a woman who had begun dating Nowak's former lover. Nowak had driven from Texas to Florida in order to track down the new girlfriend. A police report on the attack said Nowak told a detective she wore adult diapers so she would not need to make rest stops. Nowak later received a plea deal and avoided prison.

→ **Sahel Kazemi.** In 2009, 20-year-old waitress Kazemi shot and killed Tennessee Titans quarterback Steve McNair, with whom she was involved, before turning the gun on herself. She was reportedly distraught because she suspected that the married McNair was involved with yet another mistress.

BORED TO DEATH

SHE WAS BLONDE, BEAUTIFUL—AND THE ULTIMATE DESPERATE HOUSEWIFE.

In 1925, Ruth Snyder was living in Queens with her older husband, Albert, a magazine editor, and their nine-year-old daughter, Lorraine. They seemed to be a typical family, but Ruth, 30, was climbing the walls. She liked going out; Albert preferred to stay in. She wanted to be rich; he was solidly middle class. And, though Ruth was quite a looker, Albert yearned for a lost, long-ago girlfriend and wouldn't let his wife forget it. Scratch the surface and this was hardly a storybook romance.

Mrs. Snyder wasn't the first married mother to have an affair, and under the circumstances, perhaps it isn't surprising that she did. Her lover was Henry Judd Gray, a married lingerie salesman from New Jersey. The two met in hotels, including the luxurious Waldorf in Manhattan. Sometimes Ruth would even bring Lorraine, who played in the lobby while the couple was occupied upstairs. Soon, Ruth was talking to Gray about making their relationship more permanent. The only obstacle was her husband.

'Til Death Do Us Part

A divorce is the conventional way to get rid of a husband, but Ruth had other ideas. Albert had a life insurance policy, with a signature Snyder had forged herself. Were he to

A crowd waits outside the courthouse to get a glimpse of Ruth Snyder and Henry Judd Gray before their trial.

WHO KNEW?
Ruth Snyder's $100,000 insurance payoff, had she gotten it in 1927, would have been equivalent to about $1.3 million in today's dollars.

Ruth Snyder behind bars in Queens County Jail.

die of natural causes, the policy would pay Ruth close to $50,000. If he happened to die catastrophically, the policy was worth twice that.

Conveniently enough, at least for Ruth, Albert was murdered.

On the morning of March 20, 1927, Lorraine woke to discover her mother tied up and her father dead in his bed. He had been hit in the skull with a heavy object and strangled with wire. Ruth told police that she and Albert had arrived home late from a party the night before, only to be attacked by an "Italian-looking" intruder who had taken her jewelry.

Truth and Consequences

Snyder's story fell apart almost immediately. Police discovered the supposedly stolen jewelry hidden in the Snyders' home, and when they began asking Ruth questions, she accidentally divulged her lover's name, asking if he was a suspect. When the police caught up to Gray, he, too, caved quickly, claiming that he had been a reluctant participant in the crime. The lovers pointed fingers at each other, but in the end both were convicted of murder and sentenced to the electric chair. They were executed at Sing Sing Prison in Ossining, New York, on January 12, 1928. Ruth went first.

The sordid trial was welcome fodder for newspaper readers, who were endlessly fascinated with the torrid affair and the clumsy murder. To this day the tale endures: Snyder became the model for the film noir femme fatale archetype, and parts of the story were immortalized in the 1944 movie *Double Indemnity*.

Daily News front page, Extra Edition, January 13, 1928.

Ruth Snyder is the subject of one of the most famous photographs in the history of journalism.

A grainy image of the murderess dying in the electric chair, published in the *New York Daily News* the day after her execution, was the work of a Chicago photographer named Tom Howard. Although photography wasn't allowed at executions, at the moment of Ruth's death Howard lifted the cuff of his pants and surreptitiously took a shot with a miniature camera strapped to his ankle.

A PRETTY FACE

Accused or convicted murderers make good copy—good-looking ones, even better. These attractive convicts garnered more than their share of media attention.

The Face	The Crime	The Details
Jodi Arias	Murdered her ex-lover, Travis Alexander, 2008, in Arizona. Pleaded not guilty.	Photos of Arias posing in a sexually suggestive way were found in the victim's digital camera.
Karla Homolka	Helped her husband rape and murder two school girls in the early 1990s. She pleaded guilty to manslaughter in exchange for serving 12 years in prison.	The Canadian's long blonde hair and pert features earned her comparisons to Barbie.
Joran van der Sloot	Pleaded guilty to the murder of Peruvian Stephany Flores Ramirez, 2010; was key suspect in the disappearance of American Natalee Holloway in Aruba, 2005, but never charged with any crime.	The 6'4" square-jawed Dutch national is a former star athlete.
Ted Bundy	American serial killer of at least 30 women and girls, 1974–1978.	Bundy's pretty-boy looks made it easy for him to lure in unsuspecting young victims.

A KILLER CALLED
ZODIAC

THIS ARROGANT SERIAL SLAYER TAUNTED POLICE AND TERRORIZED THE BAY AREA. HE ALSO EVADED CAPTURE.

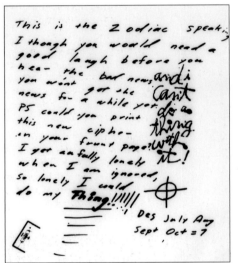

A greeting card mailed to the San Francisco *Chronicle* by the killer who called himself Zodiac.

During the late 1960s and early 70s, a serial murderer known as the Zodiac Killer terrified the people of San Francisco with claims of having committed 37 grisly homicides. He appeared to crave publicity as much as blood, phoning the local police following each fatal stabbing and taunting the press and law enforcement with arrogant letters. "I like killing people because it is so much fun," he wrote in one.

Sometimes Zodiac communicated in cryptograms or ciphers, which he dared police to decode. Often he included a symbol that resembled Taurus the Bull, prompting some to theorize that it was his astrological sign. Others suggested that Zodiac's "nom de crime" was inspired by his belief that he was acting on the orders of the stars. To this day, Zodiac's true identify is unknown. Law enforcement has not determined if he is dead or alive, and many case files in Zodiac murders remain open.

Tenuous Links

Law enforcement has only established a link to Zodiac in a handful of the 37 murders he claimed to have executed. For example, Zodiac took responsibility for the fatal stabbing in 1966 of a female college student in Southern California, but his connection to the murder has never been proven. Police do believe he struck a number of times between 1968 and 1969. Zodiac is credited with shooting two teenage couples, killing both women and injuring the males in that time frame. He is believed to have brutally stabbed a third couple where the male managed to survive. Police also believe Zodiac was involved in the 1969 killing of a San Francisco cab driver and the 1970 kidnapping attempt of a mother and baby.

According to witnesses, Zodiac appeared to be in his late twenties to early thirties, heavyset, and strong. He wore a black hooded outfit during his gruesome attacks. At the time, police investigated more than 2,500 potential suspects. Today, people continue to confess to the crimes or claim knowledge of Zodiac's true identity.

Organized, Intelligent, Meticulous

Zodiac's psychology and personality have been studied for decades, with everyone from armchair sleuths to FBI profilers weighing in speculating on who he was.

Gregg O. McCrary, a former FBI profiler and expert witness who studied Zodiac's letters, has described the killer as

The wanted poster circulated by police in the search for the Zodiac killer in San Francisco, 1969.

Actor Andrew Robinson as Scorpio in *Dirty Harry*

organized, intelligent, and meticulous. In McCrary's view, Zodiac was motivated by a desire for notoriety and press attention. He also wanted to control the investigation and prove his superiority to the police. The fact that Zodiac tended to target couples rather than individuals may have indicated that he was incapable of sustaining a romantic relationship, McCrary has theorized. His "overkill" of the females, stabbing them numerous times, might mean he was impotent or simply deeply resentful of women.

While Zodiac liked to ambush his victims, his crimes were not high risk. He attacked in secluded locations and might have fantasized that he was a skilled hunter. Since Zodiac's identity remains unknown, it is difficult to know for sure.

CRACKING THE CODE

Police were unable to decipher the Zodiac's cryptograms, but in 1969, a teacher and his wife unscrambled a terrifying message.

Robert Graysmith, author of *Zodiac* and *Zodiac Unmasked*, views cryptographs used by the Zodiac killer.

A few of Zodiac's letters to the press were written in symbols whose meanings only he knew. Police were never able to decode them—but in August 1969, a high school teacher and his wife read one of the missives in the newspaper and were able to translate all but the last 18 symbols. It remains the Zodiac's only communication to be translated (all misspellings the Zodiac's own):

"I LIKE KILLING PEOPLE BECAUSE IT IS SO MUCH FUN IT IS MORE FUN THAN KILLING WILD GAME IN THE FORREST BECAUSE MAN IS THE MOST DANGEROUE ANAMAL OF ALL TO KILL SOMETHING GIVES ME THE MOST THRILLING EXPERENCE IT IS EVEN BETTER THAN GETTING YOUR ROCKS OFF WITH A GIRL THE BEST PART OF IT IS THAE WHEN I DIE I WILL BE REBORN IN PARADICE AND THEI HAVE KILLED WILL BECOME MY SLAVES I WILL NOT GIVE YOU MY NAME BECAUSE YOU WILL TRY TO SLOI DOWN OR ATOP MY COLLECTIOG OF SLAVES FOR MY AFTERLIFE EBEORIETEMETHHPITI."

THE LEGEND OF D.B. COOPER

A MYSTERIOUS CONMAN PULLS OFF A HIJACKING AND PARACHUTES INTO THE WILDS OF WASHINGTON STATE WITH $200,000 IN $20 BILLS.

On November 24, 1971, on a plane bound for Seattle, flight attendant Florence Schaffner served a bourbon-and-soda to a male passenger who a few minutes later handed her a slip of paper. Assuming it was a businessman's come-on, Schaffner dropped the message into her purse without a glance.

"Miss," the man whispered. "You'd better look at that note. I have a bomb."

Thus began one of the most notorious skyjackings in American history. The case not only remains unsolved to this day, it has also turned the perpetrator, known as D.B. Cooper, into a folk hero celebrated for beating the system.

From Cooper's first move that Thanksgiving eve, it was clear he was no ordinary hijacker. Neatly dressed in a suit and tie, Cooper spoke courteously and calmly to Schaffner. He invited the flight attendant to sit next to him to receive instructions on how to proceed, and provided her with a quick glimpse of the red cylinders and wiring inside his attaché case. Cooper even paid his drink tab.

Yet the hijacker meant business. Cooper told Schaffner he wanted $200,000 in cash by 5:00 PM, delivered in a knapsack. He also asked for four parachutes and a truck prepared to refuel the Boeing 727 on the runway. "No funny stuff or I'll do the job," he threatened. After allowing Schaffner to quietly alert

THE REAL MCCOY—OR THE REAL COOPER?

D.B. Cooper has had many imitators. Meet one of the most puzzling ones.

In 1971, Richard McCoy was a highly decorated Vietnam veteran living in Utah with his wife and two kids. He was studying law enforcement and working on a thesis about preventing skyjackings. McCoy was also an avid skydiver and hoped eventually to use his skills at the FBI or CIA. But his life changed on November 24, when he heard reports of D.B. Cooper hijacking a plane. Knowing how fragile airline security systems were at the time, McCoy hatched a plan of his own.

On April 7, 1972, disguised in a wig and dark-toned makeup, McCoy took over United Airlines flight #855 with an empty pistol and a novelty hand grenade. He demanded and was paid $500,000 in ransom, then escaped mid-flight, leaping from the rear stairs.

McCoy's jump was successful, but investigators located him two days later using fingerprints from an airline magazine and handwriting analysis. He was arrested, tried, and sentenced to 45 years at the federal penitentiary in Lewisville, Pennsylvania.

In 1974, McCoy and three other convicts took control of a prison garbage truck and staged an escape. After three months on the run, McCoy was tracked down by the FBI in Virginia Beach. When he opened fire on the agents, he was fatally shot.

Federal agents Bernie Rhodes and Russell P. Calame published *D.B. Cooper: The Real McCoy*, which claimed that D.B. Cooper and Richard McCoy were one and the same man. McCoy's widow sued and accepted a settlement.

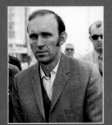

Richard Floyd McCoy Jr. in Salt Lake City, 1972.

This undated artist's sketch provided by the Federal Bureau of Investigation shows a rendering of the skyjacker known as "Dan Cooper" and "D.B. Cooper."

the cockpit, Cooper retreated behind a pair of dark sunglasses.

The plane, Northwest Airlines flight #305, circled Puget Sound for two hours while the Federal Bureau of Investigation and the Seattle police gathered the ransom. Once the aircraft landed at Seattle-Tacoma Airport, the parachutes and knapsack packed with 21 pounds of unmarked $20 bills were delivered to Cooper. He allowed the passengers to be released, and after the plane was refueled Cooper and the crew took off again.

Gone!

Northwest #305 headed south with two F-106 fighter jets and an Air Force training plane shadowing it. As Cooper readied his parachutes and strapped the $200,000-packed knapsack to his chest, he ordered the crew to the cockpit. At 8:24 PM, the pilot noticed a slight dip and correction in the plane's trajectory. The stairs in the rear of the plane had been opened. Outside, it was 7 degrees below zero and raining. Below lay miles of southwest Washington's most treacherous terrain. The plane was traveling at 195 miles per hour.

At 10:15 AM, the Northwest craft landed in Reno, Nevada. The passenger cabin was empty.

The Pursuit

For almost three weeks, the FBI and local law enforcement searched for Cooper in the wilderness of southwest Washington. They turned up two of the parachutes, eight of Cooper's Raleigh cigarette butts, his black clip-on tie and mother-of-pearl tie clip, but nothing else.

Did Cooper escape? Most FBI investigators and experts believe in the "splatter theory": that the hijacker was unable to open his chute and died in the fall. The thesis was bolstered in 1980 when three packets of $20 bills were found on the banks of the Columbia River, leading some to conclude that Cooper's body was somewhere on the bottom of the river.

Every few years, new suspects in the case emerge. In 2007, *New York Magazine* published an article focusing on deceased paratrooper Kenneth Christiansen. According to the article, Christiansen's brother Lyle was convinced that his late sibling was Cooper. Flight attendant Florence Schaffner said the photos of Kenneth Christiansen closely resembled Cooper, but she couldn't confirm it was the skyjacker.

Today, in Ariel, Washington, residents celebrate an annual "Cooper Day."

A PICNIC PAYS OFF

How a young boy made off with some of D.B. Cooper's cash.

On February 10, 1980, eight-year-old Brian Ingram was picnicking with his family on a beach north of Portland, Oregon, when he found three bundles of frayed 20-dollar bills wrapped in rubber bands, totaling $5,800. The serial numbers on the bills matched those of a $200,000 ransom paid in the D.B. Cooper skyjacking case. Federal authorities, after keeping a few bills for evidence, allowed Ingram to split his find with the insurance company that had reimbursed Northwest Airlines.

FINDING THE SON OF SAM

BRINGING NEW YORK'S MOST NOTORIOUS SERIAL KILLER TO JUSTICE TOOK OLD-FASHIONED POLICE WORK AND SOME LUCK.

"No One Is Safe from the Son of Sam," the *New York Post* headline screamed. It was the summer of 1977 and a shadowy serial killer had been terrorizing New York City for over a year, murdering six and wounding seven. He had gunned down his two most recent victims on July 31, as they sat in a car in Bensonhurst, Brooklyn. The assailant had killed Stacy Moskowitz and partially blinded Moskowitz's date, Robert Violante, with a bullet to the eye.

A City on Alert

The attacks began in the Bronx in July 1976, when someone opened fire on two women sitting in a car talking, and killed one. Other, almost identical shootings soon followed. Already roiled by unemployment, blackouts, and riots, the city went on high alert. Because the killer seemed to target victims with long, dark hair, women got short cuts or dyed their hair blonde. Couples stopped going out or avoided sitting in cars. The police deployed some 300 officers, including 50 detectives, to find the gunman.

The New York City Police Department was soon overwhelmed. Anxious citizens, each sure his or her angry coworker or unbalanced neighbor was the murderer, inundated the NYPD with false tips. It took hours to review every report, and when a nervous witness gave a new description of the killer, police often released an alternate sketch that was markedly different from the last.

As the search progressed, the killer sent taunting letters to the police; he also contacted *New York Daily News* columnist Jimmy Breslin, saying a mysterious "Father Sam" was commanding him to kill. Psychologists were unable to come up with a definitive profile of Son of Sam. One concluded that he was "neurotic, schizophrenic, and paranoid" and had trouble forming relationships with women. Another described him as "very polite, extremely intelligent, and probably a college-educated Catholic white-collar worker."

Progress at Last

The first big break in the case came when a woman who had been walking her dog near the Moskowitz murder scene reported seeing a suspicious man. She also mentioned that a police officer had been issuing parking tickets in the area that day. That prompted detective James Justus to contact everyone who had gotten a ticket, hoping to find another witness.

New York Post headline on the capture of the Son of Sam

Unidentified officers of the 84th Precinct in Brooklyn read news of the capture of David Berkowitz, August 11, 1977.

As it turned out, one $35 ticket had been issued to a David Berkowitz from Yonkers, who had parked his cream-colored Ford Galaxie too close to a fire hydrant. After repeatedly calling Berkowitz and getting no answer, Justus contacted the Yonkers police to see if they could get in touch with him. In a lucky coincidence, the dispatcher who answered the phone recognized Berkowitz's name: He was the crazy man who had shot her father's neighbor's dog, she said.

On August 10, detectives went to Yonkers to confront Berkowitz. The first to arrive was Edward Zigo, who spotted the Ford Galaxie and looked inside. On the seat was a duffel bag with a rifle sticking out of it. In the glove compartment was a letter with a threat to open fire on a discotheque. When Berkowitz emerged from his building, detective John Falotico raised his pistol to Berkowitz's temple.

"You got me," Berkowitz said. "I'm the Son of Sam."

When newspapers printed photographs of Berkowitz the next day, the public greeted them with equal parts relief and shock. The Son of Sam turned out to be a disheveled 24-year-old with a pudgy face, bushy hair, and long sideburns—a far cry from the figure with a "good, athletic build" that had been pictured in the wanted poster released just a day before his arrest. Berkowitz confessed to the crimes and is serving six life sentences.

WHO'S THE HERO?

Many detectives collaborated on Son of Sam's capture; only one got a TV movie.

In 2011, the death of former New York City detective Edward Zigo prompted a barrage of obituaries, hailing his work in bringing the "Son of Sam" killer to justice. The *New York Post* interviewed Zigo's son about his father's role in the case.

"According to my father, he introduced himself to Berkowitz and said, 'Hi, David. I'm Detective Ed Zigo.' Berkowitz said to him, 'Hi, Ed, I'm the Son of Sam,'" the son related.

Yet in many accounts of Berkowitz's arrest, it was Detective John Falotico, not Zigo, who conducted a version of this conversation. How did Zigo end up getting the credit? Most likely because of a 1985 television movie about the manhunt, *Out of the Darkness*. The producer, Sonny Grosso, was a former narcotics officer who had attended the New York police academy with Zigo and hired him as an advisor on the film. Grasso said he was interested in Zigo because he was on the Son of Sam case while dealing with the death of his wife.

The movie caused a stir when it aired, with critics claiming the story strayed from the facts. Falotico, who died in 2006, was one of the most vocal. "It is my contention that this program is like a travesty of justice. It's a hoax played on the public because, as you know, in any major investigation no one person is a hero," Falotico told the *Los Angeles Times*.

David Berkowitz with Detective Edward Zigo

A WOMAN SCORNED

JILTED FOR A YOUNGER MISTRESS, JEAN HARRIS KILLED HER UNFAITHFUL LOVER—THOUGH SHE SWORE HE WASN'T HER INTENDED TARGET.

She had been dating him for 14 years, couldn't get him to marry her, and now was being thrown over for a younger, prettier replacement. When Jean Harris, 56, shot her lover Herman Tarnower, the public wasn't entirely unsympathetic. "We were thrilled," Nora Ephron later wrote of the 1980 murder. "When I say we, I mean me, but I also mean every woman who has ever wanted to kill a bad boyfriend."

For Harris, the dignified headmistress of the Madeira School, a girls' boarding school outside of Washington, D.C., it was a relationship that had gone terribly wrong. For over a decade, the well-bred, divorced mother of two had been romantically involved with Tarnower, a New York cardiologist and the author of *The Complete Scarsdale Medical Diet*, a bestselling phenomenon of its day.

Though Tarnower was not particularly good-looking, he was wealthy, successful, and an unapologetic philanderer. Harris tolerated his behavior in exchange for the perks of being his primary girlfriend: Fancy trips, expensive presents, and social prestige.

Their relationship worked for a while. Then Tarnower began two-timing Harris with his 37-year-old office assistant, taking his new girlfriend to dinner parties and on vacations. Upset that she had been so publicly upstaged, Harris composed and mailed

THE BEDFORD BUNCH

New York's only maximum-security women's prison has had its share of infamous inmates.

Notable prisoners of the Bedford Hills Correctional Facility for Women have included Jean Harris, "Long Island Lolita" Amy Fisher, and these four convicted murderers:

Judy Clark and Kathy Boudin
(Boudin shown above)
Radical activists

Sentence: Felony murder, for the 1981 robbery of $1.6 million from a Brink's armored vehicle during which two police officers and a Brink's guard were killed.

Clark refused to participate in her trial. She is serving 75 years to life. Boudin got a plea deal, was paroled in 2003, and is an adjunct professor at the Columbia University School of Social Work.

Carolyn Warmus
Heiress and schoolteacher

Sentence: Second-degree murder, for the *Fatal Attraction*–style 1989 shooting of her lover's wife.

Warmus, who pleaded not guilty, is serving 25 years to life. She will be eligible for parole in 2017. While in prison, she has sued correctional officers for sexual harassment.

Pamela Smart
High school administrator

Sentence: Conspiracy to commit murder and other charges, for seducing a 15-year-old and persuading him to kill her husband in 1990.

Smart denied taking part in the murder; she is serving a life sentence without possibility of parole. She has completed two master's degrees in prison.

Jean Harris had been headmistress of the Thomas School in Rowayton, Connecticut, before taking the position at Madeira.

WHO KNEW?

Herman Tarnower's best-selling *The Complete Scarsdale Medical Diet* had a surge in sales after his murder.

Tarnower a rambling, vulgar, and furious letter and, she later told the court, decided to visit him one last time before killing herself.

On a rainy night in March, Harris, armed with a handgun, made the five-hour drive to Tarnower's

Dr. Herman Tarnower

house in Purchase, New York. When she discovered her rival's belongings, including a negligee and hair curlers, she allegedly flew into a rage and shot Tarnower dead.

Harris later said that she had pointed the gun at herself but in the ensuing struggle, she accidentally killed her lover. Her letter proved damning, though, as did forensic evidence. She was convicted of second-degree murder and sentenced to 15 years at a maximum security prison in New York.

Redemption and Forgiveness

While serving time, Harris worked tirelessly to improve the lives of fellow inmates, particularly mothers. In 1993, she was granted clemency by Governor Mario Cuomo and released early. She went on to live a quiet life and died in 2012 at 89, at an assisted-living facility in Connecticut.

Opinions about Harris have always been divided. Her "passionate defenders saw her plight as epitomizing the fragile position of an aging but fiercely independent woman who, because of limited options, was dependent on a man who mistreated her," said her *New York Times* obituary. Still, the true victim was Tarnower, shot four times and left for dead in his own bed.

WHO KNEW?
In 2013, Pamela Smart was among the cast of *Amazing Grace*, an original musical performed by and for inmates of Bedford Hills Correctional Facility for Women.

This photo of Pamela Smart was given to her teenage lover to be developed, according to the prosecution.

SEX, LIES, AND VIDEOTAPE

TELEGENIC AND SEDUCTIVE, PAMELA SMART TOOK A TEENAGE LOVER AND TRADED HER BODY FOR A DEADLY FAVOR.

The night Pamela Smart seduced Billy Flynn, she brought him to her bedroom and reenacted a scene from the steamy film *9½ Weeks*, performing a striptease to one of her favorite Van Halen songs. It was March 1990. Smart was 23, married, and worked at a New Hampshire high school. Flynn was 15, a student at the school, and a virgin. The pair had just taken the first step on the path to murder.

Camera Ready

Two months later, when Pamela's 24-year-old husband Gregory Smart was found shot to death in the couple's condominium, it seemed like a simple case of robbery gone wrong. In television interviews, Pamela made tearful appeals to witnesses for any information they might have about the crime. But gradually, her facade crumbled. Police grew suspicious of the young widow's eagerness to speak to the press and noted that she showed little emotion when the cameras weren't trained on her.

Five weeks after the murder, a local teenager came forward and pointed a finger at a group of four friends who had admitted to killing Gregory. The boys, including Billy Flynn, were arrested, and filled in the details: Pamela, wanting out of her marriage, had seduced Flynn, then pushed him to shoot her husband. When Flynn balked, Pamela threatened to stop having sex with him.

The sordid tale of a sexy, manipulative teacher and the hapless students who fell under her spell was perfect fodder for tabloid journalists and Hollywood. The fully televised trial became a national sensation.

Pamela, a former cheerleader and college-radio DJ who aspired to work in broadcasting, seemed to come alive in front of the camera. While the media portrayed her as instigating the crime in order to become famous, the prosecution had a more straightforward theory: Pamela wanted $140,000 in life-insurance money and custody of the couple's dog, a Shih Tzu named Halen. In the case of a divorce, Pamela would not have received either.

Lifelong Punishment

Three of the boys cut a deal with the state, including Flynn, who was the triggerman and who agreed to serve at least 28 years for the crime. Two other boys got prison time; a fourth pleaded not guilty. Pamela maintained her innocence, but was sent away for life, a term she is serving at the maximum-security Bedford Hills Correctional Facility for Women in New York. "I live every day with the ominous realization that I will only leave here in a casket," she wrote in 2005.

Pamela appeared on *Oprah* in 2010 and has an official website, run by a friend, that keeps "fans" up to date on her life behind bars.

Billy Flynn, 17, points out Pamela Smart to jurors in Exeter, New Hampshire, 1991.

THE GIRL WHO WORE A WIRE

To prove that Pamela Smart had masterminded her husband's demise, the authorities sought help from an unusual informant.

A break in Gregory Smart's homicide case came when one of Billy Flynn's young accomplices told a friend about the murder. Without hard evidence, however, the police could not arrest Pamela Smart. That changed when Cecelia Pierce, a 16-year-old former student intern of Pamela's, agreed to wear a wire. In four secretly recorded conversations, Pierce captured Pamela incriminating herself. "If you tell the truth," Smart said to Pierce, "you're gonna have to send me to the (expletive) slammer." It was reported that Pierce agreed to sell the film rights to her story for $100,000.

THE LONG ISLAND LOLITA

AMY FISHER WAS STILL IN HIGH SCHOOL WHEN SHE SHOT HER LOVER'S WIFE IN THE FACE AND LAUNCHED A TABLOID FEEDING FRENZY.

In the early 1990s, it was impossible to get away from the bizarre story of high school student Amy Fisher and her married lover, the auto mechanic Joey Buttafuoco. Fisher, a sullen, pouty-lipped teen, became a national phenomenon after she rang Buttafuoco's doorbell, then shot and nearly killed his wife Mary Jo on the porch of the couple's Massapequa, New York, home. The media pounced, dubbing Fisher the Long Island Lolita. In spite of the seriousness of the crime, the situation was parodied relentlessly on NBC's *Saturday Night Live*. After endless coverage, the sordid saga became the subject of competing made-for-television movies, one starring Drew Barrymore, the other Alyssa Milano.

They Met in His Auto Shop

The 16-year-old Fisher first met Buttafuoco in May 1991 at the auto shop he owned. She had damaged the family car and hoped to get it repaired before her father, of whom she later said she was terrified, found out. Fisher and Buttafuoco, a 35-year-old, married father of two, began a friendship that soon included trysts in local motels.

A few months into their relationship, Fisher told her lover that she needed money. He allegedly suggested that she contact an escort service, and by fall of 1991 she was working as a prostitute. At the same time, Fisher was becoming more and more obsessed with Buttafuoco, and in November she insisted that he choose between her and his wife. She was devastated when he chose Mary Jo, and the lovers broke up. After the two reunited in January 1992, Fisher began hatching a plan to get rid of Mary Jo forever.

On May 19, 1992, Fisher showed up at the Buttafuocos' house to confront Mary Jo. The two spoke for almost 15 minutes before Fisher pulled out a .25 caliber semi-automatic gun and shot Mary Jo in the face.

Severely wounded, Mary Jo miraculously survived and, a few days later, identified Fisher as the shooter. Fisher pleaded guilty to reckless assault and agreed to cooperate with the prosecution of Buttafuoco. She served nearly seven years in prison and Buttafuoco served six months for statutory rape.

Victims on Both Sides

As salacious as the case was, the incident was tragic. The shooting left Mary Jo with partial facial paralysis and deaf in her right ear. Fisher reported that she was raped by guards and harassed relentlessly by other inmates during her time in prison. She has subsequently struggled with addiction and worked in the pornography industry.

What was going through her mind all those years ago? Some, including Fisher herself, believe that she was a victim of the predatory Buttafuoco. "I was lonely and so scared of my father," she told the *New York Times Magazine* in 1996, "and here's this older man and he takes care of me and he tells me I'm beautiful. I felt honored."

Lou Bellera and Amy Fisher at the "Celebrity Fight Night" in 2011.

94

Amy Fisher as she left Nassau County Court after a hearing, September 1992.

Joey Buttafuoco with his wife, Mary Jo, in May 1993 as they arrived at court, where he faced charges of statutory rape.

WHERE ARE THEY NOW?

The major players in the Amy Fisher saga are all still alive.

→ **Amy Fisher** was paroled in 1999 and married Louis Bellera in 2003; the couple has three children. Bellera, who has described himself as a photographer and event-video producer, went on to direct Fisher in a sex tape released in 2007. Fisher has made numerous other pornographic videos. She appeared on *Dr. Drew's Celebrity Rehab* in 2011.

→ **Mary Jo Buttafuoco** stayed with her husband for another decade before filing for divorce in 2003. She underwent surgery to help regain function in her face. In 2009 she wrote a memoir, *Getting It Through My Thick Skull: Why I Stayed, What I Learned, and What Millions of People Involved with Sociopaths Need to Know*. She remarried in 2012.

→ **Joey Buttafuoco** was subsequently sentenced to a year in jail after pleading no contest to possessing ammunition as a felon.

MURDEROUS GEOGRAPHY

From serial killers to a shooter on a commuter train, Long Island, east of New York City, seemed to have had more than its share of horrible crimes in the late 1980s and early 1990s.

- ● Mineola
- ● Garden City
- ● Valley Stream
- ● Commack
- ● Bay Shore
- ● Medford

Mineola
JUNE 28, 1993

Joel Rifkin was driving a pickup truck without license plates when he hit a pole trying to outrun state troopers. A dead body was found in his trunk, and investigators suspected Rifkin was a serial killer. He was convicted of nine murders and is now serving 203 years to life.

Garden City
DECEMBER 7, 1993

Aboard a crowded Long Island Rail Road train, passenger Colin Ferguson pulled a gun and began firing, killing six people and wounding 19. Ferguson represented himself at trial, cross-examining his own victims. He will be eligible for parole in 2309.

Bay Shore
DECEMBER 28, 1992

Missing for over two weeks, Katie Beers, 10, was found shaken but alive in a concrete room under the garage of family friend John Esposito. Twenty years later, Beers wrote a book about her ordeal. Esposito died in prison in 2013.

Medford
DECEMBER 8, 1994

The dismembered body of a woman found under a railroad overpass became the first of five grisly murders ultimately linked to a former postal worker named Robert Yale Schulman. Only three victims were ever identified. Schulman died a prisoner in 2006.

Valley Stream
MARCH 4, 1989

Kelly Ann Tinyes, 13, was found stabbed to death in a home five doors from her own. DNA evidence pointed to Robert Golub, 21, a bodybuilder who lived there. Sentenced to 25 years to life, Golub professed innocence until 2013, when he finally copped to the murder.

Commack
JULY 22, 1994

Steven Chaifetz, 50, was shot and killed by an unidentified man. In the days that followed, the "Suffolk County Sniper" struck twice more, injuring another victim. A massive manhunt resulted in the capture of Peter Sylvester, a local who admitted to committing the attacks to impress a topless dancer. He was sentenced to 35 years to life.

ANGELS OF DEATH

EVERYONE AGREED THAT KRISTEN GILBERT'S NURSING SKILLS WERE TOP-NOTCH. SO WAS HER KNACK FOR KILLING.

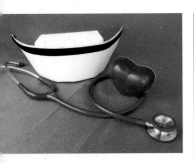

DARK MOTIVES
What do killer nurses want?

According to *Murder Most Rare*, a book about female serial killers, nurses end the lives of their patients out of "ego and a compulsion for domination." They often have a desperate need to control those who are dependent on them.

In the mid-1990s, the nurses at Veterans Administration medical center in Northampton, Massachusetts, were whispering about the unusually high number of deaths on Ward C. At least 350 patients had expired between 1989 and February 1996, a sharp spike from the previous seven years. What's more, half of the deaths had occurred during the shift of a cheerful, attractive young nurse by the name of Kristen Gilbert. Her story would end with multiple convictions for murder and a sentence of life without parole.

"Twisted But Not Stupid"
Kristen Strickland, born November 13, 1967, grew up in a quiet and loving household in Groton, Massachusetts. She was attractive and popular, seemingly wise beyond her years, according to *Perfect Poison*, a book that chronicled the case. What many of Kristen's admiring schoolmates didn't realize was that she was a compulsive liar and a petty thief. She also had a temper. Those who got to know her well learned to keep their distance.

As Kristen got older, she grew more volatile. Her exes would later describe her in interviews with the media as "twisted, but not stupid" and capable of everything from tampering with their cars to leaving fake suicide notes.

Death Shift
In 1988, Kristen married Glenn Gilbert, and the young couple settled in Northampton.

Their marriage was troubled from the start: Once Kristen even chased after Glenn with a butcher knife, according to court documents.

The following year, Kristen took a job at the local Veterans Administration hospital, where her colleagues described her as friendly, fun, and a highly skilled and competent nurse. The only thing that seemed odd to Kristen's coworkers was the way she seemed to get excited during life-or-death situations.

Yet things went smoothly on Ward C until late 1990, when Kristen, who had just given birth, returned from maternity leave. Soon, patients in the ward mysteriously started dying of cardiac arrest. Still, no one suspected Kristen of foul play. Why would they? By all appearances, she was a professional and caring nurse.

Meanwhile, the Gilberts' marriage was crumbling. In August of 1995 Kristen began an affair with James Perrault, a security guard at the hospital.

"You're Killing Me"
As deaths on Ward C continued into the fall of 1995, Kristen's coworkers jokingly began to refer to her as "The Angel of Death." Quietly, some of them began monitoring the drugs that might induce cardiac arrest, and discovered frequent shortages of epinephrine, or adrenaline.

On August 22, 1995, a nurse reported hearing a male patient screaming, "Ow! It hurts! You're killing me!" as Kristen attended him. Another time, Kristen al-

WHO KNEW?
In 1986, after Kristen Gilbert faked a suicide attempt at Bridgewater State College in Massachusetts, school authorities ordered her to undergo psychiatric treatment. She transferred instead, according to the Associated Press.

NURSES WHO KILL

Kristen Gilbert was not the first nurse to murder multiple patients.

GENENE JONES This pediatric nurse pleaded not guilty, but was convicted in 1981 of murdering one child and attempting to murder another. Police determined that Jones had been injecting patients with saline to induce seizures, then reviving them for the attendant praise. She was sentenced to 99 years in prison.

CHARLES CULLEN A nurse who was also perhaps the most prolific serial killer in history; some investigators estimate he was responsible for the deaths of more than 300 patients from 1988 to 2003; he pleaded guilty to killing 29.

legedly asked her superior, "If my patient dies, can I leave early?"

But it wasn't until February 15, 1996, when Kristen flushed the intravenous lines of an AIDS patient who then died, that the hospital grew so suspicious it contacted the police who began an investigation.

When Kristen was put on leave by VA administrators, she seemed to come undone. In June, Perrault ended their relationship and the following month, Kristen overdosed on drugs. She was admitted to a hospital psychiatric ward and, according to Perrault's testimony, called her former lover from the facility, telling him, "You know I did it. I did it. You wanted to know. I killed those guys."

"Shell of a Human"

Following her release in September 1996, Kristen disguised her voice and phoned in a bomb threat to the VA hospital. She was arrested and sentenced to 15 months in prison. Over the next few years, the investigation by the Massachusetts police about her activities at the VA hospital proceeded.

The bodies of four patients who had died under Kristen's care were exhumed and epinephrine was found in each of them. Enough evidence was collected to charge the nurse with multiple counts of murder. Prosecutors, calling her a "shell of a human," pushed for the death penalty. They asserted that Kristen had been inducing cardiac arrest with epinephrine so that Perrault would be summoned to the intensive care unit and she could show off her skills for him.

Kristen pleaded not guilty, but on March 14, 2001, she was convicted of three counts of first-degree murder, one count of second-degree murder, and two counts of attempted murder. She avoided the death penalty but was sentenced to life plus 20 years.

BAD MOTHER

WOULD YOU KILL FOR A TOWNHOUSE IN MANHATTAN? SANTE AND KENNY KIMES DID JUST THAT.

Kenneth Kimes testifies against his mother, Sante Kimes.

Irene Silverman's multimillion-dollar townhouse.

Irene Silverman's wasn't the first life destroyed by the murderous mother-son duo Sante and Kenneth Kimes Jr. By the time the law caught up with the Kimes in 1998, the pair had spent years crisscrossing the United States, conning, scheming, and killing.

Like the Kimes's other victims, Silverman, a tiny, energetic former ballerina, didn't deserve her fate. The 82-year-old simply had the misfortune of meeting up with two depraved "ingenious, evil con artists," as one law-enforcement official described them.

Silverman owned a townhouse valued between $7 and $10 million on the upscale Upper East Side of Manhattan, and Sante wanted it. The 63-year-old and her son, Kenny, 23, didn't live anywhere near New York City, but they had heard stories of a rich widow who operated an exclusive bed-and-breakfast and boardinghouse for A-listers like actors Daniel Day-Lewis and Jennifer Grey. In June 1998, Kenny rented a room from Silverman. Soon, Sante secretly moved in with him and they began hatching a plot to swindle the octogenarian out of her property.

Silverman suspected the Kimes were up to no good, and it didn't take long for the mother and son to decide to end her life. On July 5, Sante knocked Silverman out with a stun gun and Kenny strangled her, stashed her body in a duffel bag, and drove it to a dumpster in Hoboken, New Jersey. The corpse was never found, but police tracked down Sante and Kenny, who were arrested, tried, and imprisoned. Kenny, who confessed to three murders, is serving a life sentence in California; Sante died of natural causes in a New York State prison in May 2014. She was 79.

Just a Game

The sensational crime captivated and horrified the public. But the Kimes affair raised some particularly baffling questions. Sante didn't need the money: Her third husband, Kenny's father, was a very successful businessman who had died in 1994 and left her very well off. Why did Sante pursue a life of crime so zealously? And why did Kenny become her accomplice? "He hated her," one of Kenny's childhood neighbors told the New York Times. "It's unbelievable that she could make him do these crimes."

As for Sante, she freely admitted that she was a criminal, a former family accountant told the New York Times. "She thought it was funny. To her it was like a game of Monopoly. She just liked to do it, and when she got away with it, she was as happy and excited as a little kid."

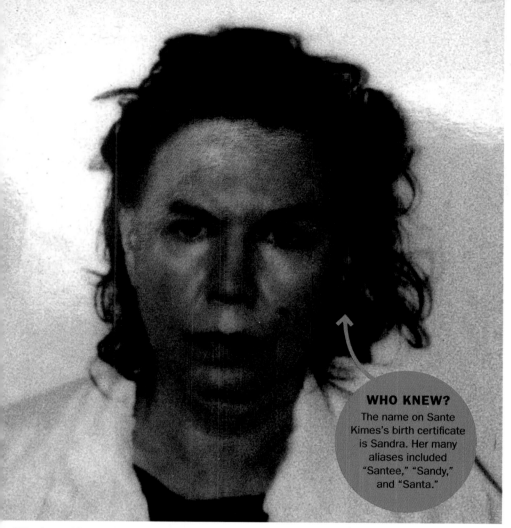

Sante Kimes never dressed to blend in; she easily stood out in a crowd.

Sometimes described as a tacky Elizabeth Taylor type, Kimes had an over-the-top personal style. She favored big diamonds, heavy perfume, pancake makeup, and pink lipstick. She also sported a variety of headwear, including turbans, wide-brimmed hats, and voluminous wigs. She once stole a mink coat from a bar by putting it on, then covering it up with her own fur coat.

WHO KNEW?

The name on Sante Kimes's birth certificate is Sandra. Her many aliases included "Santee," "Sandy," and "Santa."

This photo of Sante Kimes was released Friday, July 10, 1998, by the New York Police Department.

A LIFE OF CRIME

Born in 1934 and the mother of two sons by different fathers, Sante Kimes bounced around from husband to husband and city to city, committing scams, cons, and dirty deeds, according a 2001 book by her first son, Kent Walker.

1955: Opened a credit card account in the name of her best friend's boyfriend's father, charged $400 on it, then vanished.

1960: Set fire to her house to collect the insurance money.

1965: Using phony credit cards, racked up a $20,000 debt and was charged with grand theft.

1966: Burned two more houses for the insurance money.

1974: Crashed a reception for President Gerald Ford in Washington, D.C., by posing as a wealthy philanthropist.

1978: Burned down yet another house.

1979: Enslaved several illegal aliens in her home and forced them to work as maids.

1980: Stole a $6,500 mink coat from a bar in Washington, D.C.

1991: Suspected of murdering Elmer Holmgren, an accomplice in an arson scheme, with a hammer. The body was never found.

1996: In the Bahamas, she met a businessman for dinner. He was never seen again.

1998: Sent Kenny to kill an associate, David Kazdin, after he discovered she had used his name in a forgery scam. Kazdin was shot in the back of the head; his body was discovered in a Los Angeles trash bin.

1998: With Kenny, murdered Irene Silverman.

Irene Silverman

THE SOUND OF
MURDER

IN THE MUSIC WORLD, PHIL SPECTOR WAS FAMOUS FOR HIS SIGNATURE PRODUCTION TECHNIQUE. THEN HE BECAME A KILLER.

Before Phil Spector became notorious as a murder suspect with wild eyes and even wilder hair, he was widely considered a music-industry genius. An innovative record producer in the 1960s and 70s, Spector had been the force behind some of rock-and-roll's all-time greatest songs, including the Beatles' "Let it Be" and the Righteous Brothers' "Unchained Melody." By the 2000s, however, Spector had faded into lonely but re-spectable obscurity. He had been inducted into the Rock and Roll Hall of Fame, was living in a secluded mansion east of Los Angeles, and occasionally dropped by local nightclubs. One night at the House of Blues, a Hollywood hot spot, Spector met the woman whose death would make him famous as a cold-blooded killer.

Fateful Date

Lana Clarkson was a statuesque actress, blonde, and beautiful. At 40, she had had a few bit parts but was still trying to make it in Hollywood, and had taken a job as a hostess at the House of Blues to pay the bills. When the eccentric, diminutive Spector walked into the venue on the night of February 2, 2003, one of Clarkson's coworkers had to tell her who he was. Later that evening, when Spector asked Clarkson back to his house for a drink, she reluctantly agreed to go. Perhaps she thought that the wealthy, connected legend could help her get a break.

Only Spector knows for certain what happened that night. But at 5 AM, the producer's chauffeur, who was waiting outside to take Clarkson home, thought he heard a popping sound. Soon afterward, Spector emerged with a gun in his hand and said, "I think I killed somebody," according to the driver.

Police arrived on the scene to find Clarkson's body sprawled backward in a chair. She had been shot in the mouth; the force had knocked her teeth out. The defense later insisted that the chauffeur had misheard him and that Clarkson had killed herself. But the crime writer Dominick Dunne, for one, didn't believe that story: A beautiful woman, he wrote, would never shoot herself in the face.

Violent Pattern

During Spector's 2007 murder trial, the producer pleaded not guilty. Several women came forward to testify that he had threatened them with a gun and the case ended in a hung jury. During the second trial, in 2009, the defense argued the prosecution's case hinged on circumstantial evidence.

Government lawyers argued Spector may have been a creative genius, but his encounters with women often ended with heavy drinking and threats at gunpoint. A gun fanatic for decades, he had brandished a gun during encounters with various people including Beatle John Lennon, members of the Ramones, and singer-songwriter Leonard Cohen. Prosecutor Alan Jackson described Clarkson as "simply the latest in a very long line of women who had suffered abuse at the hands of Philip Spector."

In April 2009, a Los Angeles jury convicted Spector of second-degree murder. He was sentenced to 19 years to life and is currently in prison in Stockton, California.

Lana Clarkson

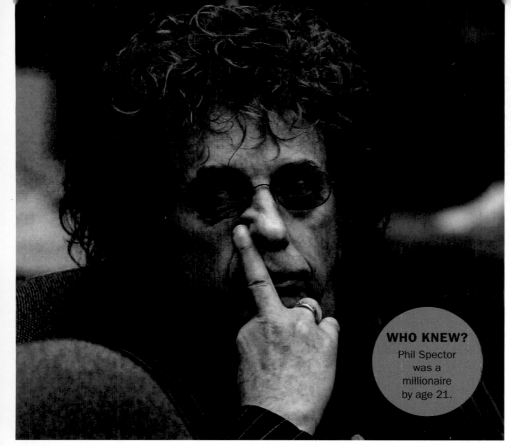

WHO KNEW?

Phil Spector was a millionaire by age 21.

Phil Spector gestures during a hearing, 2004.

Phil Spector with his then-fiancée, Rachelle Marie Short.

THE MARRYING KIND

A murder rap didn't get in the way of Phil Spector's love life.

When Rachelle Short first laid eyes on Phil Spector at a Hollywood watering hole in 2003, he was on the verge of being indicted for the murder of Lana Clarkson. He was also four decades her senior. But Short, a 23-year old aspiring singer who had just come to Los Angeles from Beaver Falls, Pennsylvania, hit it off with the infamous producer. The couple was married in 2006, and Rachelle became a regular presence at her husband's murder trials. These days, she keeps busy visiting him in prison and making music. In 2013 she released a single, "P.S. I Love You," in honor of her man.

UNFORTUNATE HISTORIES

Some showcase homes of Los Angeles can hide a grisly past. These two mansions will be forever tainted by what happened inside.

PHIL HARTMAN'S HOUSE

The 4,000-square-foot residence in Encino, California, boasts four bedrooms, five bathrooms, and a pool. It also became the home in which Brynn Hartman shot and killed her husband, the beloved *Saturday Night Live* comedian Phil Hartman, before turning the gun on herself in 1998. The house sold the next year for $1.1 million.

JOSE AND KITTY MENENDEZ'S MANSION

Located in the tony neighborhood of Beverly Hills, this six-bedroom, eight-bathroom Mediterranean home would be worth almost $8 million if it were to go on the market today. In 1989, it was a bloody crime scene where Erik and Lyle Menendez shot their parents to death execution-style. The case became a nationwide sensation following the brothers' trial on Court TV.

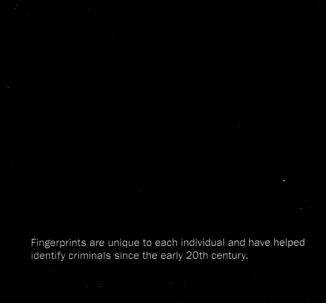

Fingerprints are unique to each individual and have helped
identify criminals since the early 20th century.

CHAPTER 5

KILLERS
AND CAPTORS

KIDNAPPERS CAN RANGE FROM TRUSTED AUTHORITY
FIGURES TO DERANGED OR POLITICALLY MOTIVATED
STRANGERS. WHAT DO THEY HAVE IN COMMON?

THE BABY
MOURNED BY MILLIONS

JOURNALIST H.L. MENCKEN DESCRIBED THE 1932 KIDNAPPING OF CHARLES LINDBERGH'S SON AS "THE BIGGEST STORY SINCE THE RESURRECTION."

Charles Lindbergh

Anne Morrow Lindbergh holding her son.

On March 1, 1932, the famous aviator Charles Lindbergh and his wife, Anne, were at home in their secluded New Jersey mansion. When Charles heard an odd noise, he shrugged it off as the snapping of the slats from an orange crate in the kitchen. But a little while later, when the Lindberghs' baby nurse went to check on 20-month-old Charles Lindbergh Jr., the crib was empty.

Lindbergh ran upstairs to search for Charles Jr. and noticed muddy footprints and an open window in the nursery. He grabbed a rifle and hurried out into the moonlit woods. The police were summoned and soon found a homemade ladder on the grounds of the Lindbergh home. A ransom note was on a windowsill. The message was rife with grammatical errors and misspellings ("the child is in gute care"), leading investigators to believe that the kidnapper might be an immigrant.

Crime of the Century

News of the Lindbergh kidnapping, later described by journalist H.L. Mencken as "the biggest story since the Resurrection," swept the country. Readers eager to follow every development in the case were captivated. At one point, President Herbert Hoover issued a statement saying he would "move heaven and earth" to find the stolen child. New Jersey state officials offered $25,000 for the return of "Little Lindy,"

with the Lindbergh family adding another $50,000 to the reward. The Bureau of Investigation, the precursor to the FBI, began working on the case.

Eight days after the abduction, a 72-year-old retired teacher and Bronx native, John Condon, contacted the Lindberghs. Accounts differ on the exact sequence of events, but Condon told the Lindberghs that he had published a letter in a local newspaper offering to act as an intermediary in the case. He said he received a reply and also had been sent the baby's sleeping suit by post. The Lindberghs confirmed the outfit belonged to their son and agreed to let Condon communicate with the abductor and pay the ransom.

On the night of April 2, 1932, Condon and Charles Lindbergh recorded the serial numbers on $50,000 in ransom money.

One of the ransom notes sent to Colonel Charles Lindbergh after the kidnapping of his son.

WANTED
INFORMATION AS TO THE WHEREABOUTS OF

CHAS. A. LINDBERGH, JR.
OF HOPEWELL, N. J.

Detail of a poster seeking information on the whereabouts of Charles A. Lindbergh Jr.

They drove to St. Raymond's Cemetery, where Condon was to meet a contact for the kidnapper while Lindbergh waited in the car. Condon said he turned over the bills to an unknown cab driver and was given a note that supposedly revealed the baby's location—but it turned out to be false.

More than a month later, on May 12, a truck driver and his assistant pulled over a few miles from the Lindbergh estate to relieve themselves in the woods, and one of them found the decomposed body of a toddler whose skull had been fractured. The remains were soon identified as the body of Charles Jr.

Police believed that the child had been fatally dropped during his kidnapper's climb down the ladder. The family and nation were devastated and newspaper editorials cried out for justice.

Trail of a Kidnapper
For 30 months, the New York Police Department and FBI tracked the ransom money as it was spent around New York City, much of it along the Lexington Avenue subway route. Eventually, a bill was traced to a gas station where the manager had recorded the license plate of a suspicious customer. He was identified as Bruno Richard Hauptmann, a German immigrant with a criminal record who lived in the Bronx. At the time of his arrest, Hauptmann had one of the ransom bills on his person.

Among the evidence collected at Hauptmann's apartment was a notebook with a sketch of the ladder. John Condon's phone number and address were written on a wall. Most damning were the missing floorboards in Hauptmann's attic, which matched the wood of the ladder. His handwriting also matched that of the ransom notes.

Hauptmann claimed that he was innocent and that a friend and business partner had left him the money, but he was sentenced to die by a New Jersey court. He was electrocuted on April 3, 1936.

Bruno Hauptmann, 1934

COULD HAUPTMANN HAVE BEEN INNOCENT?

The accused kidnapper refused to confess and was sent to the electric chair.

The case against Bruno Hauptmann seemed to be open and shut, but following his execution, facts emerged that called the verdict into question:

→ *New York Times* reporter Tom Cassidy revealed that he had scrawled Condon's phone number on Hauptmann's closet wall in order to get a "scoop." Hauptmann did not own a phone.

→ Fingerprint expert Erastus Hudson alerted the New Jersey police that he had not found any of Hauptmann's prints on the ladder. The police, who then washed the ladder, did not disclose Hudson's findings.

→ Witnesses who claimed to have seen Hauptmann on the Lindbergh property the day before the kidnapping were later discredited. One was partially blind and the other, labeled a "chronic liar" by neighbors, had only come forward after reward money was offered.

WHO KNEW?
Bruno Hauptmann's widow sued the state of New Jersey twice for the wrongful execution of her husband. The suit was dismissed both times.

THE HEIRESS
WHO ROBBED A BANK

PATTY HEARST WAS KIDNAPPED, SEXUALLY ASSAULTED, AND BRAINWASHED. THEN SHE WAS SENT TO PRISON.

Donald David DeFreeze called himself General Field Marshall Cinque.

Around 9 PM on February 4, 1974, 19-year-old Patty Hearst heard a knock on the door of the Berkeley, California, apartment she shared with her fiancé, Steven Weed. Within moments, gun-toting men and women burst in. The intruders assaulted Weed, then grabbed Hearst, granddaughter of newspaper mogul William Randolph Hearst, wrestled her into the trunk of a car, and drove off.

The young heiress's fate was unknown. Her father, Randolph, the publisher of the *San Francisco Examiner*, waited anxiously with his family to hear from Patty's abductors. Contact finally came a few days later, in the form of a tape delivered to a local radio station. Two people spoke: Patty, telling her parents she was okay, and a man who called himself General Field Marshall Cinque. The "general" announced that he and the authorities he represented held Patty's fate in their hands.

General Cinque was actually an escaped convict named Donald Defreeze. He was also a key member of the left-wing guerilla group called the Symbionese Liberation Army, or SLA, which was bent on destroying the "capitalist state." The group issued an ultimatum to Randolph Hearst: To secure Patty's release, he would have to feed California's poor. Hearst distributed $6 million worth of food to the Bay Area, but it was not enough for the SLA.

Systematic Torture

The terrorists kept Patty in a closet-size space and forced her to participate in indoctrination sessions so that she would accept their goals and philosophy. She said she was also sexually assaulted. "I mean, if you are going to break somebody down," Patty told *Dateline NBC* in 1997, "you clearly use everything that is at your disposal—and obviously sexual molestation is a really powerful way to attack a woman."

Eventually, Patty's captors wore her down. In taped messages released to her father, she began to voice her support of the SLA. On April 3, after weeks of silence, Patty recorded an announcement that shocked her parents and supporters across the nation.

"I have been given the choice of (1) being released in a safe area; or (2) joining the forces of the Symbionese Liberation Army and fighting for my freedom and the freedom of all oppressed people. I have chosen to stay and fight." Patty said her new name was Tania, in honor of a cohort of the Argentine revolutionary Che Guevara.

Less than two weeks later, images of Tania toting a machine gun were captured by security cameras at a San Francisco bank that was held up by the SLA. She was barking orders to bystanders and watching out for her colleagues. Nine days later, the SLA released a new tape in which Tania addressed the public, claiming that her gun had been loaded and that she had acted of her own free will during the robbery. She also asserted that the idea of brainwashing was "ridiculous to the point of being beyond belief."

Police escape gunfire from a house believed to be occupied by the SLA in 1974.

A teenager was forced at gunpoint to lend his van.

High school senior Tom Matthews had just finished dinner on the evening of May 16, 1974, when a woman showed up to ask about test-driving a van he had for sale. Once in the vehicle, the woman asked Matthews if they could pick up some of her friends. He agreed, only to find himself face-to-face with a gun-toting SLA member and a wigged companion Matthews recognized as Patty Hearst. The three collaborators informed Matthews they were borrowing the van. Nothing would happen to him as long as he cooperated, they said.

Hearst and her companions took Matthews to a drive-in movie for a rendezvous, but their cohorts never showed up. After being driven around for hours, Matthews was finally given back his van once Hearst and her friends stole another vehicle. He returned to his family's home at 7 AM the next day.

A poster issued by the Symbionese Liberation Army shows Patricia Hearst, as "Tania," holding a machine gun.

WHO KNEW?

In the years following her release, Patty tried her hand at acting, most famously in the films of director John Waters.

Capture

The SLA relocated to Los Angeles and quickly resumed criminal activities. They attempted but failed to rob a sporting goods store, spraying the place with bullets. One evening while Patty and SLA members William and Emily Harris were out stealing vehicles, the Los Angeles Police Department raided the house the radical group had been using as its headquarters. The small bungalow caught fire during the assault and all inside were killed.

After a summer on the run, Patty made the news again when she drove the getaway car for a bank robbery near Sacramento in which a mother of four was shot and killed. She was soon tracked down by the FBI, who found her hiding in a safe house.

Despite Patty's claims that she had been brainwashed, a jury found her guilty of armed robbery, and she was sentenced to seven years in prison. She served just 22 months before President Jimmy Carter commuted her sentence in 1979. In 2001, Bill Clinton granted her a presidential pardon. "So much anger was directed at me because of the war, Watergate, the whole '60s generation that had disappointed their parents so badly," Patty told *Dateline*. "I wouldn't even be charged today, because people don't charge kidnap victims for crimes they committed while in the company of their kidnappers."

THE GIRL IN THE BOX

KIDNAPPING VICTIM COLLEEN STAN WAS HELD CAPTIVE FOR SEVEN YEARS IN HORRIFIC CONDITIONS. HOW DID SHE SURVIVE THE ORDEAL?

A VIOLENT CONNECTION

The brother of a kidnapping victim became a murderer.

Kidnapping victim Steven Stayner's older brother, Cary, pleaded guilty to killing three women in Yosemite National Park in 1999. When questioned about the connection between his own crimes and the captivity of his brother, Cary said he thought that Steven's kidnapper had gotten off too easy, and that he was still angry at the hit-and-run driver who subsequently took his brother's life in 1989. He was given the death penalty.

Every year, about 260,000 children are abducted in the United States. Sometimes the kidnapper is a deranged stranger—the proverbial drifter—in other cases, the crime is committed by a trusted authority figure: it could be a bus driver, minister, or relative. The psychological relationship between captive and captor is complicated, as it was for 20-year-old Colleen Stan and her tormentor of seven years.

Fateful Decision

On May 19, 1977, Colleen Stan was trying to get a ride to a friend's birthday party in northern California when a blue van driven by Cameron Hooker pulled up to the side of the road. An experienced hitchhiker, Stan decided it was safe to get in because Hooker was accompanied by his wife and young child.

She was wrong. Hooker drove to an isolated area, held a knife to Stan's throat, and

Cameron Hooker as he is sentenced to 104 years in prison at his trial, 1985.

put a 20-pound insulated box over her head. Stan could hardly breathe. Once they arrived at Hooker's house in Red Bluff, California, he chained Stan to the basement ceiling by her wrists and

physically abused her for days at a time. He soon began keeping her in the head box or a coffinlike carton under the bed where he and his wife slept, letting Stan out for only one hour a day.

Eventually, Hooker coerced Stan into signing a contract agreeing to be his slave. He made her believe that if she escaped, an organization of white slave owners known as the Company would come after Stan and her family, according to later interviews she gave. "I'm in control," he told her. "Colleen no longer exists. You are now K. You are my slave."

Wanting to Be a "Good Slave"

Stan fell so completely under Hooker's control that at one point he posed as her boyfriend, and the two visited Stan's family and stayed overnight. Throughout her captivity, Stan never attempted to escape or contact anyone who might help her. She just wanted to be a "good slave," she told an interviewer.

Stan's behavior is described by therapists as "Stockholm syndrome," in which a captive develops feelings of trust or affection toward the captor. "People who have not been through this type of experience just don't understand all the threats, and all the torture, and just all the mind control that goes on.... Your abductor just conditions you...by torture and rape and abuse and threats," Stan later told an interviewer.

Colleen Stan now lives in Southern California. "I have to accept the fact that it happened because it did," she has said. "I don't let it affect my life now."

Hooker held Stan until his wife, Janice, learned of his plans to take five more "slaves" and decided to free Stan. While Hooker was at work, Janice put Stan on a bus home, explaining that her husband was not part of any Company. Bewildered, Stan continued to contact Hooker for months, never telling authorities what had happened to her. Hooker was arrested only after Janice turned him in, alerting police about the kidnapping and of a murder Hooker had allegedly committed in 1976.

Janice was granted immunity for testifying against her husband, who was sentenced to 104 years in prison.

Patty Hearst leaving the federal building in San Francisco.

THE STOCKHOLM SYNDROME

When a captive begins to see his captor as a protector or ally, the phenomenon is referred to as Stockholm syndrome. It is considered a complex unconscious act of self-preservation.

→ **Where it got its name** The term was coined in the 1970s to describe the reactions of four employees held captive following the robbery of a Stockholm bank. After being treated with intermittent kindness for six days, the kidnapping victims strongly resisted rescue efforts.

→ **Conditions** The prisoner must believe there is no possible means of escape; the captor must wield supreme power, leveling threats of torture or death if disobeyed.

→ **The trigger** Any small act of kindness on the part of the captor—or even the absence of violence—can seem like a sign of friendship.

→ **Aftereffects** Freed victims often mourn the loss of their captors, defend their actions to others, and try to contact them.

→ **A famous case** In 1974, newspaper heiress Patty Hearst was kidnapped by a group of political extremists. Within weeks, Hearst joined the organization, helped it rob a bank, and even became engaged to a member.

AFTERSCHOOL TERROR

A young boy accepted a ride home and became a pedophile's captive for seven years. Then he made a daring escape.

Seven-year-old Steven Stayner of Merced, California, was walking home from school on December 4, 1972, when a man in a white Buick pulled up and offered the boy a ride. The driver, Kenneth Parnell, was a 41-year-old convicted pedophile and rapist. He took Stayner to a remote cabin in Catheys Valley and kept him there for seven years.

Parnell convinced Stayner that his parents couldn't take care of him anymore and that he was now the child's legal guardian. As Stayner got older, he began to question Parnell's story, scanning articles for any mention of his parents' searching for him. "I'd ask myself, 'Mom and Dad, where the hell are you?'" he told *Newsweek* magazine in 1984. But it wasn't until Parnell brought home five-year-old Timmy White that Stayner knew he had to get out. While Parnell was out one day, Stayner escaped, taking White with him, and hitchhiked some 40 miles to a police station in Ukiah, California.

Stayner would go on to marry and have a family before dying in a motorcycle accident in 1989, at age 24.

Parnell served five years of an eight-year sentence, and in 2003 he was arrested again for trying to buy a four-year-old boy for $500. He died in prison in 2008.

Steven Stayner (right), with Kenneth Parnell

KILL AND TELL

"I MADE THE POLICE LOOK STUPID. I WAS OUT TO WRECK TEXAS LAW ENFORCEMENT." —Henry Lee Lucas

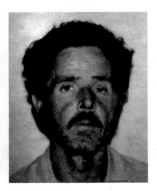

Henry Lee Lucas

THE MIND OF A SERIAL LIAR

What would have prompted Henry Lee Lucas to confess to so many crimes? He explained himself this way:

→ To get special treatment in prison. The strategy worked: He got cigarettes, milkshakes, restaurant meals, and more.

→ As long as he kept confessing, he wouldn't get transferred to death row.

→ It was a publicity stunt—he liked the media attention.

→ He wanted to die, he told one journalist; his execution would be a suicide.

Henry Lee Lucas is one of America's most heinous serial killers, convicted of slaying 11 people. But the Virginia-born Lucas grew more famous for the hundreds of murders he confessed to but didn't commit.

When Lucas was arrested in 1983, it was for the gruesome slaying of an 82-year-old Texas woman as well as the niece of an acquaintance from Florida. In the year and a half that followed, Lucas went on a confession binge that offered eager police departments the opportunity to clear their books of more than 200 unsolved murders. He took credit for killings in both Texas and West Virginia and as far afield as Japan and Spain. The public was fascinated by Lucas's lurid descriptions, and the diagnosed psychopath became a media celebrity. Then it was discovered that he'd made all or most of it up.

Rough Beginning

Born in 1936, Henry Lee Lucas was raised in backwoods Virginia. His mother, a prostitute, beat him, according to media accounts. His father, a bootlegger who had lost both legs in a train accident, died of pneumonia after passing out, drunk, in a blizzard. When Henry was ten, one of his brothers accidentally slashed his eye with a knife, and doctors had to replace it with a glass one. At 13, Henry ran away from home, became a vagrant, and eventually

spent five years in prison for burglary, according to accounts of his life published in biographies.

Although Lucas later claimed he started killing at the age of 15, he wasn't charged in a murder case until he was 24, when he stabbed his 74-year-old mother during a drunken argument. Lucas claimed he was acting in self-defense, but was sentenced to 20 to 40 years in prison. After attempting suicide, he was transferred to a forensic psychiatric hospital, and in 1970, ten years into his sentence, he was released on parole.

Deadly Drifter

Following another stretch in prison on weapons charges, Lucas met arsonist and serial killer Ottis Toole and his niece, 12-year-old Frieda "Becky" Powell, in Florida. For the next six years the three drifted from state to state. Lucas and Powell then settled in with a Pentecostal cult in Texas, but in a 1982 argument Lucas stabbed Powell to death. A few weeks later, he claimed another victim, 82-year-old Kate Rich.

It wasn't until 1983, when Lucas was serving time on weapons charges, that Lucas confessed to killing Powell and Rich and led investigators to the murder sites. They found corroborating evidence in the form of clothing, bones, and decomposing remains, and charged Lucas with both murders. Later that year, he entered

Henry Lee Lucas, left, with police at the site of a double homicide on September 6, 1984, in San Luis Obispo County.

a guilty plea, then announced a shocker in court: "I got a hundred more out there somewhere," Lucas said, referring to his alleged victims.

The Lucas Task Force

With hundreds of unsolved murder cases on the books, the Texas Rangers swung into action, forming the Lucas Task Force to investigate the killer's claims. During interviews with police, he often declared, "Oh, yeah, I got me some there in your area." Investigators eager to wrap up their open cases dropped clues allowing Lucas to describe crimes he hadn't committed. More than 200 cases were put to bed.

In all, Lucas officially confessed to murdering 600 people, but it is unknown how many of those he made up. It is likely that the killing that landed Lucas on death row in Florida was one he did not commit.

The slaying involved an unnamed hitchhiker whose body was discovered near a Texas interstate on Halloween 1979.

While interrogating Lucas about the murder, police provided Lucas with key details, and he was able to accurately describe the slaying and victim, dubbed "Orange Socks" by police because that was all she was wearing when she was found. During the trial, Lucas's attorneys presented strong evidence that he'd been in Florida, not Texas, on the night in question, but the jury convicted him anyway and sentenced him to death.

The Texas attorney general later dubbed it "highly unlikely" that Lucas was guilty, and even the county prosecutor who had secured his conviction believed the evidence didn't support a guilty verdict. In 1998, Texas Governor George W. Bush commuted Lucas's sentence to life in prison. Lucas died in prison in 2001, at the age of 64.

Ottis Toole

CONFESSIONS BY NUMBERS

How many murders did Henry Lee Lucas actually commit? The ultimate tally remains unclear, but here are statistics.

→ Murders for which he was irrefutably shown responsible: **3**

→ Murders for which he was convicted, but may not have committed: **11**

→ Murders to which he officially confessed: **600** across 27 states

→ Murders to which he confessed unofficially: **3,000**

→ Number of his confessions considered "believable" by the investigating task force: **350**

→ Number of cold cases closed based on his confessions: **213**

111

HOUSE OF HORRORS

IN THE ANNALS OF CRIME, THERE MAY BE NO MORE DERANGED SERIAL ABDUCTOR THAN GARY HEIDNIK.

Gary Heidnik after being sentenced to die.

"I went to the execution but it was too calm and serene for me.... They just stuck a needle in his arm. He never looked at us. Never acknowledged us. Never said he was sorry. He didn't say anything. He didn't even look in our direction."

—*Tracey Lomax, sister of Heidnik's victim Sandra Lindsay*

On March 24, 1987, Philadelphia police officers David Savidge and John Cannon responded to a 911 phone call from a woman who claimed that she and a group of other women were being held in chains in the basement of a local home. Although initially skeptical, the officers followed up, and after interviewing the woman in person, they arrested the man she identified as her captor, Gary Heidnik, who was parked nearby in his Cadillac.

Savidge and Cannon next drove to Heidnik's house, which had barred windows festooned with crucifixes and an entrance secured by numerous metal doors. Inside, the officers found exactly what their informant had described: half-naked women chained in the cellar and human body parts in the freezer.

The nation soon learned the details of the grisly kidnappings, which had been executed over a period of nine months. During that time, Heidnik had abducted, tortured, and sexually abused six women. He kept them in a pit he'd dug in his cellar, sometimes filling it with water and giving them electric shocks. He ultimately murdered two of them, one of whom he dismembered, cooked, and fed to the others.

IQ of 148

Born in Ohio in 1943, Heidnik was raised by his mother before moving in with an allegedly emotionally abusive father. After dropping out of high school, he joined the army and was stationed in Germany.

There, he trained as a medic, but suffered a nervous breakdown. To qualify for disability payments from the federal government, Heidnik, who had an IQ of 148, claimed that he was schizophrenic. He later started his own church in Philadelphia as a tax scam. He invested his disability checks in the stock market and parleyed them into over half a million dollars.

In 1978, Heidnik was imprisoned for kidnapping and raping his girlfriend's mentally impaired sister, whom he signed out of an institution. He was sentenced to seven years for the crime, serving only three in a mental institution. Upon his release, Heidnik took a Philippine mail-order bride. "He thought he was getting hooked up with a nice subservient [woman], but he wasn't," his friend John Cassidy told *Philadelphia Magazine* in 2007. After the wife became pregnant, she left Heidnik when his beatings became unbearable.

A Prison Basement

Heidnik turned to kidnapping and torture in November 1986. His first victim was Josefina Rivera, a prostitute he picked up on the street, brought to his basement, and kept chained to a pipe. He would eventually bring five other women to join Rivera as his sex slaves, whom he kept in freezing cold and hellish conditions. Heidnik beat and raped the women regularly and drowned out their screams with a loud radio turned to a hard rock station.

WHO KNEW?
Gary Heidnik allegedly kept women captive in a pit in his basement, furnished with mattresses and a portable toilet.

The Philadelphia house where three women were found, chained to a sewer pipe, and a human arm was found in a freezer.

Homicide and Cannibalism

Conditions in the basement turned deadly in early February 1987, when Heidnik caught one of the girls, Sandra Lindsay, trying to escape. He hung her from a ceiling beam by a single handcuff for days. When Lindsay stopped eating and died, Heidnik cooked her remains, mixed them with dog food, and fed the concoction to the others. He soon tortured and killed another of his victims, Deborah Dudley, electrocuting her with a stripped extension cord.

The Horror Ends

Over time, Rivera, Heidnik's first victim, gained his trust by informing him about the actions of the other prisoners. She became Heidnik's constant com-panion, accompanying him on errands and sleeping in his bed. On March 24, 1987, Rivera convinced her captor to let her go see her family, with the promise she would bring him back a new girl in return. While free, Rivera went to her boyfriend's house and made the 911 call to the police.

Heidnik was executed by lethal injection on July 6, 1999. His surviv-ing victims were present for the proceedings.

HOMEMADE PRISONS

THE DUNGEONS BUILT BY SOME KIDNAPPERS CAN RESEMBLE TORTURE CHAMBERS FROM ANOTHER ERA.

John Jamelske's first victim was only 14 years old. The 52-year-old handyman lured the girl into his car and made her his captive—first in a well near his mother's house, and then in a dank, windowless underground bunker he built at his garbage-strewn Syracuse, New York, home. Over the next two years, Jamelske repeatedly raped his young prisoner, until he finally set her free. It was a pattern he would repeat with five girls and women from 1988 to 2003, when he was captured by law enforcement.

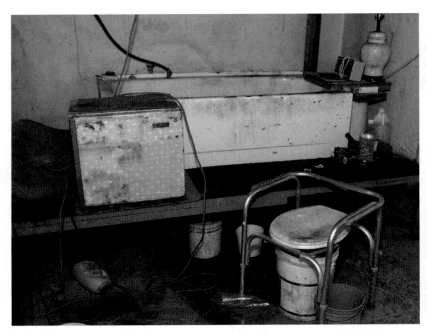

Part of the underground bunker where Jamelske kept five women as sex slaves

Serial kidnapper John Jamelske admitted keeping five women as slaves and was sentenced to 18 years to life for his crimes.

Josef Fritzl kept his daughter Elisabeth and their children captive for 24 years in a space that was less than 600 square feet.

Josef Fritzl

BLUEPRINT FOR A BUNKER

Josef Fritzl's captive children grew up underground and never saw sunlight.

In 1978, Josef Fritzl applied for a building permit for an "extension" in his basement. He began construction around 1981, and over time created a 590-square-foot space with two sleeping areas, a cooking area, and bathroom facilities. Fritzl installed a series of eight doors, two of which locked electronically, to hide the rooms. The ceilings were only 5½ feet high, and as his captive children grew, they developed posture and spine problems.

Such a scenario, where a captor holds a prisoner almost in plain sight, is exceedingly rare, with fewer than 100 cases each year, according to CNN. But when cases come to light, they are the stuff of nightmares.

Almost Unfathomable

One of the most infamous incidents involved Elisabeth Fritzl, a teenager from Amstetten, Austria. Elisabeth was home one day in 1984 when her abusive father, Josef Fritzl, called her to come down to the basement. When Elisabeth went to meet her father, he knocked her out with an ether-soaked cloth and locked her in the underground dungeon he had been secretly building for years.

Fritzl told his wife Rosemarie and their children that Elisabeth had run away, an explanation that seemed plausible since the teen had done so once before. For the next 24 years, Fritzl kept his daughter prisoner, raping her repeatedly while the family went on with their lives upstairs. During that time, Elisabeth gave birth to seven children. One died shortly after birth, a victim of Fritzl's neglect. Three were raised by Fritzl and Rosemarie, who believed they were foundlings. The other three children lived in the rat-infested basement with their mother. All were abused by Fritzl.

The imprisonment finally came to an end when the 19-year-old child who lived in the basement developed kidney failure and had to be taken to the hospital. The staff thought Fritzl acted suspiciously and notified the police, who found the subterranean chamber. Fritzl was convicted of negligent homicide, rape, incest, and enslavement. He was sentenced to life in an Austrian prison, where he remains.

MANHUNT

WHEN PURSUING A KIDNAPPER, TIME IS OF THE ESSENCE. TECHNOLOGY INCREASINGLY HELPS SOLVE ABDUCTIONS.

Donna Norris touches a photograph of her daughter, Amber Hagerman.

THE REAL AMBER

The little girl behind the national kidnapping-prevention program AMBER Alert

On January 13, 1996, nine-year-old Amber Hagerman vanished while riding her bicycle in Arlington, Texas. According to the only witness, the abductor grabbed the child and drove away in a black truck. Four days later, Amber's body was found in a drainage ditch. After the tragedy, Amber's parents became activists, suggesting a system through which law enforcement authorities could work efficiently with the media to help find missing children. The AMBER Alert program was launched in Dallas on a local radio station in October 1996, and by 2005 it was a coordinated program in all 50 states. Amber Hagerman's abductor has never been caught.

When 12-year-old Polly Klaas was kidnapped in 1993, her family distributed flyers. *America's Most Wanted* aired a segment about her. Neighbors formed search parties, rewards were offered, and bloodhounds and even psychics were enlisted. In the end, however, the manhunt for Polly's abductor and murderer pivoted on a simple tip from a local property owner. Sadly, police had already missed several opportunities to catch him, including one that might have saved the young girl's life. If any good can be said to have come from Polly's case, it is that it inspired significant improvements in the way law enforcement investigates and apprehends kidnappers.

A Missed Opportunity

Polly lived with her mother, Eve Nichol, in an affluent Northern California neighborhood. The night the 12-year-old was abducted, she had been hosting a slumber party for two friends. As Nichol slept, a stranger broke in to the house, threatened the girls with a knife, and carried Polly away.

That same night, 25 miles away, police responded to a call from a landowner about a trespasser. Officers confronted the man, whose car had gotten stuck in some mud on the property, and recorded his name, Richard Allen Davis. Unaware of an all-points bulletin (APB) about Polly's abduc-

tion, the police concluded that Davis was not a threat, helped him free his car, and let him go. Davis was arrested again a couple of weeks later for drunk driving, but again, police failed to connect him to the kidnapping. It was only in late November, when the property owner discovered some of Polly's clothing on her land, that the police put two and two together and arrested Davis, a lifelong criminal. He confessed to the killing and is now on death row in California.

Changes in the System

The Klaas abduction altered the way law enforcement approaches kidnapping cases. APBs are now issued on all police channels, instead of just certain frequencies as they

Advances in computer technology have helped efforts to catch suspects.

An electronic sign shows an AMBER Alert over Interstate 80 in Omaha, Nebraska.

were back then. More states have adopted strict punishments for habitual offenders like Davis; and the national AMBER Alert system, which broadcasts real-time information about abducted children through a variety of public systems, has been introduced in phases nationally. Since its inception, more than 675 children featured in AMBER Alerts have been recovered.

Technology has also come a long way since 1993. The prevalence of security cameras has helped lead to some suspects, including a gunman who in 2014 tried to kidnap a Tennessee community-college student. She managed to escape, and police were later able to identify the offender through video footage.

In a number of recent cases, police have traced kidnappers through their or their victims' cell phones. In 2009, police apprehended a woman who had kidnapped her granddaughter in Massachusetts by using GPS to track the missing girl's phone. But the strategy can be even simpler than that. In 2014, after a woman abducted her infant nephew in Wisconsin, police simply called her cell phone and asked her to meet them for questioning. The woman, who was in Iowa by that time, agreed to stop, and the baby was safely recovered from a nearby gas station where she'd hidden him.

DEATH OF A LITTLE BEAUTY

THE DAY AFTER CHRISTMAS 1996, SIX-YEAR-OLD JONBENET RAMSEY WAS FOUND MURDERED IN THE BASEMENT OF HER COLORADO HOME

John and Patsy Ramsey hold a reward sign for information leading to the arrest of their daughter's murderer.

EVIDENCE OF A STRANGER

As the investigation of JonBenet Ramsey's murder proceeded, the police were widely criticized for being so fixated on the Ramseys' guilt that they failed to pursue evidence pointing to other suspects. Among other discoveries:

➜ **A stranger's** DNA was found on the blanket Jon-Benet's body was wrapped in.

➜ **An unidentified** palm print was found on the door of the wine cellar.

➜ **An unidentified** boot print was found in the cellar's concrete dust.

On the morning of December 26, 1996, Patsy Ramsey was heading to the kitchen of her Boulder, Colorado, home when she spotted a letter on the staircase. One glance told her it was a ransom note for her young daughter, JonBenet, a six-year-old beauty-pageant contestant. As she bolted upstairs to JonBenet's room, Patsy yelled for her husband, John. Sure enough, JonBenet was gone. Ignoring instructions in the ransom message not to call law enforcement, the couple contacted the police.

Faulty Investigation

Instead of immediately sealing off the house and declaring it an official crime scene, investigators allowed family members and visitors to enter and leave for hours, a decision that would later come to haunt the inquiry. It wasn't until the Ramseys had scrambled to put together the $118,000 in ransom—coincidentally, the precise amount of John's bonus the previous year—that a proper search of the house was conducted. That afternoon, John made the grisly discovery: JonBenet's body under a white blanket in the wine cellar.

"As I was walking through the basement," he later said, "I opened the door to a room and knew immediately that I'd found her. . . . Her eyes were closed; I feared the worst, but yet—I'd found her."

An autopsy revealed that JonBenet had died from strangulation and a skull fracture.

The murder sent the press into a frenzy, and local authorities made the situation worse by stating that they strongly suspected JonBenet's parents were responsible for her death. One policeman even questioned Patsy's grief, telling *Vanity Fair* magazine that she'd been watching him through "splayed fingers" while crying.

The Ramseys pleaded their innocence. Both parents submitted to polygraph tests and passed them, but the results were dis-

> Mr. Ramsey,
>
> Listen carefully! We are a group of individuals that represent a small foreign faction. We do respect your bussiness but not the country that it serves. At this time we have your daughter in our posession. She is safe and unharmed and if you want her to see 1997, you must follow our instructions to the letter.
>
> You will withdraw $118,000.00 from your account. $100,000 will be in $100 bills and the remaining $18,000 in $20 bills. Make sure that you bring an adequate size attache to the bank. When you get home you will put the money in a brown paper bag. I will call you between 8 and 10 am tomorrow to instruct you on delivery. The delivery will be exhausting so I advise you to be rested. If we monitor you getting the money early, we might call you early to arrange an earlier delivery of the

The first page of the original ransom note found in the Ramsey home.

JonBenet Ramsey

Boulder sheriffs stand guard outside the Ramsey home.

missed as inconclusive because the FBI had not supervised the process. Many observers pointed to the fact that Patsy had enrolled JonBenet in a number of children's beauty pageants, thus "sexualizing" the six-year-old. Police were also criticized for their sloppy supervision of the Ramsey home.

No Closure for the Ramseys

Several grand juries reviewed the evidence, but the Ramseys were never formally named as suspects and no criminal charges were ever brought against them. The couple was officially cleared in 2008, based on DNA evidence pointing to an unknown assailant.

As tips and leads in the case continued to trickle in over the years, the Boulder Police Department decided to reopen the investigation in 2009. Court papers revealed in the wake of that process indicated that one grand jury had voted to indict Patsy and John as accessories to the crime, but that District Attorney Alex Hunter had declined to prosecute. The revelation of the indictment spurred another round of media coverage and speculation about JonBenet's murder, which remains unsolved. A lawyer for John Ramsey criticized the unsealed documents as "nonsensical."

Patsy Ramsey died in 2006 of ovarian cancer. John Ramsey ran for a seat in the Michigan House of Representatives in 2004 and 2008 and lost both times. In 2011, he married Jan Rousseaux.

HIDDEN
IN PLAIN SIGHT

ARIEL CASTRO KIDNAPPED THREE WOMEN AND HELD THEM CAPTIVE FOR OVER A DECADE, JUST THREE MILES FROM WHERE THEY WERE TAKEN.

Between 2002 and 2013, Ariel Castro, a one-time bus driver and sometime musician, kidnapped three young women and kept them as sexual prisoners in the bedrooms of his Cleveland home. Castro's victims included 21-year-old Michelle Knight, a single mother. He also abducted Amanda Berry, in 2003, just one day shy of her 17th birthday. His third victim was Gina DeJesus, the 14-year-old best friend of Castro's daughter Angie, who was taken while walking home from school.

Castro had grown up and raised his four children in the Tremont neighborhood of Cleveland, and worked around the area for more than 20 years. In each kidnapping, he offered the woman a ride, gained her trust, then lured her into his house and restrained her. After his arrest, Castro insisted that the kidnappings were always "crimes of opportunity," never premeditated.

Horrendous Abuse

While in captivity, the three women kept journals, which later would shed light on their treatment and horrendous abuse. They were shackled by the ankles and held in two adjoining upstairs bedrooms where the windows were blacked out and the only ventilation was provided by a small hole in the door.

The portable plastic toilets made available to them were seldom emptied, and the women were allowed to shower at most twice a week.

Castro beat and sexually assaulted his victims regularly. He was said by Knight to be "obsessed with prostitutes" and would give the women money after each rape. Knight, Berry, and

DeJesus then had to pay if they wanted anything from the outside world. Knight became pregnant more than once over the years, but after being beaten, miscarried each time.

Castro taunted Berry and DeJesus by making them watch news reports about searches and local vigils for them. He told Knight that no one was

---

"I'M NOT A MONSTER, I'M JUST SICK"

In court proceedings, Ariel Castro claimed that his only fault was that he was a sex addict.

After pleading guilty to more than 937 criminal counts of abduction and assault over the course of a decade, Ariel Castro made a rambling 16-minute statement to the court in which he showed no remorse. "Most of the sex in the house was consensual," he claimed. "There was harmony." He added, "I'm not a monster, I'm just sick."

At Castro's sentencing hearing, one forensic psychiatrist testified that Castro suffered "no psychiatric illness whatsoever." Retired FBI criminal profiler Mary Ellen O'Toole agreed, saying that Castro exhibited traits of psychopathy: "Psychopathy's not a mental illness, it's a personality disorder...distinguished by a stunning lack of consciences—no remorse or empathy for what they do. They're very arrogant individuals," she said.

Ariel Castro

WHO KNEW?
Ariel Castro's daughter Angie had dinner at her father's house just hours before the rescue of his captives. She only learned of his crimes afterward.

Ariel Castro's Cleveland home was surrounded by a ten-foot chain link fence.

RESCUER ROCKS THE INTERNET

Ariel Castro's neighbor Charles Ramsey helped rescue Knight, Berry, and DeJesus. His colorful interviews went viral in social media outlets. Among his comments:

→ **About race relations** "Bro, I knew something was wrong when a little pretty white girl ran into a black man's arms. Something is wrong here. Dead giveaway."

→ **About being a hero** "I'm a Christian, an American, and just like you. We bleed same blood, put our pants on the same way. It's just that you got to put that—being a coward, and 'I don't want to get in no-body's business'—you got to put that away for a minute."

→ **About what he's going to do with the reward** "I tell you what you do, give [the reward money] to [the victims]. Because, if folks been following this case since last night, you been following me since last night, you know I got a job anyway."

looking for her or cared if she was dead or alive.

On Christmas Day 2006, Berry, pregnant with Castro's child, went into labor. Castro forced Knight to deliver the baby and threatened to kill Knight if the child died. At one point, she revived the infant using CPR, but Castro neverthe-less viciously assaulted Knight following the birth.

Eventually, Castro allowed the women to walk around unshackled, but only in the upstairs rooms. He seemed to believe he had created a new family and appeared to enjoy celebrating holidays and raising the baby, whom he doted on. Castro even let Knight, Berry, and DeJesus out into the backyard on occasion, though only at night, while wearing wigs.

No Exit Strategy

Around the end of 2012, Castro told Berry that the end was near. He had been fired from his job and his house was in foreclosure. He said he would not kill any of them, because of the baby—but could not let them go either, or turn himself in to police.

On May 6, 2013, Berry took a chance and opened an inside door between the house and porch, then walked out onto the porch with her daughter. Her yells for help attracted the attention of neighbors, who kicked in the bottom of the porch door. After Berry and her daughter crawled through the opening, the police were summoned to rescue Knight and DeJesus. Castro was arrested the same day and later sentenced to three consecutive life terms, plus 1,000 years. After a month in prison, Castro committed suicide by hanging himself with a bed-sheet. The city of Cleveland tore down 2207 Seymour Avenue in August 2013.

NINE MONTHS IN HELL

AT 14, ELIZABETH SMART WAS KIDNAPPED AND ABUSED BY A SELF-PROCLAIMED RELIGIOUS PROPHET AND HIS WIFE.

Elizabeth Smart at a signing of her book, *My Story*, in 2013.

On the night of June 5, 2002, in Salt Lake City, Utah, 14-year-old Elizabeth Smart was sleeping in the bedroom she shared with her sister when she felt a beard against her face. "I have a knife at your neck," a man's voice said. "Don't make a sound, get up, and come with me." Paralyzed with fear, Elizabeth complied as her sister, nine-year-old Mary Katherine, watched. Later, Mary Katherine would recall the man as polite, calm, and nicely dressed, with a voice she thought sounded familiar.

He was Brian David Mitchell, a 57-year-old self-proclaimed religious prophet, familiar on the streets of Salt Lake City as a panhandler. Mitchell escorted Smart to a nearby camp on a steep mountainside. "There were tarps on the ground and then right here the tent was set up," she told NBC News upon revisiting the site later. "Out of this area walked a woman, she had on long linen robes."

The woman, Wanda Barzee, was Mitchell's wife.

She ordered Smart into the tent, where she washed her feet and dressed her in a similar robe. After a brief "wedding" ceremony, Mitchell pushed Smart to the ground and raped her. It was the horrifying beginning of nine months of abuse.

Life in Captivity

Smart was being held just five miles from her home, but whenever the trio went out in public, people kept their distance, in part because of their bizarre appearance: All three dressed in religious garb, and Smart and Barzee wore

Surrounded by families of kidnapped victims, including Elizabeth Smart (far left), U.S. President George W. Bush signs the Amber Alert law at the Rose Garden of the White House on April 30, 2003.

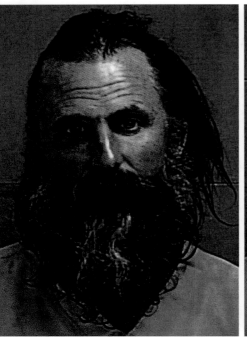

Brian Mitchell, left, and his wife, Wanda Barzee.

veils. Early on in Smart's ordeal, Mitchell told her that he had planned her kidnapping from the moment her mother gave him five dollars one day on the street.

During her captivity, Smart was raped multiple times each day. Mitchell often forced her to drink alcohol and starved her. Barzee, too, abused Smart, treating her as a slave. "She would have me sweep out the tent, sweep off the tarps," Smart told NPR in an interview. "Because our plates would be sitting outside, it wouldn't be rare in the middle of the night for mice or rodents to be running across our plates and leave their business on the plates, and so then she would have me wipe off and wash the dishes from rodent feces." According to Smart, Barzee was jealous of the young girl and fought with her husband about her constantly.

Close Calls

Smart came close to being rescued at least twice. Only days after being kidnapped, a helicopter searching for her hovered above the camp, but Mitchell and Barzee forced Smart inside. She said her heart sank as she heard the chopper fly away, never to return. Mitchell took this as a "sign from God."

On another occasion, a policeman confronted the threesome at a downtown library. As the detective questioned Mitchell, Barzee clamped "iron" fingers on Smart's thigh under the table. The teenager said she kept quiet out of fear Mitchell would make good on his constant threats to murder her family.

Rescued

Ultimately, Smart helped maneuver her own release after Mitchell and Barzee brought her to California for the winter. Realizing her only chance at being recognized was returning to Utah, Smart told Mitchell that God wanted them to go back. "You are His servant, you're His prophet," she told him. "You're practically His best friend. Could you please ask Him?" In March 2003, after the three moved again to the Salt Lake City area, multiple witnesses recognized Mitchell from a police sketch. Soon, the police raided the camp where Smart was being held. Today, Smart is an activist who works to educate the public about violent and sexual crime.

PROPHET OF EVIL

One of the big breaks in the Elizabeth Smart case came when Smart's sister, Mary Katherine, suddenly recalled where she'd heard the voice of her sister's kidnapper. "I think I know who it is," she told her parents. "Emmanuel."

Emmanuel was the strange, bearded man her mother had given money to on the street and had hired to do a few hours' work around the house. His real name was Brian David Mitchell, and he claimed to be an angel who was being groomed by God to prepare the world for the second coming of Christ. In reality, he was a manipulative pedophile, rapist, stalker, and kidnapper.

Twice divorced, Mitchell married Wanda Barzee in 1985. When he kidnapped Smart, he planned for her to be the first of 350 wives. A clinical psychologist who examined Mitchell in 2008 diagnosed him as having paranoid schizophrenia. He was found competent to stand trial in 2010. In December of that year, a jury deliberated for about five hours before finding him guilty.

THE STRENGTH TO RISE

HOW DO VICTIMS OF CRIME AND THEIR LOVED ONES MOVE ON WITH THEIR LIVES AFTER THE UNTHINKABLE HAS HAPPENED?

THE AFTERMATH

Survivors of violent crimes are likely to experience after-effects for anywhere from a few hours to years afterward, according to the National Center for Victims of Crime. Their troubles may manifest themselves as:

→ **Physical injuries.** Internal trauma, cuts and bruises, broken bones, sexually transmitted diseases

→ **Stress.** Headaches, tension, high blood pressure, racing pulse, difficulty breathing, insomnia, stomach problems

→ **Emotional trauma.** Flashbacks, anxiety, nightmares, anger, memory problems, trouble concentrating, difficulty making decisions, emotional numbness, revenge fantasies

In May 2014, Richard Martinez's only son, Christopher, was shot dead during a killing rampage near the University of California, Santa Barbara. In the aftermath, Martinez channeled his anguish into gun control activism. "Chris died because of craven, irresponsible politicians and the NRA," Martinez said at a press conference following the massacre. "Too many have died. We should say to ourselves, 'not one more.'"

Jaycee Dugard, who was abducted in 1991 at age 11, repeatedly raped, and held captive for 18 years, started the JAYC Foundation to serve other abduction victims and their families. Salt Lake City, Utah, abduction survivor Elizabeth Smart (see pages 122–123) became a victim's-rights activist, as did Cleveland kidnapping survivor Michelle Knight (see pages 120–121).

In media reports about crime and criminals, victims often get overlooked in favor of sensational stories about the offenders. But sometimes victims themselves make news, particularly when they emerge from a seemingly unbearable experience with resilience and the determination to make a difference.

Moving Forward

Some less sensational crimes yield inspiring stories as well, including that of Paul Traub of Burnsville, Minnesota. In 2008, a pair of home-invasion burglars stabbed Traub 20 times in the back, head, and face before setting his house on fire and taking off with his car. After running through the flames to safety, Traub's first thought was to make sure the rest of the neighbors in his build-

Elizabeth Smart-Gilmour speaks on overcoming adversity and of being kidnapped at age 14.

Richard Martinez speaks about the loss of his son, Christopher, who was killed during a May 2014 shooting at the U.C. Santa Barbara campus.

ing were all right. Traub won a 2014 Special Courage Award from the U.S. Department of Justice for his bravery, and for cooperating with police and prosecutors to solve the crime. "I believe I have a fairly strong faith, and I believe that that is what carried me through that night," he said.

Many survivors say that their faith or positive outlook on life is what has helped them move forward. And they often cite a refusal to define themselves by their offenders' inhuman actions. After Dugard's rescue in 2009, Smart said she hoped Dugard wouldn't let "this horrible event take over and consume the rest of your life."

Thankfully, Smart's wish seems to have come true. "I don't think of myself as a victim," Dugard wrote in her 2012 book, *A Stolen Life*. "I simply survived an intolerable situation."

EASING THE BURDEN

Money can't eliminate their suffering, but financial assistance can help victims get back on their feet.

Crime doesn't just take an emotional and physical toll; it can take a financial one as well. Medical care, crime scene cleanup, lost wages, and funeral expenses are just some of the costs associated with being a victim. To help, each state has a crime-victim compensation fund to defray costs. In all, such programs pay about $500 million a year to more than 200,000 victims; the maximum benefit averages about $25,000. Most of the money comes out of the fines and fees charged to criminal offenders. The families of homicide victims, as well as victims of rape, assault, child sexual abuse, domestic violence, and drunk driving are eligible for compensation. To qualify, applicants must have reported the incident promptly to law enforcement and cooperated with investigators and prosecutors.

The majority of stalking victims are women.

CHAPTER 6

GOING AFTER WOMEN AND CHILDREN

FROM JACK THE RIPPER TO TED BUNDY, SERIAL
MURDERERS HAVE SOUGHT OUT VICTIMS WHO WERE
TRUSTING, AVAILABLE, AND VULNERABLE.

MONSTERS
AMONG US

FEW CRIMINALS ARE MORE TERRIFYING THAN SERIAL MURDERERS. BUT SOME POPULAR GENERALIZATIONS ABOUT THEM ARE JUST PLAIN WRONG.

Real-life serial killers may be rare, but they've been the subject of countless articles, books, movies and television shows, and are part of our collective nightmares. Over the years, the media has assembled an almost generic profile for such murderers: They're white male outcasts. They're evil geniuses and sexual predators who target women and children. They keep "trophies," or souvenirs, from their kills. Yet the reality is more complicated and nuanced.

As defined by the FBI, serial murder is "the unlawful killing of two or more victims by the same offender(s), in separate events." Criminals who fit this description are racially diverse; according to the agency, the distribution of ethnicities basically matches the American population. Far from being loners, these people are often contributing members of society who appear normal. Their motives can include anger, hatred of a specific category of people or of society in general, financial gain, and a desire for fame. A killer's rationale can change or evolve over time.

Certainly, sexual satisfaction is a common motive. Serial killers tend to choose

THE BEAST

One of the worst serial killers in history confessed to killing 140 boys in Colombia and Ecuador in the 1990s.

Luis Eduardo Garavito of Colombia confessed to killing 140 children in a five-year nationwide spree.

Luis Garavito, a drifter and alcoholic from Colombia, admitted to torturing and murdering 140 boys in a brutal seven-year spree in the 1990s after prosecutors presented overwhelming evidence against him. He was sentenced to 52 years in prison for two of the crimes. One was the killing of a 14-year boy, whose tortured body was found outside Tunja, Colombia in 1996. The other was the attempted rape of another boy in the western city of Villavicencio, the crime that led to Garavito's arrest in 1999.

The killer was sentenced to the country's maximum prison term of 60 years, but in a plea bargain, the sentence was reduced to 52 years and six months in exchange for Garavito agreeing not to contest any of the charges against him.

A 1982 mug shot shows Gary Leon Ridgway, who targeted prostitutes and runaways.

WHO KNEW?
Serial murders make up less than 1 percent of the approximately 15,000 American homicides a year.

An engraving of accused killer Gilles de Rais, shown invoking the devil

UNFAIRLY ACCUSED?

Today, some experts suspect there are historical killers who were the victims of sinister plots.

→ **Gilles de Rais.** The wealthy French lord was said to have kidnapped, tortured, and killed hundreds of peasant children from nearby villages. Rais confessed to the crimes and was hanged in 1440. Despite the confession, some modern theorists believe de Rais was the target of a plot—especially since, after his death, his prosecutor was awarded all of his land.

→ **Gilles Garnier.** Called the Werewolf of Dole, this French hermit was blamed for and confessed to the death and mutilation of several children in 1572. Believed to be a werewolf, Garner was burned at the stake. Historians now think he was the innocent scapegoat in a case of witchcraft hysteria.

→ **Peter Stumpp.** A prosperous German farmer, Stumpp was accused of killing and eating 14 victims. Under torture, he confessed and was beheaded in 1589, in a particularly brutal execution. Historians still debate Stumpp's guilt, with some arguing that he was a victim of political intrigue.

victims who are available and vulnerable, and more than half of the 25 most ferocious modern serial killers hunted—or are still hunting—women and children.

Domination and Anger

Nevertheless, there are certain traits that repeat. The predator who targets women and children is usually male and tends to come from an abusive background. His father may have been sadistic or overly strict; his mother may have been promiscuous or smothering. In murder, the killer is believed to be retreating from the pain of his boyhood into a world in which he is in control. He is seeking gratification in the violent domination of others, especially of the people who symbolize those who abused him. A serial murderer who targets women may be trying to destroy someone who represents his cruel mother;

a child-slayer may be going after those who embody what he despises in himself, especially cracks in his own masculinity.

Gary Leon Ridgway, America's most voracious serial killer to date, seems to have been motivated in part by a hatred of prostitutes, an insatiable desire for sex, and an obsession with necrophilia. Dubbed the Green River Killer, Ridgway confessed to murdering 71 prostitutes and runaways in Washington State and California in the 1980s and 1990s. He is now serving 48 life sentences plus 480 years without parole. But even Ridgway, a classic serial killer, doesn't fit neatly into the supposed profile.

"When I read up on serial killers…they always keep stuff," he told interrogators who asked whether he had kept souvenirs from his victims, "and that's why I didn't keep stuff."

An engraving showing what Jack the Ripper might have looked like

THE INFAMOUS WHITECHAPEL MURDERS

MORE THAN 100 YEARS AGO, JACK THE RIPPER TERRORIZED LONDON WITH VICIOUS ACTS. HIS IDENTITY REMAINS UNKNOWN.

There have been many more prolific serial killers than Jack the Ripper, but few have achieved his grisly renown. Between August and November of 1888, the Ripper terrorized the overcrowded, impoverished Whitechapel section of London's East End, slashing the throats of victims and savagely mutilating their bodies. All of the killer's victims were women, and all were prostitutes. As the attacks became progressively more violent, they were publicized in London and around the world. The killer was never apprehended, and the case remains one of the most famous unsolved mysteries of all time.

The Women

Though some speculate that Jack the Ripper murdered as many as a dozen women, only five are accepted as definitive victims:

MARY ANN "POLLY" NICHOLS, 43. Her body was found on August 31. Her throat was slashed, and there were deep cuts on her abdomen.

ANNIE CHAPMAN, 47. She was severely mutilated and disemboweled on September 8. Her corpse led investigators to suspect that the perpetrator had medical training of some sort.

ELIZABETH "LONG LIZ" STRIDE, 44. She was discovered on September 30. Her throat had been cut, but she was not otherwise violated, leading investigators to think that the killer may have been interrupted.

CATHERINE EDDOWES, 46. Also discovered on September 30. She had been disemboweled and her kidney removed; the autopsy noted that "there was great disfigurement of the face" as well.

MARY JANE KELLY, 25. Found in her bed on November 9, Kelly is believed to have been Jack the Ripper's last victim.

Scotland Yard photograph of Elizabeth Stride, one of Jack the Ripper's victims

A portrait of Prince Albert Victor, c. 1890s, one of the people suspected of being Jack the Ripper

The Investigation

Almost from the first Whitechapel murder, theories and suspects abounded. The gruesome nature of the slaying, coupled with the profession of the victims, provided endless fodder for the newspapers, which tried to outdo one another with gory details and outlandish theories. During the fall of 1888, hundreds of letters poured in to the police and the press from people claiming to be the killer. Some were signed "Jack the Ripper," providing the murderer with his moniker for posterity. Credible suspects included a barber who poisoned three of his wives, an insane Polish Jew who professed hatred of women, and a mentally ill lawyer.

Yet none of Scotland Yard's efforts led to an arrest, prompting a number of high-profile resignations from the force. The case became the greatest whodunit of all time. To this day, so-called Ripperologists continue to work the angles: Over the years, the Ripper's crimes have been attributed to Lewis Carroll, author of *Alice in Wonderland*; Prince Albert Victor, possibly driven insane from syphilis; and Mary Pearcey, a murderous midwife. In the century-and-a-quarter since he committed his foul acts, Jack the Ripper has been the subject of many articles, books, paintings, films, television shows, graphic novels, and even musicals.

CASE CLOSED?

Novelist Patricia Cornwell is convinced she has figured out the identity of Jack the Ripper.

"I feel that I have cracked it," best-selling novelist Patricia Cornwell told the *London Evening Standard* in November 2013. "I believe it's Sickert, and I believe it now more than ever."

Cornwell, obsessed with Jack the Ripper for years, first shared her thoughts about the Whitechapel fiend in her 2002 book *Portrait of a Killer: Jack the Ripper Case Closed*. Others, too, have identified William Sickert, a German-born artist who often depicted London prostitutes in his images, as the perpetrator. But few have gone as far as Cornwell in their sleuthing. She has purchased 32 of Sickert's works, along with some of his letters and even his writing desk. Her proof of his guilt? Cornwell told the *Standard* that "confessional and violent" letters sent to the police at the time of the murders were written on paper bearing the same watermark as that used by Sickert. In her interview in the *Standard*, Cornwell said she will publish her new findings soon.

This illustration shows one of the victims, Catherine Eddowes, and a sketch of a man thought to be implicated in the case.

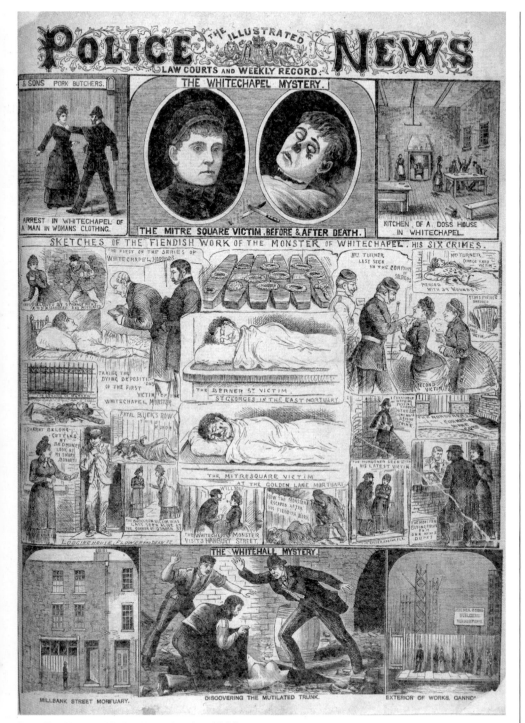

From *The Illustrated Police News*, London, 1888

→ Starting in the 1860s, Bristol, England, midwife Amelia Dyer took in babies from impoverished unmarried mothers with the understanding that she would find homes for them. Over 30 years, Dyer is believed to have killed as many as 400 infants. Some have speculated that Amelia Dyer and Jack the Ripper were one and the same.

→ In 1853, traveling salesman Manuel Blanco Romasanta, Spain's first known serial killer, confessed to murdering 13 people and using their body fat to make soap. It is now believed that Romasanta, who was initially raised as a girl, may have suffered from a gender disorder known as pseudohermaphroditism.

→ In 1897, drifter Joseph Vacher, who came to be known as the French Ripper, was charged with the strangulation and evisceration of a 17-year-old shepherd boy. Vacher ultimately confessed to killing ten girls and boys and one woman between 1894 and 1897. In some cases, he sexually assaulted and mutilated the bodies.

→ Between 1884 and 1908, Norwegian-born Belle Gunness, aka Lady Bluebeard, murdered multiple husbands, children, and several suitors, typically for financial gain. After Gunness's farmhouse burned to the ground in 1908, the remains of 40 people were exhumed on her property.

In September 2014, Russell Edwards, an author and amateur sleuth, professed to have conclusively identified Jack the Ripper as Aaron Kosminski, a young Polish immigrant who was committed to an asylum soon after the killings. Although Kosminski has long been a suspect, Edwards claimed to have done DNA testing that proves Kosminski's guilt. Skeptics were not convinced, and the riddle of the Ripper remains unsolved.

REAL-LIFE
PSYCHO-KILLER

THE GHOULISH INSPIRATION FOR ALFRED HITCHCOCK'S CLASSIC FILM WAS A SHY MIDWESTERN FARM BOY.

The house belonging to Ed Gein, where he lived a deceptively quiet life and where parts of his victim's bodies were found.

In Alfred Hitchcock's classic 1960 horror film *Psycho*, creepy Norman Bates runs an isolated motel where guest Marion Crane is murdered as she showers by a knife-wielding old woman. Spoiler alert: The killer turns out to be Bates, dressed up as the domineering mother he had slain years earlier. Bates wasn't just a figment of Hitchcock's imagination. The director modeled him on an actual serial killer named Ed Gein.

Driven Crazy

Born in 1906, Gein grew up on an isolated Plainfield, Wisconsin, farm. His mother, Augusta, kept him busy reading the Bible and doing chores with his brother, Henry. The two were only allowed to leave the house to attend school. Though Augusta was verbally abusive, shy Ed was devoted to her. His father died of alcoholism in 1940, and Henry was killed in a suspicious brush fire on the farm four years later. Some Plainfield residents suspected Ed of murdering his sibling, but no investigation was undertaken.

Gein continued to live with his mother into adulthood, caring for her after two strokes that ultimately led to her death in 1945. He then shut up much of the house, leaving Augusta's things undisturbed. Known locally as "weird old Eddie," Gein

lived as a reclusive, in just two rooms, and supported himself doing occasional odd jobs. On one occasion, Gein showed some shrunken heads to a young boy who stopped by the house, claiming they came from the South Seas.

Crafty Killer

In 1957, Gein was identified as the last person to see 50-year-old hardware store owner Bernice Worden before she disappeared. During a search of Gein's farm, police found Worden's body in a shed. It was hanging upside down from a beam, slashed open and decapitated. When they entered Gein's rooms, officers discovered rotting, refrigerated, and preserved human body parts, including at least one head. There were bowls made of human skulls, lampshades and chair seats made of human skin, and trophies and trinkets made of various other body parts. Most chilling of all were the skins of female victims that Gein had removed and sewn together into a "woman suit" that he wore while pretending to be Augusta.

All told, police found the partial remains of ten women on the premises, and Gein confessed to robbing the graves of eight women in the local cemeteries between 1947 and 1952. Police knew that Worden's body was the ninth, but were uncertain of the identity of the 10th victim. They focused on

More than 90 percent of necrophiliacs are men.

WHO KNEW?

A hardcore punk band in the 1980s was named Ed Gein's Car.

Waushara County Sheriff Art Schley, left, escorts Ed Gein into Central State Hospital for the Criminally Insane in Milwaukee, 1957.

five unsolved Plainfield-area missing-persons cases dating from 1947 to 1952. Eventually evidence suggested that the unidentified parts belonged to Plainfield tavern keeper Mary Hogan, who had disappeared in the winter of 1954. After an intensive search of Gein's farm and neighboring land, Gein finally admitted he had killed Hogan.

Home Again

During a month-long evaluation, Gein was found to be a schizophrenic, a sexual psychopath, and mentally incompetent. As such, he couldn't be tried for murder and was instead committed to a state hospital. After ten years passed, Gein was reevaluated, declared competent, and in 1968 tried for Worden's murder. Found guilty, he was sentenced to life in a mental hospital, but was never tried for Hogan's murder.

Gein died in 1984 at the age of 77, and was buried beside his mother in Plainfield, near the graves he had robbed. His story inspired not only *Psycho* but also *The Texas Chainsaw Massacre* and *The Silence of the Lambs.*

SIMPLY IRRESISTIBLE

THE SCARIEST KILLERS ARE THE ONES YOU LEAST SUSPECT.

B ut he was such a nice man," the neighbors sometimes say after the arrest of the killer next door. They've been duped by a criminal who, in fact, has no conscience or compassion. He's manipulative and predatory, but he's also a chameleon who knows how to play the part of the good—or at least normal—guy. He is often invited willingly into the lives of his victims. Children and women may trust him. But his crimes, premeditated and deliberately cruel, defy understanding.

Becoming Bundy

The most famous American example of the irresistible psychopath is Ted Bundy, who murdered at least 36 women in the 1970s. Why did he do it? According to prison psychologists, Bundy had a deep-seated fear of being humiliated by women. He may have felt wronged by his mother, who bore him out of wedlock and pretended for years that she was his older sister.

Bundy exhibited an early taste for revenge at the University of Washington, where he wooed then dumped a girlfriend who had broken up with him, an event that has been described as pivotal in his psychological development. Yet he fit in seamlessly on campus. A psychology major, Bundy was a high achiever, a snappy dresser, and an emerging leader. He was admitted into two law schools and became active in the Republican Party while working on Governor Daniel J. Evans's 1973 reelection campaign.

Bundy committed his first confirmed murder in 1974, when he was a 27-year-

---

THE DATING GAME MURDERER

A photographer with a violent past makes an appearance on prime-time TV.

In 1978, a handsome man with thick, dark hair and smiling eyes appeared on the TV show *The Dating Game*, where unmarried contestants interviewed potential dates from behind a partition. The host introduced the unseen man as a successful photographer who enjoyed skydiving and motorcycling. But once "bachelorette" Cheryl Bradshaw selected the photographer and met him backstage, she changed her mind, finding him "creepy."

In fact, just a few weeks earlier, Rodney Alcala had been released from prison for raping a 13-year-old girl. After being rejected by Bradshaw, he went on a killing spree, raping and bludgeoning to death a series of women. In all, Alcala was convicted of seven murders, though it is suspected he committed many more.

A 2010 *Los Angeles Times* profile of Alcala, then 66 years old, described him as a "brilliant, persuasive serial murderer in the mold of Ted Bundy," and a "once-dashing ladies' man [with] a near-genius IQ of 135." A graduate of the UCLA School of Fine Arts, Alcala had studied with director Roman Polanski.

Rodney Alcala in court in New York, 2013

During his 1979 murder trial in Miami, Florida, Ted Bundy presents a motion before circuit judge Edward Cowart.

old law student. Breaking into a Seattle apartment, he beat to death a coed from the University of Washington. He soon dropped out of school and started killing in earnest. Sometimes slipping a fake cast onto his arm or leg, he tricked female college students into helping him with his books or packages; sometimes he posed as a police officer or firefighter. He would kidnap and sexually assault his victims, then beat or strangle them to death.

In 16 months, Bundy killed 17 women in the Pacific Northwest and Rocky Mountain states, convinced no one would ever see through his handsome facade. But one of his intended victims escaped, and in 1976 her testimony sent him to prison for aggravated kidnapping.

Duping the Pros

Bundy's charm continued to serve him when prison psychologists found that he was neither psychotic nor sexually deviant. Prison staff relaxed their guard, and in 1977, facing trial for a 1975 murder, Bundy escaped, ending up in Tallahassee, Florida. There, in the early morning hours of January 15, 1978, he broke into the Chi Omega sorority house at Florida State University and slaughtered five women in 15 minutes. He was arrested on Valentine's Day, five days after killing 12-year-old Kimberly Leach, his last victim.

Bundy stood trial for two of the Chi Omega murders in June 1979. Exhibiting characteristic self-confidence, he acted as his own attorney. When the jury foreman read the guilty verdicts and the judge handed down two death sentences, Bundy remained impassive. After receiving a third death sentence for the murder of Leach, he was executed on January 24, 1989. Investigators suspect that he killed at least 100 women.

KILLER CLOWN

A CONSTRUCTION CONTRACTOR AND COMMUNITY VOLUNTEER LIVED A DOUBLE LIFE AS A SERIAL MURDERER.

Two members of the hip-hop group Insane Clown Posse, whose fans pretend to be obsessed with murder.

The creepy case of John Wayne Gacy made the killer clown a pop culture icon.

→ **Insane Clown Posse.** Recording since 1992, this "horrorcore" hip-hop group performs in clown makeup and incorporates circus imagery into their concerts. Devoted fans called Juggalos wear clown makeup and affect an obsession with murder.

→ **It.** Stephen King's novel was the basis for a 1990 television miniseries of the same title. The villain is a clown with sharp fangs and claws who lives in the sewers and preys on children.

→ **Killer Klowns from Outer Space.** This 1988 cult favorite features aliens dressed as clowns who collect humans by encasing them in cotton-candy cocoons, then transport their catch to the home planet.

In the 1970s, Pogo the Clown was a favorite character at fundraisers and parades in Norwood Park, a tidy Chicago suburb. He was the creation of construction contractor John Wayne Gacy, who volunteered with a civic group. But Gacy troubled some of his acquaintances when, still in full makeup and costume, he would drop into the Good Luck Lounge and throw back a few drinks. Gacy's neighbors were right to worry.

Rise and Fall

Born in Chicago in 1942, John Wayne Gacy was shy and awkward throughout his school years and suffered from a minor heart condition that kept him from playing sports. At nine, he was molested by a family friend, and after a playground accident at 11, he began to suffer occasional blackouts. Gacy struggled to fit in at four different high schools, dropped out, ran away briefly, then returned home and graduated from business college in 1963. He soon took a position as a management trainee at the Nunn-Bush Shoe Company.

Gacy married Marilynn Myers in 1964 and the couple settled in Waterloo, Iowa, where Gacy managed his father-in-law's Kentucky Fried Chicken franchises. The Gacys had two children, and from the outside their life looked good.

But John was troubled by his sexual attraction to teenage boys. In 1967, he lured a 15-year-old to his house with promises of porn movies and alcohol, then sexually assaulted him. Other attacks followed, and in 1968 Gacy was arrested and charged on two counts of sodomy. Gacy pled guilty and received a sentence of ten years in prison. Though his life in Waterloo and his marriage were over, Gacy became a model prisoner and was released on parole after 18 months.

Regular Guy, Dark Secret

In the summer of 1970, 28-year-old Gacy returned to Chicago to start over. He got a job as a cook, and his mother helped him buy a two-bedroom house in Nor-

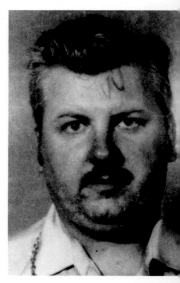

John Wayne Gacy

Original artwork by John Wayne Gacy

friendly meals with the police officers tasked with following him. On December 19, he invited two of the detectives into his home, which was filled with a putrid stench. Stressed and jittery, Gacy was arrested.

On December 21, investigators examining the crawl space under his house immediately found human remains. Gacy confessed to Piest's murder and as many others as he could recall, guessing the number to be at least 45. Although Gacy never claimed that the character Pogo was involved with the murders, the media dubbed Gacy the Killer Clown.

Pleading Insanity

The excavation of Gacy's property took two months and unearthed 29 bodies, 26 of them in the crawl space. The youngest victim was nine years old and the oldest in his mid-20s.

At his trial in early 1980, Gacy pled not guilty by reason of insanity. Gacy received 12 death sentences and 21 life sentences, and was executed by lethal injection on May 10, 1994.

wood Park. Two years later, he married Carole Hoff. In 1974, he started his own business, PDM Contractors, and began volunteering as a charity clown.

Gacy was soon living a double life. While raping 15-year-old Timothy McCoy in 1972, he committed his first murder. Gacy took his second victim in 1974 and his third in 1975. Over the next three years he assault-ed, tortured, and murdered at least 30 more boys—all in his own home. He stashed the bodies in the crawl space under the house.

Despite the disgusting odors, the Gacys entertained friends and family, blam-ing the smell on humidity. Eventually, Gacy admitted to his wife that he preferred boys to women. She di-vorced him in 1976 and his spree continued.

Unmasked

On December 11, 1978, after 15-year-old Robert Piest didn't return from a job interview with Gacy's firm, Piest's mother reported him missing. Local police ques-tioned Gacy and let him go, but they continued to moni-tor him because three other employees of PDM Contrac-tors had disappeared.

The killer seemed unconcerned, even having

LOVE IN THE TIME OF MR. GOODBAR

THE CLUB SCENE OF THE 1970S AND 80S WAS AN ENDLESS PARTY—BUT SINGLES HANGOUTS COULD BE DEADLY.

Filmmaker William Friedkin, center, tries to elude reporters, 1979.

OUTRAGED REACTION

A film about the gay club scene is attacked as homophobic.

Director William Friedkin's sexually explicit movie *Cruising*, based on a novel by the same name and inspired by true events, was largely panned by reviewers when it was released in 1980. But the story, about a cop played by Al Pacino, also caused outrage within the gay community. Protestors objected to the plot, which followed Pacino as he went undercover to infiltrate Manhattan's gay S&M scene to track down a serial killer. It was criticized as homophobic and exploitative, equating homosexuals with depravity and criminal behavior.

One of the most controversial novels of the 1970s, Judith Rossner's best-selling *Looking for Mr. Goodbar* caused a stir when it was published in 1975 and a bigger one when the film based on it was released in 1977. The story explored the double life of a repressed schoolteacher, Theresa Dunn: During the day, Dunn works with deaf children, but by night she frequents New York City singles bars, cruising for casual rough-sex partners. It can't end well, and it doesn't.

Though Dunn's character is complicated—she wants a liberated life but she's self-destructive and has father issues—the film was largely interpreted as a cautionary tale: Engaging in promiscuous behavior with strangers can be deadly. Based on real-life events, *Looking for Mr. Goodbar* terrified a generation raised on the ideal of free love. For many, the party was over, at least for a little while.

The Real "Mr. Goodbar"

In early January 1973, 28-year-old RoseAnn Quinn didn't show up for work one morning at the St. Joseph's School for Deaf Children in the Bronx. Concerned, a colleague went to her apartment, where she and the building superintendent discovered Quinn's blood-covered body. She had been stabbed repeatedly, and evidence of sexual activity was found on the body. In the *New York Daily News*, a neighbor described Quinn as "very nice and quiet and shy. She wore skirts and blouses, not this hippie stuff." Neighbors also noted that she was "the type of girl who would have a guy in if he brought her home," and indicated delicately that from what they'd heard, she may have enjoyed rough sex.

Serial killer Glen Rogers after being captured, 1995

Lounges have long served as hunting grounds for serial killers.

Serial killers seek their prey in all corners, but taverns were especially popular with these three pickup artists.

→ **Glen Rogers, aka the Casanova Killer,** was a blue-eyed smooth talker who picked up blondes and redheads in bars, persuaded them to drive him home, then stabbed or strangled them. He has been sentenced to death in two separate trials.

→ **George Russell, "the Bellevue Yuppie Murderer,"** was an attractive young man who frequented the yuppie nightclubs of Bellevue, Washington, in the summer of 1990. Russell's crimes were notable for their savagery and for the degrading ways he posed the corpses. He was convicted on three charges of first-degree murder.

→ **Michael Lupo,** a flower shop manager in London, cruised the city's homosexual bars in 1986. Having contracted the HIV virus, Lupo was on a campaign to exact revenge against the gay population. He strangled four men and attempted to murder two others before he was apprehended. Lupo died in prison in 1995 while serving four life sentences.

WHO KNEW?
The number of serial killers in the U.S. spiked dramatically in the 1970s and 1980s, according to *Extreme Killing: Understanding Serial and Mass Murder.*

Richard Gere sits with Diane Keaton at a bar in a scene from the film *Looking For Mr. Goodbar*, 1977.

A few days after Quinn's body was found, police apprehended a 23-year-old drifter named John Wayne Wilson. He soon confessed that he had met Quinn in a singles bar and gone home with her. He became enraged when she insulted him, and murdered her. Wilson was diagnosed as severely mentally ill, and committed suicide while awaiting trial.

The Pickup Artist
The straight, single women of New York weren't the only ones thinking twice about their dating habits in the 1970s. Between 1974 and September 1975, 14 gay men in San Francisco were murdered by a serial killer nicknamed "the Doodler." He cruised gay bars to find victims and would draw sketches of them to break the ice. Once he got them alone, he'd stab them to death. The Doodler didn't have a type: His victims included drag queens, leather-bar denizens, businessmen, and lawyers. At one point, the police were fairly certain they had identified the killer, but two men who survived attacks were reluctant to cooperate. They were worried about testifying in court, not wanting to admit publicly that they were gay. The Doodler was never caught.

REIGN OF THE ROSTOV RIPPER

WHEN RUSSIA'S FIRST KNOWN SERIAL KILLER WAS APPREHENDED AFTER A 12-YEAR MURDER SPREE, HE ANNOUNCED, "I WAS A MISTAKE OF NATURE."

Andrei Chikatilo languishes in a cell after his conviction.

OTHER VICTIMS

Before the real Rostov Ripper was apprehended, several men paid for his crimes.

Chikatilo not only murdered 52 women and children, he also caused the deaths of others suspected of the killings.

➔ **1978** A young laborer, Aleksandr Kravchencko, was arrested after Chikatilo's first murder. Kravchencko had only one arrest on his record, for vandalism. But as the case progressed, he lost hope and confessed. He was found guilty and was executed.

➔ **1982** A former sex offender arrested for one of the murders hanged himself rather than face interrogation and trial.

➔ **Late 80s** Three gay suspects in the slayings committed suicide.

It was a frigid December 1978 in Shakhty, a coal-mining town in southern Russia, when a clean-shaven, neatly dressed man in his 40s invited nine-year-old Yelena Zakotnova into a cabin. The man promised to let Yelena use the bathroom, but once he got the young girl inside he raped, strangled, and stabbed her to death. He then threw Yelena's body into a nearby river.

So began the sadistic career of Andrei Romanovich Chikatilo. Over the next 12 years Chikatilo would sexually assault, murder, and mutilate at least 14 girls, 21 boys, and 18 women, before being stopped by the police.

Born in 1936 in famine-ravaged Ukraine, Chikatilo as a child was beaten by his mother and bullied by his schoolmates. When he began having sex at age 15, he found satisfaction only when the girl struggled. Nevertheless, Chikatilo married in 1963 and later fathered two children. He became a schoolteacher in 1971, and although he was repeatedly accused of molesting his students, he was never fired. In 1978, Chikatilo took a new teaching position and moved to Shakhty.

Vicious Pattern

In September, 1981, almost three years after murdering Yelena Zakotnova, Chikatilo struck again. This time his victim was a 17-year-old boarding school student Larisa Tkachenko, whom he lured into the woods to drink vodka, then raped and killed. He started prowling bus and railway stations for schoolchildren, prostitutes, and the homeless. After enticing his prey to secluded spots with offers of food, alcohol, or help, Chikatilo would sexually assault, stab, and sometimes strangle and mutilate them. When he was finished, he made little effort to hide the bodies.

Even as Chikatilo's murderous tally rose, Soviet authorities were reluctant to admit there might be a serial killer at large. But by 1982, police had linked six of 17 murder victims to a single killer, and a profile began to emerge. The media, transfixed by the ghoulish details, stepped up its coverage of the case and dubbed the unidenti-

Andrei Chikatilo, who was found guilty on 52 counts of murder, is seen here before his 1992 trial.

known victim was 22-year-old Svetlana Korostik, murdered on November 6, 1990, in a forested area near the Donleskhoz station.

Technical Surprise

As Chikatilo emerged from the woods, he was spotted by an undercover police-man and soon apprehended for suspicious behavior. Yet again, Chikatilo was seemingly exonerated by his blood test, which showed him to be an A, not the incriminating AB. When the Rostov police learned that there were extremely unusual cases in which men could have different blood and semen types, they tested Chikatilo's semen. It was AB.

Chikatilo quickly admitted to 34 of the 36 murders attributed to the Rostov Ripper and described them in detail. He then surprised the police by confessing to 22 more unsolved homicides and leading them to the crime scenes. The prosecutor charged Chikatilo with 53 of the 56 slayings he described, and psychiatrists found him competent to stand trial.

During the 1992 proceedings, Chikatilo was confined to a cage in the courtroom. Sometimes refusing to answer questions, sometimes shouting, singing, or exposing himself, he was suspected of attempting to fake insanity—but if that was the case, it did little to help him. He was found guilty on 52 counts of murder, sentenced to death, and executed by a gunshot to the head on Valentine's Day, 1994.

fied butcher the "Rostov Ripper," after the Rostov district, where many of the slayings took place.

Chikatilo's most savage year was 1984, when he took the lives of 15 people, ranging from a ten-year-old boy to a 45-year-old woman. Eyewitnesses began to come forward, and the police found some physical evidence, including semen that pegged the killer's blood type as the rare AB. In September, a plainclothes police officer noticed a man fitting the killer's description at a bus station and arrested Chikatilo. Though a knife and rope were found in Chikatilo's briefcase, lab tests showed that the suspect's blood type was A, and he was allowed to go.

Profiles in Murder

For a period, Chikatilo seemed to withdraw. By early summer 1986, only two other murders fitting Chikatilo's signature had been recorded and authorities feared the trail was running cold.

Chikatilo resumed killing in August 1986, when he took the life of an 18-year-old girl. In 1987, he murdered three teenage boys, then another two boys and a young woman in 1988. In 1989 he killed five times, and in 1990, eight. His final

VICTIMS WANTED

THE DIGITAL AGE HAS MADE LIFE EASIER FOR JUST ABOUT EVERYONE, INCLUDING WOULD-BE MURDERERS.

Murderer Richard Beasley received the death penalty; his accomplice was sentenced to life in prison.

COLD BLOODED

Three men who responded to online help-wanted listings ended up dead.

In 2011, 52-year-old Richard Beasley and 16-year-old Brogan Rafferty placed an ad offering $300 a week and a free trailer to "watch over a 688-acre patch of hilly farmland and feed a few cows" in Ohio. Beasley and Rafferty murdered three men who responded to the ad. Both were convicted.

B ack in the 1970s, when the internet was emerging, not even the most visionary minds could have predicted the ways in which our lives would be transformed. Today, users take for granted all of the things the web offers, whether buying or selling things, paying bills, playing games, or making friends. But the online world, with its thin promise of anonymity, also presents opportunities for predators, pedophiles, scammers, and even murderers.

Killers Anonymous

One of the many liberating wonders of the internet is how it allows users to speak freely in web forums and chat rooms without fear of recourse. But that same feature provides cover for some depraved, mentally ill, and criminal members of society. Amateurs can pretend to be authorities, pedophiles can pose as teenagers, and people claiming to look for kinky sex can actually be looking for someone to murder.

In the 1990s, John Edward Robinson used the nickname "the Slavemaster" in the sadomasochistic chat rooms he trolled, ostensibly seeking women to play submissive roles during sex. A convicted embezzler, Robinson would meet and develop relationships with the women, who would then disappear. Eventually Robinson's name began to appear in missing persons investigations, and he was was convicted of murdering three women in Kansas and Missouri. Today, Robinson is called "the internet's first serial killer."

Alternatively, online criminals seek their prey in innocuous places, such as chat rooms for animal lovers. In 2004, 36-year-old Lisa Montgomery used a fake name when she made contact with 23-year-old Bobbie Jo Stinnett in an online forum devoted to rat terriers. On December 16, Montgomery strangled the eight-months-pregnant Stinnett in her Missouri home, cut the unborn baby out of her womb, and showed off the child as her own.

Lisa Montgomery was convicted of the 2004 murder of a pregnant woman.

144

The various labels on the bulletin board read:

- Marriott Hotel, Copley Square, 4/14/09 10:06 pm
- Marriott Hotel, Room 2034 Broken Glass, Blood stain, spent shell casing
- Philip Markoff Left profile
- Holiday Inn Express Warwick, RI 10:52:31
- Clothing matches description by Warwick victim
- Markoff profile
- Westin ...es
- Philip Markoff
- Purchasing form from 2/23/09 murder weapon purchase. Bears Markoff's fingerprints, signed by "Andrew Miller"
- Ball gag recovered from boxspring. Described by victim, bears victim and...
- Andrew Miller driver's license recovered from Markoff's wallet
- DRIVER LICENSE, ID:287 376 091, DOB: 04-21-82, MILLER,ANDREW,H, 944 ALLENS CREEK RD, ROCHESTER NY 14618, SEX M EYES: BL HT: 6-02 CLASS: D, ISSUED: 12-06-03 EXPIRES: 04-21-11
- Baseball cap, XD-9 holster, duct tape, zip ties from backpack in Markoff's home. Cap bought with Westin victim's gift card. Tape identical to gag of Westin victim. Holster fits murder weapon
- Springfield Armory XD-9

A detail of a bulletin board created by police officials that features photographs of Philip Markoff, who targeted women he met through the website Craigslist.

Craigslist Killers

One site that has won notoriety for allegedly enabling criminals to connect with unsuspecting victims is the classified advertisement website Craigslist. The site is operated as a sort of bulletin board where users are allowed to post information. After a number of homicides in which perpetrators met their victims through the classified site, the media coined the phrase "Craigslist Killers."

Philip Markoff, for example, was a clean-cut, 22-year-old Boston University medical student who frequented the erotic services section of Craigslist. In April of 2009, Markoff answered an ad for massage services posted by 26-year-old Julissa Brisman, and the two arranged a meeting at Boston's Copley Marriott. When Brisman was discovered at the hotel, she was bound and unconscious, with multiple gunshot wounds; she died later that night. Police investigating the case soon linked Markoff though an earlier assault on an erotic dancer he also had met on Craigslist. Markoff was arrested and charged with murder and robbery, but committed suicide in jail before he could be tried. (The erotic services section of Craigslist has since been discontinued.)

Self-proclaimed Satanists Miranda Barbour, 19, and Elytte Barbour, 22, were newlyweds when Miranda placed an ad on Craigslist looking for "companionship" in exchange for $100. Troy LaFerrara, 42, of Sunbury, Pennsylvania, responded to the posting and agreed to meet Miranda in a parking lot. According to Miranda, the original plan was for Elytte, who was hiding under a blanket in the backseat of their car, to kill Ferrara. Instead, Miranda did it herself, stabbing her victim 20 times. The two have pleaded guilty to murder. Elytte told police that they slew LaFerrara because they wanted to take someone's life together.

Raymond Martinez Fernandez found his victims through personal ads.

TARGETING SINGLE WOMEN

In the pre-digital era, one killer sought out the vulnerable through Lonely Hearts Club ads.

Before the era of dating sites, single men and women seeking companionship often turned to personal ads. For Raymond Martinez Fernandez, a former merchant marine, this was an opportunity. In the 1940s, Fernandez began responding to so-called Lonely Hearts Club listings, finding vulnerable women, building their trust, then robbing them.

He met Martha Beck this way, but instead of robbing her, Fernandez enlisted her as an accomplice. Beck soon became so jealous of the attention Fernandez gave their targets that the pair turned to murder. It wasn't until February 1949, after murdering as many as 20 victims, that Fernandez and Beck were caught. They signed a lengthy confession, were tried, and were sentenced to death.

IN LOVE WITH THE INCARCERATED

FOR WOMEN WITH A PECULIAR PSYCHOLOGICAL DISORDER, CONVICTED MEN HAVE A SPECIAL APPEAL.

If most of us found out a potential love interest had a criminal record, we would probably think twice about getting involved. So what explains the attraction so many women have for convicted felons they have never met?

Consider Scott Peterson, the adulterous husband convicted in 1995 of murdering his pregnant wife, Laci.

Death row inmate Scott Peterson

No sooner had he settled in on death row at San Quentin Penitentiary than Peterson began to get fan letters, phone calls, and even marriage proposals. Or Drew Peterson (no relation), convicted in 2012 of the murder of his third wife and suspected in the disappearance of his fourth, whose attorney said he received a "truckload" of mail from women while he was on trial.

Hot for Bad Guys

It's sometimes called Bonnie and Clyde syndrome, but the clinical term for the attraction some people have for violent criminals is *hybristophilia*. Though research on this psychological disorder is limited, more women seem to have it than men. In profound cases, a hybristophiliac might end up a co-conspirator in her paramour's crimes. The so-called prison groupies

who develop crushes on high-profile killers are said to have a lesser form of the condition.

Experts suggest a number of reasons that women fall for felons. Some are simply attracted to famous men, and a love letter to a prisoner is much more likely to get a response than one to a movie star. Other women may sincerely believe that the object of their affections is innocent, or may want to save him. Women who communicate with prisoners often suffer from low self-esteem and may have suffered sexual or physical abuse; they see a relationship with an incarcerated criminal as perversely safe, because the criminal is behind bars and can never get out.

If you are wondering how they manage to initiate contact, it's fairly easy to get in touch with any incarcerated person. Government

databases, accessible via the internet, list the location of many inmates, and websites such as WriteAPrisoner.com facilitate email correspondence between those in the outside world and those behind bars. Prisoners do not have access to the internet, so WriteAPrisoner.com prints out the emails it receives and forwards them to the addressees, who reply via regular mail.

It's not particularly difficult to marry a convict, either: The prisoner must request a marriage packet, and the bride- or groom-to-be on the outside must provide proof of citizenship and legal age. Though conjugal visits aren't allowed in federal prison, a few states allow them in medium or minimum-security facilities.

Testimonial letters from pen pals who met through a website WriteAPrisoner.com, which helps inmates receive letters from correspondents

WHO KNEW?
Some believe that writing to convicts provides a social good by keeping them connected to the outside world.

Manson cult member Susan Atkins, left, with her husband, attorney James Whitehouse

ISN'T IT ROMANTIC?

Their inhuman deeds didn't stop them from finding love—or what passes for it—behind bars.

→ **"Bolin the Butcher."** Oscar Ray Bolin was on death row in Florida for raping, beating, and stabbing three young women, but when Rosalie Martinez, a social worker, met him in 1995, she was so bewitched that she gave up a wealthy husband and four daughters to marry him. They made it legal over the telephone in 1996.

→ **Susan Atkins.** This Manson Family murderess and eventual born-again Christian scored not one but two husbands while in the slammer. In 1981 she wed Donald Lee Laisure, a Texan who claimed to be a multimillionaire and spelled his name "Lai$ure." The marriage lasted a few months. In 1987 she married James Whitehouse, 15 years her junior. That one stuck: The two remained a couple until Atkins's death from brain cancer in 2009.

→ **The Hillside Stranglers.** Cousins Kenneth Bianchi and Angelo Buono Jr. raped and murdered ten women and girls in Los Angeles in the late 1970s. The duo was imprisoned for life, but each found a bride. In 1986 Buono married Christine Kizuka, a government employee. In 1989 Bianchi married Shirlee Book, a Louisiana woman who had corresponded with a number of convicts and had reportedly been rejected by Ted Bundy.

A CONTROVERSIAL REQUEST

The internet helps some criminals connect with pen pals. Others have no such luck.

In 2003, Susan Smith, convicted eight years earlier of drowning her two sons, posted the following profile on WriteAPrisoner.com. It garnered so much negative media attention that Smith asked that it be taken down a few weeks later:

"I am 31 years old. My birthday is September 26. I am looking to meet new people and, hopefully, become friends. During my spare time, I enjoy reading, working puzzles, and writing. I love rainbows, Mickey Mouse, the beach, the mountains, and waterfalls. My favorite color is navy blue and my favorite flower is the daisy. I am a Christian and I enjoy attending church. I consider myself to be sensitive, caring, and kind-hearted. I'm currently serving a life sentence on the charge of murder. I have grown and matured alot since my incarceration, but

I will always hurt for the pain I've caused so many, especially my children. I hope to receive letters from those who are not judgmental and who are sincere. I look forward to hearing from new people and, hopefully, finding new friends. May God bless each one of you!"

Susan Smith during a preliminary hearing, 1995

Female killers may use guns to
level differences in strength.

CHAPTER 7
THE LETHAL FEMALE

WOMEN COMMIT ONLY ABOUT 10 PERCENT OF MURDERS IN THE UNITED STATES, BUT WHEN THEY KILL, THEY CAN BE JUST AS RUTHLESS AS MEN.

WOMEN WHO KILL

BOTH SEXES ARE CAPABLE OF EXTREME VIOLENCE, BUT THEY TEND TO MURDER DIFFERENTLY, AND FOR DISSIMILAR REASONS.

Police said Amy Bishop shot and killed her brother in this house in Braintree, Massachusetts. More than two decades later, she would be convicted of a workplace shooting.

The professor had been denied tenure and feared losing a job. During a routine staff meeting, the academic stood, pulled out a handgun, and began firing. A few moments later, three innocent co-workers were dead and three others were injured.

The circumstances behind this 2010 incident are chillingly familiar, but there was a twist: The shooter was a woman. Amy Bishop, a biology professor at the University of Alabama in Huntsville, didn't fit the profile of a workplace killer. Her actions, for which she was sentenced to life in prison without parole, prompted a re-examination of whether women are capable of the kind of violence usually associated with men.

The answer is yes, but much less often. Only about ten percent of U.S. homicide offenders are female, and they tend to commit their crimes for different reasons than men do, often out of self-defense or in response to abuse. Like men, women kill people they know more frequently than they kill strangers. But women usually go after those with whom they have had an intimate emotional relationship, while men are more apt to kill acquaintances.

Lethal Choices

Guns are the preferred weapon for men. Women are more likely to use a knife, a blunt object, or other implement. Contrary to conventional wisdom, women are less likely than men to poison their victims: men committed 60 percent of the deadly poisonings reported between 1980 and 2008, according to the U.S. Department of Justice.

About 15 percent of serial killers are female. They tend to use less violent means to kill, are less likely to torture their victims, and usually target people close to them, including spouses and children. But not always.

In England in 2014, Joanne Dennehy, 31, was sentenced to life in prison for methodically propositioning and stabbing to death three men she knew over the course of ten days, dumping their corpses, and then traveling to a different town in search of more men to kill. She jumped and knifed two random strangers, who survived to identify her. Dennehy, diagnosed as a sadistic psychopath, said she killed "to see if I was as cold as I thought I was."

There have even been a few female sex killers. Between 1976 and 2007, there were just over 200 homicides committed by a woman that featured a sexual element such as evidence of intercourse or provocative positioning of the victim's body, according to the Federal Bureau of Investigation. That compares to 3,684 sexual homicides carried out by men over

WHO KNEW?
There are 200,000 women behind bars and another mill on on probation for all types of crime.

Amy Bishop pleaded guilty and was sentenced to life for murdering three co-workers.

the same time period. Women sex killers tend to favor guns, using them over half the time—whereas male sexual killers tend to use other methods, such as strangulation. Researchers suggest that the female offenders choose guns in order to level differences in strength and make the crime less personal.

Tianle Li at her arraignment, 2011

TOXIC RELATIONSHIPS

Cases like these reinforce the mistaken idea that women turn to poison more often than men do.

→ **Tianle Li** A New Jersey chemist, Li was going through a divorce in 2011. But before the split became final, her husband developed stomach pains and checked himself into a New Jersey hospital. He died 12 days later from what doctors discovered was a lethal dose of thallium, a water-soluble, tasteless toxin. Li, who pleaded not guilty, got life in prison.

→ **Vickie Jo Mills** A 33-year-old from Pennsylvania, Mills was hoping her longtime boyfriend would pay more attention to her when she spiked his water with Visine multiple times between 2009 and 2012. Though the boyfriend lived, he suffered chronic symptoms including breathing trouble and vomiting. Mills pleaded guilty to aggravated assault and was sentenced to two-to-four years in prison.

CHARACTER ASSASSINATION

On television, fictional females get killed more brutally than their male counterparts do.

TV land is a cruel and ruthless place for women, at least according to a 2012 survey by Hollywood.com and Funeralwise.com. Though fictional men were the victims in 77 percent of television homicides, female characters were much more likely to be killed in savage and intimate ways, such as by strangulation, stabbing, or beating. Presenting these kinds of up-close-and-personal murder methods as entertainment, critics say, reinforces the notion of women as weak and helpless. It also desensitizes our culture to violence against women and makes killing women seem sexy. Besides, the fictionalized small-screen mayhem is an inaccurate representation of how women are most often murdered in real life. According to the Violence Policy Center, more homicides against females are committed with firearms than with all other weapons combined.

A RENAISSANCE STORY

WAS LUCREZIA BORGIA REALLY A BLOODTHIRSTY FEMME FATALE, OR SIMPLY A PAWN OF HER SCHEMING FAMILY?

A MUSE FOR THE AGES

Countless artists, writers, composers, and filmmakers have been inspired by Lucrezia's tale.

→ In Friedrich Maximilian von Klinger's 1791 novel *Faust's Life, Deeds, and Journey to Hell*, the scholar Faust, who has made a pact with the devil, has an affair with the seductive Lucrezia.

→ Gaetano Donizetti's tragic 1833 opera *Lucrezia Borgia* is a swirling cauldron of incest, adultery, and murder. In it, Lucrezia poisons a group of men, realizing too late that her own son, who doesn't know she is his mother, is among them.

→ Abel Gance's 1935 film *Lucrèce Borgia* depicts Lucrezia as a pawn of her power-grasping, sex-mad brother Cesare.

→ Jean Plaidy's 1958 novels, *Madonna of the Seven Hills* and *Light on Lucrezia*, fictionalize Borgia family intrigue. Highlights include Pope Alexander bedding adolescent girls and the brutal murder of Lucrezia's second husband, Alfonso.

→ In Showtime's 2011–2013 *The Borgias*, Lucrezia is manipulated by her scheming family. Oscar-winner Jeremy Irons starred as her ruthless father.

In 1480, as the Italian Renaissance was transforming Europe, Lucrezia Borgia was born into a ruthless noble clan with ties to the papacy. Her father was Spanish cardinal Rodrigo Borgia; her mother, his Roman consort Vannozza Catanei. Lucrezia reportedly spoke several languages, including Italian, French, and Latin. She was often described as having a regal air, thick blonde hair, bewitching eyes, and a fair complexion.

Troubled First Marriage

At the time, the daughters of aristocratic families were expected to enter into strategically advantageous marriages and bear children to cement political bonds. When Lucrezia's father was elected as Pope Alexander VI in 1492, the Borgias aligned with the Sforza clan of Milan and arranged for Lucrezia to wed Giovanni Sforza. But the marriage quickly faltered when Alexander switched political allegiances and sought to eliminate Sforza. Lucrezia possibly supported the plan, but nevertheless warned her new husband that her family planned to have him murdered. Sforza fled and Alexander sought to have his daughter's marriage annulled.

During the next few years, the Borgias were involved in a number of notorious incidents. In mid-1497, a servant of Lucrezia's brother Giovanni was found mortally wounded, and the mutilated corpse of Giovanni himself later turned up in the Tiber River. Rumors followed that Lucrezia's eldest brother, Cesare, murdered Giovanni in order to inherit his land and titles. Some historians attribute the murder to jealousy over the brothers' alleged incestuous relations with Lucrezia.

Lucrezia withdrew to a convent. As the annulment process continued, Sforza was pressured into confessing impotence in exchange for keeping Lucrezia's substantial dowry. Ironically, when the marriage was officially voided in December 1497, Lucrezia was six months pregnant, and in March 1498 she gave birth to a son, Giovanni. Two conflicting papal decrees were issued to identify the child's father; neither acknowledged Lucrezia as the mother. The first declared that the child was the illegitimate son of Cesare. The second stated that Giovanni had been sired by Alexander himself. The statements captivated Rome's gossips, but the child's true paternity was never established.

Murderous Second Marriage

Later in 1498, Lucrezia wed Alfonso of Aragon, a 17-year-old son of the late king

Lucrezia Borgia, daughter of Pope Alexander VI, in a painting by Bartolomea Veneto

WHO KNEW?

In 1501, at a famous banquet hosted by Lucrezia's brother Cesare, 50 of Rome's most beautiful prostitutes reportedly entertained guests with nude sexual antics, culminating in an orgy.

Portrait of Cesare Borgia by Altobello Melone

HOW BAD WAS SHE?

Lucrezia Borgia has survived in the popular imagination as the ultimate symbol of feminine evil, thanks largely to rumors circulated by her family's enemies.

Some creators of the hostile stories:

→ Pope Julius II, who succeeded Alexander and became an adversary of Lucrezia's third husband.

→ Niccolò Machiavelli, who singled out Cesare as a model of ruthlessness in his 1513 political manifesto *The Prince.*

→ Historians Johann Burchard and Francesco Guicciardini, contemporaries of Machiavelli, who reported the incest and other scandalous rumors.

→ Victor Hugo, whose 1833 play *Lucrèce Borgia* fueled the fire; and Alexandre Dumas, whose 1839 *Crimes Célèbres* series included a semi-fictional account of the Borgias's murderous poisonings.

of Naples. Political machinations forced the couple to flee Rome; after their return, Alfonso was brutally stabbed on the steps of St. Peter's Basilica. While recovering under Lucrezia's care, he was strangled to death, allegedly by one of Cesare's servants.

Cesare then orchestrated Lucrezia's third marriage, to Alfonso d'Este, son of the Duke of Ferrara, in 1501. Lucrezia settled into life at the Ferrara court, eventually becoming duchess.

Today, historians debate whether Lucrezia was complicit in her family's political machinations or just a vehicle for the Borgias's ambitious power plays. Recent studies have shown she was admired by her subjects in Ferrara for building hospitals and convents. She is also depicted as a shrewd businesswoman who drained marshes for agricultural use. Following the death of her son Rodrigo, Lucrezia withdrew from public life and turned to religion.

153

THE BLOODTHIRSTY COUNTESS

ELIZABETH BÁTHORY, A BEAUTIFUL HUNGARIAN NOBLEWOMAN, LURED SERVANTS TO HER CASTLE WITH A PROMISE OF WORK. THEN SHE SLAUGHTERED THEM.

High above the Hungarian village of Cjelte lie the ruins of Čachtice Castle, a medieval fortress that once served as a prison residence for Countess Elizabeth Báthory, the world's first and most ruthless female serial killer. Well-connected but sadistic, Báthory is said to have tortured and murdered dozens or perhaps hundreds of servant girls who came from the neighboring village to work and learn the ways of the court. Her case has inspired folklore, books, comics, movies, and plays.

Temper Leads to Torture

Born in 1560 to Baron and Baroness Báthory, Elizabeth Báthory was an educated, beautiful, and highly intelligent young girl. By age 11, she was fluent in Hungarian, Latin, and Greek, but her childhood was marred by epileptic seizures followed by fits of rage. At age 15, Báthory was married to Count Ferenc Nádasdy, a skilled soldier some 15 years her senior. Nádasdy often left home for long periods on military campaigns, and his young bride's rages were said to grow more intense while he was away.

It is unknown exactly when the countess began torturing the peasants and noblewomen who worked for her, but the abuses were described as atrocious. She was said to have burned maids with red-hot irons, roasting their flesh before serving it to them as food. In a few cases, she poured boiling water on victims as they sat in an earthen tank. In others, she covered servants' naked bodies with honey and tied them up outdoors as prey to bees and ants.

What could possibly have motivated Báthory? Some say her husband taught her to brutalize the workers. Others maintain that Nádasdy had little knowledge of his wife's proclivities and may have attempted to dissuade her from them. A different theory holds that an aunt, a rumored witch, incited her niece's bloodlust.

When Nádasdy died of unknown causes in 1604 at the age of 48, rumors about his widow's vicious activities began to spread. Báthory was able to intimidate the families of peasant girls into silence, but when daughters of the local nobility were reported missing, Hungarian king Matthias II ordered Báthory's cousin, Count György Thurzó, to investigate.

Crime in Progress

When Thurzó visited Báthory at her estate in December 1610, he said he discovered her in the middle of a torture session. Numerous victims were found on the property, according to Thurzó's report. "When my men entered Csejthe Manor," he wrote, "they found a girl dead in the house; another followed in death as a result of many wounds and agonies…the other victims were kept hidden away."

The countess and four of her alleged accomplices were arrested a few days later. The following month, Báthory's cohorts were tried for the murder of 80 girls. They were found guilty and promptly executed. The countess herself was spared a trial in favor of a lifetime of captivity in a set of rooms at Čachtice Castle, where she died in August 1614.

The ruins of Čachtice Castle in the Male Karpaty hills, the prison of Elizabeth Báthory

WAS BÁTHORY FRAMED?

Revisionists think the countess could have been the victim of a vendetta against her husband.

Some modern-day historians have questioned whether Báthory was truly guilty of her crimes. One theory points to the debts her husband Ferenc Nádasdy owed Matthias II, the King of Hungary, for financing a costly military campaign against the Turks. When Nádasdy died, Elizabeth inherited the debt. Under this reading of history, Matthias ordered Thurzó to arrest Báthory and try her for crimes she did not commit.

Another theory holds that the Protestant Elizabeth was the victim of a conspiracy masterminded by Catholics intent on removing her from power.

WHO KNEW?
Jesuit scholar Laszlo Turoczi, who published an account of Báthory's trial in 1729, reported that the countess bathed in the blood of young women to keep her skin youthful. Testimony from the case does not back this up.

A portrait of Elizabeth Báthory, considered the world's first reported serial killer

THE BLACK WIDOW OF LOUDUN

IF MARIE BESNARD DIDN'T POISON 11 FAMILY MEMBERS AND TWO FRIENDS IN MID-20TH-CENTURY FRANCE, WHO DID?

Arsenic bottles exhibited at the Besnard trial

THE PROOF ISN'T IN THE POISON

In the Besnard case, a smart defense team overcame strong circumstantial evidence.

When Besnard's lawyers suggested that arsenic entered the exhumed bodies' hair through anaerobic bacteria in cemetery grounds, they put locals on the stand to back them up. These witnesses testified that the cemetery-keeper had planted potatoes near the graves and doused the plants with arsenic-containing fertilizers. The prosecution's expert witnesses were then challenged to prove that arsenic had not seeped into the bodies *after* interment.

By the late 1940s, Marie Besnard, a farmer's daughter in the historic town of Loudun, France, had inherited considerable property from relatives. She owned nine houses, three hotels, 120 acres, and several stud farms. She was a church stalwart who donated to local charities and was admired by neighbors. But Besnard was rumored to have a young lover, Alfred Deitz, a former German war prisoner in his 20s. And Leon, her second husband, a prosperous rope merchant, was reportedly also having an affair.

In the fall of 1947, Leon became gravely ill during lunch one day and passed away a few days later. On his deathbed, he asked a friend and neighbor to insist on an autopsy. Doctors initially attributed Leon's death to uremia, or urea in the blood due to kidney failure.

When Besnard's mother unexpectedly died 15 months later, some community members suspected Besnard. Given the circumstances, Leon's body was exhumed and a high level of arsenic was discovered. Soon, a local midwife who had confided in Besnard about her unhappy marriage recalled that Besnard had recommended arsenic rather than divorce. Officials then exhumed the body of Besnard's first husband, who had died two decades earlier. Tests again revealed the presence of arsenic.

More Digging

Officials exhumed the remains of eight more of Besnard's relatives and two friends who had died during the previous decades. A Marseille toxicologist, Dr. Georges Beroud, discovered arsenic in all. In July 1949, Besnard, 52, was accused by local police of poisoning 13 people, including her parents, two husbands, several family members, and two friends, all of whom had left her inheritances. She was sent to prison to await trial.

Marie Besnard conferring with her lawyers during her second trial

Marie Besnard appeared in court on February 22, 1952, charged with poisoning friends and family.

The grave of Marie Besnard

MEASURE FOR MEASURE

Everyone's body has traces of arsenic.

Most people have about 1 microgram, or 1/1000th of a milligram, of arsenic per liter of blood. The bodies of Besnard's acquaintances had thousands of times more than the norm.

→ Auguste Antigny, Besnard's first husband, died in 1927. When exhumed in 1949, his remains showed 60 mg of arsenic.

→ Toussaint Rivet, a baker and a neighbor of Besnard's, died in 1939. His body was found to have 18 mg of arsenic.

→ Besnard's father, Pierre-Eugene Davaillaud, died in 1940. A 1949 autopsy of his exhumed remains showed 36 mg of arsenic.

→ Besnard's sister-in-law Lucie Bodin died in 1941. Bodin's exhumed remains contained 30 mg of arsenic.

→ Pauline Lalleron, the cousin of one of Besnard's husbands, died in 1945. Her body was found to contain 48 mg of arsenic.

→ Pauline's sister, Virginie Lalleron, also died in 1945. Her corpse showed 24 mg of arsenic.

→ Marie's second husband, Leon Besnard, died in 1947. His exhumed corpse had 19 mg of arsenic.

→ Marie's mother died in 1949. Her remains showed 48 mg of arsenic.

Three Tries at Conviction

During Besnard's first trial, in February 1952, she was charged with 11 murders. Evidence proved inconclusive and she was returned to preventive detention while three experts spent two years reexamining remains. Several corpses were eliminated from the case. At Besnard's second trial, in 1954, her Parisian lawyer Albert Gautrat posited that the Loudon cemetery grounds contained arsenic from fertilizers. Experts battled over the evidence for 15 days, and Besnard was ultimately released on bail.

Besnard's third trial took place in 1961 and lasted 20 days. As with the previous proceedings, chemists, physicians, and physicists gave contradictory testimony. Besnard's defense team accused the prosecution of mismanaging evidence and the state backed off, dropping all but three murder charges. The jury deliberated for just a few hours, then pronounced Besnard not guilty. On December 12, 1961, after 12 years—almost five spent in prison—she was acquitted. She died in 1980, a free woman.

THE DEADLY PROSTITUTE

AILEEN WUORNOS SLEW SEVEN MEN IN 1989 AND 1990. WAS IT SELF-DEFENSE OR COLD-BLOODED MURDER?

Aileen Carol Wuornos, born in 1956 in Rochester, Michigan, grew up in troubled circumstances. Her mother, Diane Wuornos, married Leo Dale Pittman at 15, and they separated two years later, before Aileen was born. Aileen never knew her father, but he spent time in mental hospitals for child molestation and was found hanged in prison in 1969. When Wuornos abandoned Aileen and her older brother Keith in 1960, the children were adopted by their maternal grandparents. Aileen's grandfather drank heavily and violently beat his granddaughter to discipline her. She began exchanging sexual favors with men at age 12 for cigarettes and beer. Pregnant in her mid-teens, Aileen sought help at a home for unwed mothers, but after her grandmother's death, she put the child up for adoption, left high school, and began prostituting herself.

Fifteen-Year Crime Spree

In 1974, Wuornos was arrested for drunk driving and firing a weapon from a moving vehicle. In 1976, her brother died of throat cancer and her grandfather committed suicide. Hitchhiking in Florida, she met and soon married a wealthy 69-year-old yacht-club president who had the volatile marriage annulled a month later. In the late 1970s, Wuornos survived a sui-

Aileen Wuornos waits to testify in the Volusia County courthouse, Daytona Beach, Florida, 2001.

Investigator Richard Vogel holds a mug shot of Aileen Wuornos and a photo of her first victim, Richard Mallory. Other members of Vogel's team are in the background.

cide attempt. Numerous arrests followed through the 1980s for such crimes as forging checks, armed robbery, and stealing cars. In 1986, the alcoholic Wuornos began a lesbian relationship with Tyria Moore, 24. The pair lived off Wuornos's prostitution earnings.

Multiple Murders and Execution

In 1989, years of petty crime and substance abuse spiraled into something much darker, and Wuornos snapped. She murdered a number of middle-aged male motorists, shooting them repeatedly, robbing them, and hiding their bodies in desolate wooded areas along Florida highways. Law enforcement caught up with her in early 1991 at a Port Orange, Florida, bar called The Last Resort. With Moore's help, police elicited a confession. Wuornos insisted she killed her victims in self-defense after each had either threatened, assaulted, or raped her. In 1992, she was convicted of one murder and received a death sentence. She subsequently confessed to three more, eventually admitting that her motive was profit, not self-defense. Despite defense team claims of severe mental illness, Wuornos was executed by lethal injection in October 2002, in Starke, Florida.

The hearse carrying the body of convicted killer Aileen Wuornos leaves the Florida State Prison.

THE PSYCHOPATHY OF FEMALE SERIAL KILLERS

Women tend to have different motives and methods than men.

→ A 2005 *Journal of Forensic Sciences* article estimates that women are responsible for four to 14 serial killings a year.

→ In contrast to their male counterparts, whose motives are usually sexual, most women kill for financial enrichment or excitement and power.

→ Most of their victims are strangers, and poison is the most common method used to dispatch them.

→ Women serial killers' careers tend to last longer than men's, possibly because they plan more carefully and methodically.

GUILTY INNOCENTS

SHOCKING AS IT SEEMS, CHILDREN KILL FOR MANY OF THE SAME REASONS ADULTS DO.

Mary Flora Bell, circa 1968

THE CASE OF MARY BELL

A little girl known as the Tyneside Strangler left her murderous mark on England.

In the summer of 1968, the bodies of two young boys were discovered in Newcastle, England. One was found in an abandoned building, another in a wooded area. The investigations pointed to a local girl, Mary Flora Bell, who had boasted of the crime in the playground.

Neighbors described 11-year-old Mary, the daughter of a prostitute and a petty criminal, as cold and lacking empathy. Though she never confessed, Mary was convicted of manslaughter in two of the slayings. Her accomplice, Norma Bell (no relation), was acquitted when the court decided she was manipulated by the more calculating Mary.

After serving 12 years, Mary Bell was released at the age of 23. Now a grandmother, she has had no further run-ins with the law. Her legal battles resulted in a ruling known as the Mary Bell Order, which protects the identity of children arrested for violent crimes.

Examples of young children who kill, or attempt to, appear in the news all too frequently. In 2014 alone, Noel Estevez, a 14-year-old from Bronx, New York, was accused of stabbing to death a bullying classmate; 16-year-old Chris Plaskon was accused of killing a classmate from his Connecticut high school, possibly for refusing his invitation to the prom. Plaskon pleaded not guilty to manslaughter and the case is expected to be moved family court.

The Bad Seed

History is rife with examples of children who murder children. Often they exhibit patterns similar to those of adult murderers, starting with mistreating animals, progressing to bullying children, then moving on to killing them. One 19th-century example of such behavior was 14-year-old Jesse Pomeroy of Charlestown, Massachusetts. After attacking and torturing several boys in 1871–1872, Pomeroy was sent to reform school. He was released early to his mother, but within a few months viciously murdered a four-year-old boy and a ten-year-old girl. His crimes earned him the nickname the Boston Boy Fiend, and he became the youngest person in Massachusetts history to be convicted of first-degree murder. Pomeroy's excuse was simple: "I couldn't help it."

One of the most infamous and widely publicized cases of children killing children unfolded in England in 1993. In February of that year, two ten-year-olds, Jon Venables and Robert Thompson, were captured on a security video in Kirkby, Merseyside, abducting two-year-old James Bulger from a mall. They led Bulger into the woods, where they beat, sexually abused, and killed him, leaving his body on some railroad tracks. Both boys were convicted of murder and abduction.

Experts have said the case illustrates the dynamic of two culprits working together. The fact that Venables and Thomson each had a partner in crime may have given them the emotional wherewithal to carry out acts that neither would have committed alone. The boys knew that what they did was wrong. Upon confessing, Venables said to investigators, "Tell his mum I'm sorry."

What Set Them Off?

Thompson had a reputation as the more streetwise and manipulative of the two young killers. Though he had not previously exhibited much in the way of aggressive behavior, his home life was troubled. His mother was an alcoholic and his brothers were violent. Venables, portrayed as more of a follower, also came from a broken home and had exhibited behavioral issues. His teachers reported that he banged his head against walls and cut himself, and

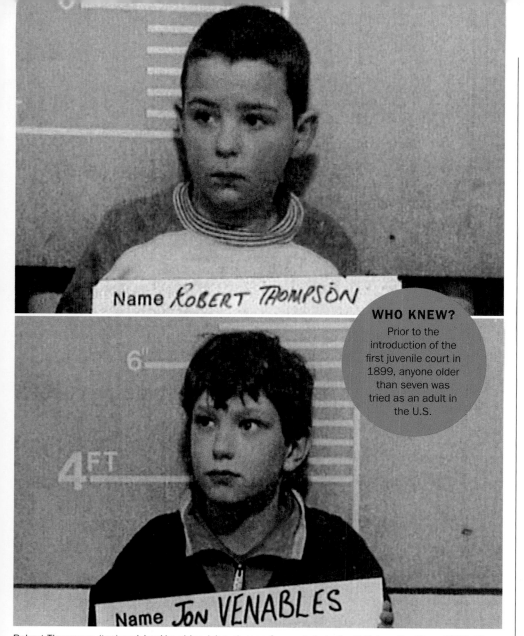

Name *ROBERT THOMPSON*

Name *JON VENABLES*

WHO KNEW?
Prior to the introduction of the first juvenile court in 1899, anyone older than seven was tried as an adult in the U.S.

Robert Thompson (top) and Jon Venables (above) pose for mug shots for British authorities, 1993. They were both ten years old when they tortured and killed two-year-old James Bulger in Bootle, England.

Lionel Tate

FROM SAD TO SENSELESS

Some defenses offered by children convicted of murder

→ **Innocence.** In 1999, 12-year-old Lionel Tate killed six-year-old Tiffany Eunuck in Broward County, Florida, while wrestling. The prosecution compared the injuries to what would be sustained by falling from a three-story building. Tate, who maintained his innocence, was convicted of second-degree murder, but the sentence was later overturned and Tate was released on house arrest. He later violated parole and eventually returned to prison for a different crime.

→ **Self-defense.** Donna Marie Wisener of Tyler, Texas, was physically and sexually abused by her father from the time she was two years old. At the age of 16, Wisener shot him six times; she was acquitted on grounds of self-defense.

→ **Peer pressure.** In August, 2012, Connor Doran, 17, Brandon Doran, 14, and Simon Evans, 14, of Liverpool, England, found a homeless man sleeping behind a grocery store. On a dare from Connor, Simon and the older boy brutally kicked 53-year-old Kevin Bennett while Brandon kept watch. Bennett later died, and all three boys were convicted.

he had gotten into trouble for attacking another student. Thompson and Venables frequently skipped school and bullied other kids together. On the day of the murder, they first attempted to abduct another child but were foiled by the child's mother.

The two were released from prison in 2001. Since then, there have been few reports of Thompson's activities. Venables returned to jail in 2010 for distributing indecent images of children.

From Abused to Abuser

A background of being bullied shows up with alarming regularity in the profile of children who kill. A typical example is 13-year-old Eric Smith, who was convicted for the 1993 murder of a four-year-old boy in Steuben County, New York. With thick glasses, red hair, and protruding ears, Smith had been relentlessly bullied. From jail years later, Smith recalled that killing felt good simply because "instead of me being hurt, I was hurting someone else."

Since 2006 the rate of mass shootings has more than doubled, according to the Federal Bureau of Investigation.

CHAPTER 8
SCHOOL SHOOTERS
AND WORKPLACE KILLERS

MANY AMERICANS ARE ALIENATED, FRUSTRATED, ANGRY, AND OFTEN DEPRESSED. BUT THEY DON'T TURN ON OTHERS WITH GUNS. WHAT TRIPS THE TRIGGER?

MURDER
BY THE NUMBERS

HOMICIDES HAPPEN IN ALL CORNERS OF THE GLOBE, BUT BY WHAT MEANS AND HOW OFTEN VARIES DRAMATICALLY.

A crime site in Honduras, where four young people were shot dead in 2013

THE WORLD'S MOST DANGEROUS PLACES

According to the United Nations, the following countries have the world's highest homicide rates:

→ **Honduras:** 90 murders per 100,000 people

→ **Venezuela:** 54 murders per 100,000 people

→ **Belize:** 45 murders per 100,000 people

→ **El Salvador:** 41 murders per 100,000 people

→ **Guatemala:** 40 murders per 100,000 people

There were 437,000 murders worldwide in 2012, according to the United Nations Office on Drugs and Crime. But any one person's likelihood of becoming a victim depends on who he is and where he lives. Most victims of murder—79 percent of them worldwide—are male. The majority are between the ages of 15 and 29, and living in the Americas. Men also make up the vast majority of perpetrators, committing 95 percent of killings globally.

Though murders of women are much less common, the biggest danger is from someone the victim knows and loves. Almost half of the 93,000 women murdered in 2012 were killed by a family member or a romantic partner. Only 6 percent of men are killed by someone close to them.

As for the most common murder weapon: It's guns, which were used in 41 percent of all murders and 70 percent of mass murders. A third of all homicides were committed by "other means," including beating, poisoning, and strangulation. Sharp objects such as knives and machetes were used in slightly less than a quarter of all homicides.

In the U.S., 60 percent of murders are committed with a gun.

Port-Au-Prince, Haiti, had 495 homicides in 2010—about 40 per 100,000 people.

Tegucigalpa, Honduras, had 1,175 homicides in 2011, more than one per 1,000 citizens.

Access to Guns

According to research, the availability of guns does affect murder rates. In one study, European countries in which fewer than ten percent of households owned a gun had about one murder per half a million people. In European countries in which more than 15 percent of households owned a gun, there were about three murders per 200,000 people.

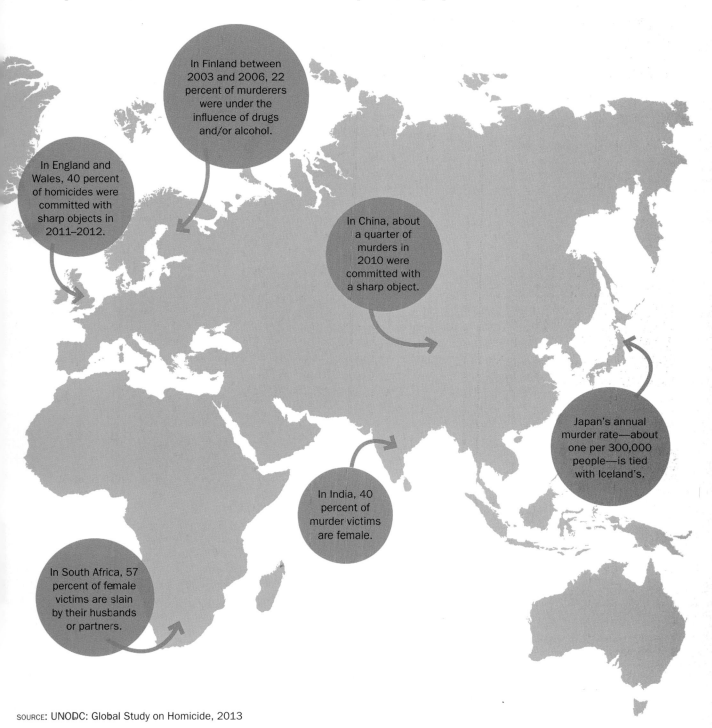

In Finland between 2003 and 2006, 22 percent of murderers were under the influence of drugs and/or alcohol.

In England and Wales, 40 percent of homicides were committed with sharp objects in 2011–2012.

In China, about a quarter of murders in 2010 were committed with a sharp object.

Japan's annual murder rate—about one per 300,000 people—is tied with Iceland's.

In India, 40 percent of murder victims are female.

In South Africa, 57 percent of female victims are slain by their husbands or partners.

SOURCE: UNODC: Global Study on Homicide, 2013

GOING POSTAL

EXPERTS CHALK UP WORKPLACES RAMPAGES TO JOB STRESS AND EASY ACCESS TO DEADLY WEAPONS.

A t about 7 AM on August 20, 1986, mail handlers in Edmond, Oklahoma, were busy sorting the letters and preparing for their morning routes when postman Patrick Sherrill, wearing his uniform and carrying three handguns, walked in. Sherrill never said a word as he strode through the building shooting employees. As he passed through each room, he locked the doors behind him so that no survivors could escape. He paused only to reload his weapons. By the time Sherrill turned one of his guns on himself, he had killed 14 people and wounded six; it was not even 7:30 AM.

The incident was one of the first of a series of violent sprees involving U.S. Postal Service workers. Soon, people began to use the expression "going postal" to refer to episodes of work-related rage that segued into violence. The stereotype of the potentially homicidal postal worker became so widespread that the U.S. government established a commission to investigate.

"Going postal is a myth, a bad rap'" concluded Joseph Califano Jr., the head of the commission. "Postal workers are no more likely to physically assault, sexually harass, or verbally abuse their coworkers than employees in the national work force." Experts went on to point out that homicides committed by postal workers simply received more press than other violent workplace incidents because of the public and commonplace nature of mail delivery. The notion of a mailman gone mad seemed to tap into some basic fear or fascination, but workplace violence has never been confined to any one occupation.

Danger: Men at Work

In the United States alone, there were 14,770 workplace homicides between 1992 and 2012; that's an average of more than 700 per year. What turns a disgruntled worker into a killer? Investigators claim to have

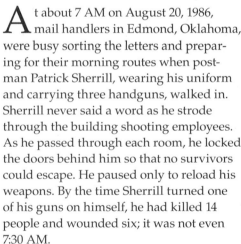

WHO KNEW?

From 2003 to 2012, more than half of workplace homicides took place in three occupation classifications: sales, protective services, and transportation and material moving.

Members of the Edmond Police Department gather in front of the Edmond Post Office, where Patrick Henry Sherrill systematically killed 14 people before killing himself, 1986.

Police investigate the crime scene at a U.S. Postal Service distribution center in Goleta, California.

THE SHOOTERS

Killings inside U.S. Postal Service offices loom large in the public imagination.

→ **Ridgewood, New Jersey.** In 1991, a former U.S. postal worker, enraged about his dismissal, killed his former supervisor and her boyfriend at their home. The next morning, the 35-year-old Navy veteran stormed the post office, armed with a machine gun, a samurai sword, three hand grenades, and some homemade bombs. Before surrendering, he killed two mail handlers.

→ **Royal Oak, Michigan.** In 1991, an ex-Marine and former postal clerk, furious that he had been dismissed, walked into a postal center and opened fire with a sawed-off .22-caliber rifle. He killed three workers and wounded six before shooting himself.

→ **Goleta, California.** In 2006, a former postal employee with a history of mental illness killed six postal employees at a mail-processing facility before committing suicide with a handgun. This was one of the deadliest American workplace shooting incidents ever carried out by a woman.

identified certain conditions that seem more likely to breed workplace violence. These include the following:

→ Contact with the public

→ Exchange of money

→ Delivery of passengers, goods, or services

→ Having a mobile workplace such as a taxi or a police car

→ Working with unstable persons in health care, social service, or criminal justice settings

→ Working alone or in small groups

→ Working late at night or during early morning hours

→ Working in high-crime areas

The most common connection among employees who become violent seems to be a change in employment status. An unfavorable review, a decrease in hours, the threat of termination, or termination itself can all trigger an unstable employee to react violently. Patrick Sherrill, for example, had been reprimanded by two supervisors the day before his murder spree. One of them was the first person he shot.

Obviously, not everyone who is scolded by a boss resorts to murderous revenge. But negative encounters with authority figures do seem to be a common link. The availability of firearms (75 percent of these incidents involve guns), combined with work-related stress and the erosion of job security, form the deadly equation of workplace violence.

COMING HOME

SOLDIERS ARE TAUGHT TO KILL IN WARTIME, BUT DO THEY BRING MURDEROUS TENDENCIES BACK?

Nidal Malik Hasan, a U.S. Army major, fatally shot 13 people and injured more than 30 at Fort Hood, Texas.

U.S. Army major Nidal Hasan's murderous shooting spree at Fort Hood in Texas was ghoulishly historic: It resulted in more casualties than any other attack by a fellow service member on a U.S. military base. At his court martial in 2013, Hasan was found guilty of premeditated murder and sentenced to death.

Post-Traumatic Stress Disorder and Violence

Although some politicians described Hasan's shootings as an act of terrorism, the U.S. Department of Defense and federal law enforcement agencies classified the event as workplace violence. In recent years, there have been several such high-profile attacks at U.S. military bases. In many of the attacks, the shooters seemed to suffer from post-traumatic stress disorder, or PTSD.

The term PTSD describes a constellation of mental health problems triggered by experiencing or witnessing terrifying events. It is most often diagnosed in soldiers returning from combat, though victims of abuse or other crimes are common sufferers as well. Symptoms of PTSD may include flashbacks, nightmares, severe anxiety, and violence. Most people who have experienced a traumatizing event will not develop PTSD, but about 7 percent of American adults suffer from the condition, including more women than men.

Multiple studies have cast light on the struggles faced by soldiers returning home.

A 2010 study funded by the U.S. Marine Corps surveyed 1,543 marines with at least one combat tour and found that those who had reported PTSD symptoms were more than six times as likely to engage in antisocial and aggressive behaviors as those who did not report PTSD symptoms.

Another study in 2012 looked at more than 1,000 combat veterans and found that about 23 percent of those with PTSD and high irritability had been arrested for a criminal offense. This was more than double the rate of all the combat veterans studied, including those with and without combat trauma.

The link between PTSD and crime is worrisome. In response to an apparent clustering of homicides at Fort Carson, Colorado, the U.S. Army's third-largest post, the military commissioned a report. Issued in 2009, the 126-page study found that the murder rate around the post had doubled, and that the number of rape arrests had tripled between 2005 and 2008.

While it is inaccurate to claim that all combat veterans have PTSD, or that PTSD causes violence, there is at least some link between PTSD and postwar homicide. Serving in a war zone exposes people to serious psychological and moral challenges, and that experience has the potential to make some people less stable and more violent than they might have otherwise been.

Bystanders and soldiers crouch for cover as law enforcement officers (upper right) run toward the sound of the gunfire at the Soldier Readiness Processing Center at Fort Hood, Texas, in 2009.

50,409 soldiers wounded in action	239,174 vets diagnosed with PTSD

WAR WOUNDS

Studies show PTSD is much more common among U.S. veterans than physical wounds. Experts have diagnosed the condition...

→ **In 11 to 20 percent** of veterans of the Iraq and Afghanistan wars.

→ **In as many as 10 percent** of Gulf War Veterans.

→ **In about 30 percent** of Vietnam veterans.

BASE ATTACKS

Although unprecedented in scale, Major Nidal Hasan's killings at Fort Hood were not unique.

Lawyers for shooter and paratrooper William Kreutzer Jr. claimed he had mental health issues.

In 1995, William Kreutzer Jr., a U.S. Army paratrooper, killed one soldier and wounded 18 others when he opened fire on a physical training formation at Fort Bragg, North Carolina.

In 2003, at Camp Pennsylvania in Kuwait, U.S. Army soldier Hasan Akbar threw hand grenades into a tent in the early morning, when most troops were sleeping. He then fired his rifle into the subsequent bedlam; two soldiers were killed.

In 2009, at Camp Liberty in Iraq, John M. Russell, a sergeant, was being escorted back to his unit after a visit to the combat stress clinic at the camp when he grabbed an unsecured rifle. He then drove back to the counseling center and opened fire on unarmed fellow service members, killing five. He survived and was convicted of the killings.

Navy subcontractor Aaron Alexis was delusional said the FBI.

In 2013, Aaron Alexis, a subcontracted technology worker at a navy facility, fatally shot 12 people and injured four others inside the Washington Navy Yard in Washington, D.C. It was the second-deadliest mass murder on a U.S. military base, behind the 2009 shooting at Fort Hood, Texas. Alexis was killed at the scene.

In 2014, there was a second mass shooting at Fort Hood, in which three were people killed and 16 others wounded. The gunman, 34-year-old Ivan Lopez, an Iraq war veteran, died of a self-inflicted wound.

CAMPUS KILLERS

MANY SCHOOL SHOOTERS SUFFER FROM SEVERE EMOTIONAL TRAUMA, PSYCHOSIS, OR MENTAL ILLNESS.

Gun control supporters and opponents gather outside the National Shooting Sports Foundation in Newtown, Connecticut, in 2013.

THE GUN QUESTION

Arming the defenders

A heated public debate on gun ownership followed the December 2012 massacre in Sandy Hook, Connecticut. The National Rifle Association responded to calls for restrictions by suggesting school-children would be safer with armed security personnel. A total of 33 states considered new bills to arm teachers and administrators, but as of August 2014 only eight had enacted such laws, while gun laws were strengthened in 15 states.

Violent media images and video games, bullying, and mental illness have all been cited as factors in school shooters' psychological profiles, but it is difficult to pinpoint a primary cause of the bloodshed. Many students are subject to these influences and don't kill classmates. It is more accurate to say that these mass attacks result from a combination of clinical and sociocultural elements.

School shooters are typically portrayed as shy, aloof loners who react violently to prolonged bullying or humiliation. But psychologist Peter Langman, who evaluates youths at risk, suggests this stereotype is wrong. Instead, Langman suggests that these individuals suffer from disturbing, unbearable, often misunderstood psychological problems. He divides them into three categories:

1. The traumatized, full of hostility and shame

2. The psychotics, driven by paranoid delusions

3. The psychopaths, mainly motivated by sadistic ideologies

Traumatized individuals tend to have violent fathers, while substance abuse and parental rejection are common among psychotics, writes Langman in *Why Kids Kill: Inside the Minds of School Shooters*. Psychopaths often are more sadistic than their peers and have been immersed in gun culture. Not all kids who commit mass murder come from difficult homes, however. And while some are loners, others are surrounded by friends.

Most school shooters kill themselves afterward and intend to do so from the beginning. This makes them especially dangerous because they are unafraid of punishment. The school environment, which represents the existing social order, becomes the target of seething anger and revenge in a bid for recognition. Some experts believe shooters attack children and teenagers because they're easier to control than adults, who appear more threatening.

Snapshots of Notorious Shooters

Violence researcher Jack Katz of the University of California, Los Angeles, says some shooters inflict "righteous slaughter" to right past wrongs. Seung-Hui Cho, the Virginia Tech student who massacred 32 and injured 17 in April 2007, was said to have had an uneasy relationship with his fellow students. In the middle of the shooting spree, Cho returned to his dorm

Thousands of Virginia Tech students wait in line to attend a memorial service in honor of those killed in the shootings of April 17, 2007, in Blacksburg, Virginia.

Eric Harris (left) watches as Dylan Klebold practices firing a gun. Both committed suicide after massacring classmates at Columbine High School in Colorado in 1999.

PREVENTING THE VIOLENCE

How should schools work to keep another Sandy Hook from happening?

A December 2013 gun-violence report from the American Psychological Association suggests the following guidelines:

→ Establish behavioral threat assessment teams.

→ Provide access to conflict-resolution programs and improved mental-health services.

→ Intervene early with at-risk families to improve parenting techniques.

→ Work with the community to train law enforcement, teachers, and mental-health professionals.

→ Improve oversight of firearms retailers, licensing of handgun purchases, and background checks.

to mail photos, writings, and homemade videos denouncing hedonism and materialism to NBC News. A note found in his room condemned "rich kids."

Columbine killers Eric Harris and Dylan Klebold were also different from their peers. Klebold was depressed and troubled. Harris, extremely self-conscious about "bodily defects," was fascinated with Nazi leader Adolph Hitler's master race concept. The two shared sadistic, suicidal fantasies. In their diaries, they depicted themselves as wrathful gods.

Some shooters develop an all-consuming rage at life and attack schools with no apparent reason. It is unknown, for example, why 20-year-old killer Adam Lanza chose his former grade school, Sandy Hook Elementary, as his target. Lanza reportedly had been diagnosed with sensory integration disorder as a child. He had a history of obsessive-compulsive behaviors, including changing his socks 20 times a day, and was interested in advocating for pedophiles' rights. He was fascinated by military and school shootings, especially Columbine.

SLAUGHTERED INNOCENTS

BRUTAL, PREMEDITATED SCHOOL SHOOTINGS ARE A GLOBAL PHENOMENON, AND COPYCAT SCENARIOS ARE COMMON.

In recent decades, there has been a rise in carefully choreographed attacks on schools around the world. No matter where the events have unfolded, the psy-chopathy and characters involved have been startlingly similar.

Typically, the perpetrator has been a young male. Of the 101 school shootings worldwide between 1974 and 2007, only four were committed by females, according to Frank J. Robertz, cofounder of Berlin's Institute for Violence Prevention and Applied Criminology.

While many young people fantasize about wreaking revenge on schoolmates for perceived wrongs done them, shooters are extremely disturbed individuals who suffer from various psychoses, psychopathy, and trauma. As they become consumed by out-of-control emotions, they gradually lose any sense of empathy; ultimately, they become cold-blooded and methodical, often planning their attacks down to the smallest detail.

Among adolescents considered at risk for such behavior are those who have experienced violence; they can develop brutal fantasies as a way to gain recognition and respect, says clinical psychologist Al Carlisle, a youth-violence researcher in Price, Utah. The ubiquitous media scrutiny of school shooters such as Eric Harris and Dylan Klebold, perpetrators of the 1999

REMEMBERING THE DEAD

While nothing can ever replace a lost loved one, a number of towns have honored victims with moving public memorials

Dunblane, Scotland. To commemorate the 1996 Dunblane Primary School massacre, relatives in 1998 dedicated a garden at the cemetery where most of the victims are buried. Mick North, whose daughter was among the slain, described the memorial: "The cheerfulness and brightness of a classroom is evoked by each one of the pebbles in the pools. You can almost hear the chatter of children in the sound of the fountain." Three years later, a commemorative tablet was unveiled for the town's cathedral. Among the quotations inscribed on it is W.H. Auden's "We are linked as children in a circle dancing."

Flower tributes line the road leading to the Dunblane Primary School.

Beslan, Russia. Memorials to the more than 330 victims of the 2004 three-day Chechen separatist school siege in Beslan, Russia, have been erected in several cities. In Beslan, a structure inspired by a mourning wreath now encircles the destroyed gymnasium, the center of the tragedy. In a sculpture in the Church of Nativity square in Moscow, bronze slabs suggesting monumental stairs rise from a memorial plaque. The steps transform into human shapes, and finally into a flock of birds.

A pile of rifles handed in for scrap in Melbourne, after Australia banned all automatic and semi-automatic rifles in the aftermath of the Port Arthur shooting, 1996.

The Australian government mandated that would-be buyers declare a "genuine reason" for needing a firearm.

ANTI-GUN LEGISLATION AND POLITICAL REFORMS

Many countries have responded to school violence and other mass shootings with regulations meant to stem the tide.

→ **Australia:** After a rampage by a deranged gunman killed 35 in Port Arthur, Tasmania, the Australian government outlawed private gun sales. An aggressive buyback program yielded some 600,000 weapons. Reports show that gun-related homicides subsequently fell by 59 percent.

→ **Great Britain:** Following the 1996 massacre in Dunblane, Scotland, a virulent anti-gun-ownership campaign culminated in a petition with almost 750,000 signatures. By fall 1997, lawmakers had banned private ownership of handguns.

→ **Russia:** In 2004, Chechen rebels staged a siege of a school in Beslan, Russia; 334 people were killed and more than 700 wounded. Following the massacre, the national legislature approved sweeping counterterrorism measures centralizing control over Russia's various regions.

→ **European Union:** In 2007, after a spate of deadly shootings, legislators backed new gun regulations. Each member state is required to maintain a database of all firearm owners.

Columbine High massacre, also can feed a desperate yearning for recognition in violence-prone individuals with low self-esteem.

Copycats Across the Sea

Harris and Klebold, for example, were heroes of Sebastian Bosse, an emotionally disturbed 18-year-old living in Emsdetten, Germany. In November 2006, Bosse posted a video message online: "I can't f–kin' wait until I can shoot every mother-f–kin' last one of you." After driving to his former high school armed with rifles and homemade bombs, Bosse fired randomly, injuring 37 students and teachers before committing suicide.

Similarly, Harris is thought to have inspired Pekka-Eric Auvinen, the 18-year-old from Finland who became the second school shooter in Finland's history when he massacred eight and wounded one at Jokela High School in November 2007. Eleven others were injured by flying glass, and Auvinen shot himself in the head. In a rambling online message two weeks before the deadly attack, Auvinen wrote, "I, as a natural selector, will eliminate all who I see unfit, disgraces of human race and failures of natural selection." The t-shirt that Eric Harris wore at the Columbine massacre read "Natural Selection."

Thomas Hamilton, the unemployed Dunblane, Scotland, shopkeeper who killed 16 kindergarteners and an adult on March 13, 1996, is believed to have inspired Martin Bryant, the Australian mass murderer who slew 35 tourists and injured 23 others a few weeks later on a rampage in Port Arthur, Tasmania.

Quiet suburban homes can hide shocking crimes like that of Randall Engles of
Dundee, Oregon, who killed his wife and children before turning the gun on himself.

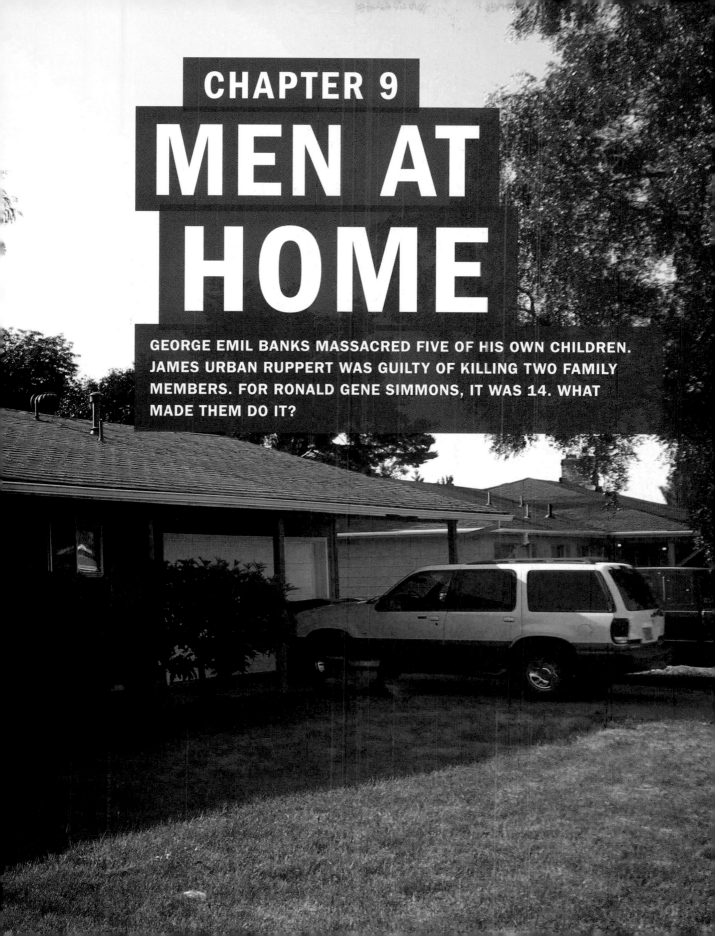

CHAPTER 9
MEN AT HOME

GEORGE EMIL BANKS MASSACRED FIVE OF HIS OWN CHILDREN. JAMES URBAN RUPPERT WAS GUILTY OF KILLING TWO FAMILY MEMBERS. FOR RONALD GENE SIMMONS, IT WAS 14. WHAT MADE THEM DO IT?

THE EASTER SUNDAY MASSACRE

IN AMERICA'S DEADLIEST HOME SHOOTING, ONE SEEMINGLY MILD-MANNERED SON TOOK OUT HIS ENTIRE CLAN.

In the aftermath of a massacre, stunned neighbors often use the same two adjectives to describe the killer: quiet and unassuming. Those are certainly the words someone might have used to characterize James Urban Ruppert until Easter Sunday, 1975, the day the 41-year-old from Hamilton, Ohio, snapped. Coming downstairs where his family was gathered, Ruppert systematically gunned down his mother, brother, sister-in-law, and eight nephews and nieces ranging in age from four to 17. It remains one of the worst family murders in American history.

Veneer of Normality

Single and unemployed, "Jimmy" Ruppert lived with his widowed mother, Charity, in a small, plain, two-story house about 35 minutes north of Cincinnati. The Rupperts were considered a nice, middle-class family. One neighbor described Charity as "the sweetest little woman who ever walked," and Jimmy's older brother, Leonard, was a successful engineer and happily married. But under the veneer of normality, something was terribly wrong.

Jimmy and Leonard's father had died when the boys were adolescents and both had grown up quickly. Jimmy believed he was unwanted and that his mother favored Leonard. Socially, he was less successful and less motivated than his brother. When Jimmy was 16, he tried to hang himself. One of the few interests he cultivated was collecting and shooting guns.

Eventually, Jimmy would begin drinking and develop paranoid delusions. He believed his mother, brother, and the FBI were trying to sabotage his reputation by telling people he was gay and a communist. And then there was the money. Jimmy's mother had grown tired of supporting her younger son and had started eviction proceedings against him—but he knew that upon her death he would inherit $340,000, the equivalent of $1.5 million today.

Thirty-one Gunshots

March 30, 1975, began normally enough for the Ruppert family. Leonard, then 42, his wife, Alma, 36, and their children arrived at Charity's house. There was an Easter egg hunt in the yard. Afterward, the adults and kids went inside to prepare a meal and relax. Jimmy, who had been up in his room, came

Leonard R. and Alma Ruppert and their eight children, 1975

WHO KNEW?

In 2007, 13 percent of family homicides involved children killing parents, up from 9.7 percent in 1980.

James Urban Ruppert, center, being taken to jail after his arraignment in Hamilton, Ohio, 1975.

downstairs carrying four weapons—three handguns and a rifle—and proceeded to fire 31 times. When he was finished, the house was littered with the bodies of adults and children. About three hours later, he called police to report a shooting. When they arrived, they found Jimmy standing in the doorway. There were no signs of a struggle in the house.

Jimmy was tried twice and eventually found guilty of the murders of his mother and brother. He was found not guilty by reason of insanity in the murders of his sister-in-law and the eight children. He was sentenced to two life terms, which he is serving in Lima, Ohio.

Peoria, Ohio, resident Nathan Leuthold shot his wife on Valentine's Day.

DISTRESSING TIMES

Family celebrations and holidays can bring up old traumas and unleash virulent emotions.

→ **Valentine's Day.** On February 14, 2013, Nathan Leuthold of Peoria, Illinois, shot his wife, Denise, in order to be with a 20-year-old foreign college student the missionary couple had sponsored. He was sentenced to 80 years in jail. Leuthold was convicted of his wife's murder in September 2014 and sentenced to 80 years in prison.

→ **Independence Day.** On July 4, 2012, Randall Engels of Dundee, Oregon, shot his estranged wife, Amy, and their two children before killing himself. Amy had filed for divorce in May, and a post on Engels's Facebook page read, "If she's gone i cant go on."

→ **Christmas.** On December 25, 1929, North Carolina tobacco farmer Charlie Lawson killed his wife, Fannie, and five of his six children before shooting himself. It is now believed that he was sexually abusing his teenage daughter.

ASSESSING THE DANGER

A straightforward test can help predict a woman's risk of being killed by an abusive husband or boyfriend.

More than a third of family homicides are committed by a spouse or former spouse, according to government statistics, but some are preventable. A questionnaire developed at the Johns Hopkins University School of Nursing can help identify which women are in imminent danger.

The assessment involves a series of 20 questions posed by a nurse, counselor, or advocate. The questioner asks whether the abuser drinks or uses certain drugs, owns a gun, forces her to have sex, or threatens to kill her. The woman is also asked for details about any beating or other abuse she'd experienced over the previous year.

Properly analyzed, the responses can accurately predict a woman's chances of becoming a victim of murder or attempted murder by her partner. Those women perceived to be in serious danger are counseled to take steps to secure the safety of themselves and their children.

"MY PEOPLE DIED BECAUSE I LOVE THEM"

THREE DECADES AFTER SLAUGHTERING HIS CHILDREN, GEORGE EMIL BANKS REMAINS A PRISONER OF HIS PSYCHOTIC DELUSIONS.

Solving the puzzle of what causes mental illness has proven elusive.

WHAT CAUSES MENTAL ILLNESS?

As much as we'd like to find one clear trigger, psychological problems are likely a result of a number of factors.

Serious mental illness is surprisingly common. In 2012, one in every 25 American adults suffered from debilitating psychological impairment not attributed to substance abuse or developmental disorders. These illnesses, including schizophrenia, psychotic disorders, and bipolar disorders, typically result from a combination of biological and environmental causes.

Some mental illness has a genetic component, but it can be triggered by abuse, trauma, neglect, or ongoing stress. Brain injuries, oxygen deprivation at birth, substance abuse, and certain infections can also affect a person's psychology.

What does society do with a condemned man who is too mentally ill to execute? George Emil Banks was given the death penalty in 1983 for slaughtering 13 people, including five of his own children, in Pennsylvania. But as the years ticked away and execution dates came and went, Banks remained in such bad psychological shape that in 2011 the Pennsylvania Supreme Court upheld a ruling that executing him in his current mental state would violate the U.S. Constitution.

"He doesn't have a rational understanding of why he's sentenced to death," his attorney, Al Flora Jr., told the Scranton *Times-Tribune*. "He doesn't have a rational understanding of the implications of the death penalty."

Today, Banks remains on death row, in a restricted unit at a maximum-security prison near Philadelphia. In prison, Banks has attempted suicide numerous times, embarked on hunger strikes that require him to be force-fed, claimed he was being attacked by a "flesh-eating demon," and insisted he was the victim of a pro-Islam conspiracy.

Irrevocably Damaged

Banks's history of psychological problems extends back before the day in September 1982 that he executed his five sons and daughters, along with his three live-in girlfriends, an ex-girlfriend, three of his lovers' relatives, and a bystander who just happened to be in the wrong place at the

wrong time. When questioned about his motive, he said he believed he was acting in the children's best interest.

The son of a black father and a white mother, Banks grew up tormented by racism, which ultimately destroyed his sanity, his lawyers said. Employed as a prison guard before he snapped, Banks told coworkers that he believed the world was soon to be engulfed in a race war and that he was worried about the effect of racism on his children. About three weeks before his killing spree, he locked himself inside a guard tower at work and threatened to shoot himself. He was put on leave.

Created a Cult

Banks reportedly admired cult leaders Jim Jones and Charles Manson, and he appeared to have mimicked some of their behaviors, creating a small cult around himself. At his home in Wilkes-Barre, Banks lived with three women, each of whom was the mother of at least one of his children.

On the day of the massacre, Banks, then 40, woke up after a night of drinking gin and taking prescription drugs and began executing the members of his household. He began with the children, who ranged in age from one to 11 years old. Then, dressed in fatigues and a t-shirt that read "Kill 'em all and let God sort 'em out," he left home, randomly shooting two men across the street, one of whom died. He drove to the home of a fourth girlfriend, who had left

George Emil Banks, center, is led to his sentencing at the Luzerne County, Pennsylvania, courthouse.

him. He shot her, their five-year-old son, and two of her family members. When he was finished, he shouted, "I killed them all!"

Banks's guilt has never been in dispute, but his well-documented mental illness has led to debates about the fairness of the death penalty. For his part, Banks said at his 2010 competency hearing that he was willing to die. Death, he believed, would deliver his soul to the Lord.

CAPITAL CRIMES?

George Emil Banks remains on death row in case he is ever declared "fit for execution." Other mentally ill inmates have met different fates.

PRISONER		CRIME	DIAGNOSIS	SYMPTOMS	STATUS
	Kelsey Patterson	Shot a business owner and his secretary for no reason	Paranoid schizophrenic	Right after the murders, stripped down to his socks; at trial, ranted about devices implanted in him	Executed in Texas, 2004
	Scott Louis Panetti	Shot his mother-in-law and father-in-law	Schizophrenic	Represented himself at trial; wanted to subpoena Jesus as a witness	Declared competent; awaiting execution in Texas
	Calvin E. Swann	Shot a man during a home-invasion robbery	Schizophrenic	As his execution date neared, was concerned only with getting money for cigarettes	Granted clemency in 1999 in Virginia

FATHER FROM HELL

A CONTROLLING LONER ABUSED HIS DAUGHTER AND RULED HIS FAMILY WITH AN IRON FIST—AND KILLED THEM ALL WHEN THEY DISPLEASED HIM.

On Monday morning, December 28, 1987, 47-year-old Ronald Gene Simmons armed himself with two pistols and systematically shot his way through the tiny town of Russellville, Arkansas, as if crossing people off a hit list—as, in fact, he was. Simmons's first stop was a law firm, where he killed Kathy Kendrick, a 24-year-old secretary he had once worked with. From there, he made the rounds to three former employers, including a mini-mart where he'd quit working just days earlier. He killed Jim Chaffin, 33, and wounded three more people. Then he calmly surrendered. "It's over," he said, before relinquishing his guns to the police.

His rampage might have been finished, but the extent of Simmons's madness was yet to be discovered. Police who entered his ramshackle home would soon find out that Simmons had methodically executed his wife, their children, and his grandchildren—14 family members in all—in four separate waves of violence over the course of several days. The first to die, on Tuesday, December 22, were Simmons's wife, a visiting adult son, and the son's three-year-old daughter. Later that day, the school bus dropped off the four Simmons children who still lived at home, and Simmons killed them one by one. The bodies all went into a pit on his property.

For three days after the murders, Simmons

THE VICTIMS

Simmons's last two victims were not related to him; the rest were family members. At the end of his spree, Simmons said he'd "gotten everyone that had hurt him," a witness recalled.

SHOT

REBECCA SIMMONS, 46
wife

GENE JR., 29
son

SHEILA, 24
daughter

DENNIS MCNULTY, 23
son-in-law

BILLY, 22
son

RENATA, 21
daughter-in-law

JIM CHAFFIN, 33
no relation

KATHY KENDRICK, 24
no relation

STRANGLED

LORETTA, 17
daughter

EDDY, 14
son

MARIANNE, 11
daughter

BECKY, 8
daughter

SYLVIA, 7
Sheila's daughter by Simmons

BARBARA, 3
granddaughter

MICHAEL, 20 months
grandson

DROWNED

WILLIAM HENRY "TRAE", 1
grandson

WHO KNEW?
Simmons's last words were, "Let the torture and suffering in me end."

Ronald Gene Simmons, who killed 16 in four waves of violence, being escorted by police in Little Rock, Arkansas, in 1987

remained at home, reportedly drinking beer and watching television. He resumed his spree on Saturday, December 26, when Simmons's older children Sheila and Billy and their families arrived for a post-holiday dinner. The two sets of guests turned up separately and Simmons murdered them as they entered, scattering their bodies around his home: two on the floor, covered with their own coats; Sheila on the dining table; the youngest babies in the trunks of cars.

Twisted History

Even before the carnage, family and neighbors had been deeply wary of Simmons, an Air Force veteran. He was so controlling that he read his family's mail before allowing them to send it. His home had no telephone or indoor plumbing; he made his children haul water to the house and dig a hole for a family outhouse—a crater that ultimately would become their own grave.

Unknown to his family at the time, he had sexually abused his daughter Sheila when she was a teenager. One of Sheila's two children, seven-year-old Sylvia, was Simmons's daughter.

Simmons's motive for the mass murder seemed to be a combination of factors. His wife, Rebecca, was reportedly planning to leave him, and Sheila had married and condemned him for molesting her. He had made repeated unwanted sexual advances toward the secretary Kathy Kendrick, with whom he had worked at a trucking company before she'd moved to the law firm. The one motive he wasn't found to have was insanity. Deemed competent to stand trial, Simmons was given the death penalty. He was executed on May 31, 1990.

WHO KNEW?
Bill Clinton, then the governor of Arkansas, signed Simmons's death warrant.

An overhead shot of the Branch Davidian religious compound, where a 50-day siege by federal authorities began on February 28, 1993, and ended violently on April 19.

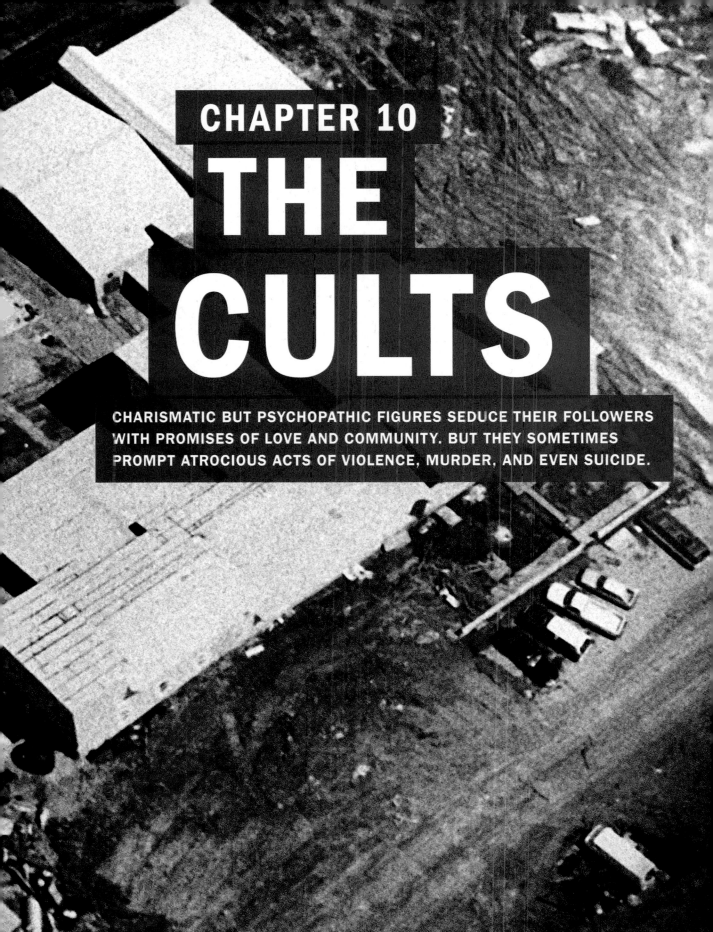

CHAPTER 10
THE
CULTS

CHARISMATIC BUT PSYCHOPATHIC FIGURES SEDUCE THEIR FOLLOWERS WITH PROMISES OF LOVE AND COMMUNITY. BUT THEY SOMETIMES PROMPT ATROCIOUS ACTS OF VIOLENCE, MURDER, AND EVEN SUICIDE.

On November 18, 1978, 900 members of the Peoples Temple lie dead around their compound in Jonestown, Guyana.

CRIMINAL CULTS AND KILLERS

PSYCHOPATHIC CULT LEADERS MAY SEDUCE PROSPECTS WITH THE PROMISE OF UNCONDITIONAL LOVE.

Violent episodes involving cults may be rare, but the image of the charismatic leader with the power to dictate what members think, whom they should trust, and even when to eat and sleep looms large in the American imagination. Because of figures such as Charles Manson and Jim Jones, who have manipulated followers into murder or suicide, the fear of the homicidal cult leader remains deeply embedded in the national psyche.

Members of the Charles Manson "family" outside the Los Angeles Hall of Justice during the Manson trial.

Captivated by Charisma

When do cult beliefs become deviant? Sociologists have argued this question for decades, debating when the label "cult" is used as a tool to marginalize groups that are merely different from societal norms. For Margaret Singer, a psychologist and expert in cults and mind control, the main criterion is simply "intense relationships between followers and a powerful idea or leader."

Successful cult leaders tend to be charismatic and exceptionally magnetic. Many may be perceived by followers as superhuman. Recruits are promised that they will find their life's purpose by joining the group.

Lethal Combination

But the combination of charisma and a psychopathic personality disorder can be quite lethal. A cult leader's charming exterior may belie an irrational or even violent nature, according to psychologist Robert D. Hare, creator of the Hare Psychopathology Checklist, a tool used to diagnose psychopaths. Often, psychopaths who become leaders of cults have a narcissistic personality disorder, meaning they are excessively preoccupied with personal adequacy, power, prestige, and vanity, according to Hare.

When Follow the Leader Turns Tragic

Over the past five decades, several cult leaders have orchestrated acts of extreme brutality, caused mass suicide, and created bizarre cult compounds.

RAISED IN A CULT

For children who grow up in cults, learning to live in the wider world can be a challenge.

Psychologists and sociologists often refer to people who have grown up within a cult, as opposed to having joined of their own volition, as second-generation adults.

These individuals face particular difficulties if they decide to break with the group. Leaving can mean being cut off from the only connections they've ever known and entering a world in which they have no experience. Many lack social skills and have never learned to think critically. They may have difficulties making decisions or even discerning right from wrong.

Charles Manson believed the Beatles song "Helter Skelter" predicted an impending race war.

LEADER **Charles Manson**

CULT NAME **The Family**

BASE OF OPERATIONS San Francisco, CA

GOAL To prompt a widespread race war

VICTIMS Drug dealer Bernard Crowe, music teacher Gary Hinman, actress Sharon Tate and her three houseguests, and Leno and Rosemary LaBianca

QUOTE "I'm Jesus Christ, whether you want to accept it or not, I don't care."

In 1967, in San Francisco, Charles Manson began building a nonreligious cult called the Family. In 1969, he ordered the brutal killings of seven people, including actress Sharon Tate, the wife of director Roman Polanski, who was more than eight months pregnant at the time. The unrepentant Manson continues to make headlines from prison, offering periodic interviews and making bizarre pronouncements prior to his parole hearings. In 2012, after Manson advised parole officers that he is a very dangerous man, he was denied parole for the 12th time. Manson will next be eligible for parole when he is 92. More details on Manson's story appear on pages 80–81.

Jim Jones was the leader of the Peoples Temple. The mass suicide of his followers was the source of the cautionary phrase "Don't drink the Kool-Aid."

LEADER **Jim Jones**

CULT NAME **The Peoples Temple**

BASE OF OPERATIONS Jonestown, Guyana

GOAL To infiltrate the church with Marxism

VICTIMS Congressman Leo Ryan and three members of his delegation and 910 Temple members

QUOTE "If you're born in capitalist America, racist America, fascist America, then you're born in sin. But if you're born in socialism, you're not born in sin."

Jim Jones is perhaps the most infamous cult leader in American history. During the 1950s, he formed the Peoples Temple in San Francisco, California, but by 1977, he'd relocated the group to Jonestown, Guyana, on the north coast of South America. When several members tried to return to the United States, Jones killed them along with members of a congressional delegation who had flown in to investigate. In the days that followed, Jones orchestrated a mass suicide in which 900 Peoples Temple members drank poison mixed with fruit punch, many at gunpoint.

Shoko Asahara founded the cult Aum Shinrikyo, which blends elements of Christianity, yoga, and the teachings of Nostradamus.

LEADER **Shoko Asahara**
CULT NAME **Aum Shinrikyo**
BASE OF OPERATIONS Tokyo, Japan
GOAL To act as "Christ" and transfer spiritual powers to his members
VICTIMS 13 people

Shoko Asahara was leader of the Japanese cult Aum Shinrikyo, which at its height had more than 5,000 adherents. Many of them were highly educated doctors, lawyers, and scientists. Asahara advised his followers that the world would end soon, but their loyalty to him would ensure their survival. In 1995, members of Aum Shinrikyo dumped toxic sarin gas into a Tokyo subway, killing a dozen people and injuring hundreds of others. Asahara was arrested and tried for masterminding the attacks. He was found guilty and remains incarcerated for the crime. The group has since reorganized under new leadership and a new name.

Heaven's Gate leaders Marshall Applewhite and Bonnie Nettles described themselves as alien entities who had entered vacated human bodies.

LEADERS **Marshall Applewhite and Bonnie Nettles**
CULT NAME **Heaven's Gate**
BASE OF OPERATIONS San Diego, CA
GOAL To ascend to the "Next Level" of existence by being taken up by aliens
VICTIMS 39 Heaven's Gate followers
QUOTE "We do in all honesty hate this world."

In 1997, 39 members of the Heaven's Gate cult committed mass suicide in Rancho Santa Fe, near San Diego, California, by taking cyanide, arsenic, and sedatives mixed with juice and alcohol. All were dressed in black, with arm patches that read Heaven's Gate Away Team, and sported identical pairs of Nike shoes. The founders of the cult, Marshall Applewhite and Bonnie Nettles, believed they were "the Two" mentioned in the Bible's book of Revelation and that believers' souls would be taken away by aliens associated with the return of the Hale-Bopp comet.

WORKING WITH SURVIVORS

Jill Mytton is a psychologist working with abuse survivors. Mytton points out that second-generation adults have to assimilate into a culture that they've been taught to hate.

In her counseling, Mytton has seen former cult members experience emotional turmoil, isolation, and difficulty transitioning to a "normal" life. Out of 262 second-generation adults counseled by Mytton:

70% lost their families upon leaving the cult

68% experienced trauma upon leaving the cult

27% reported child sexual abuse in the cult

THE FAMILY THAT KILLS TOGETHER

HALF A CENTURY AFTER CHARLES MANSON PROMPTED A KILLING SPREE, HIS NAME STILL PRODUCES SHUDDERS.

Charles Manson is escorted to his arraignment on conspiracy-murder charges in connection with the Sharon Tate murder case, 1969, Los Angeles, California.

As a symbol of evil and the macabre, it is difficult to compete with Charles Manson. In the late 1960s, the California musician and hippie-cult leader nurtured a devoted following among a band of petty criminals and drug addicts, calling them the Family, and urged them to go on a brutal killing spree. Members of the group used the victims' blood to scrawl words such as "pig" and "death to pigs" on the walls next to the bodies. For America, Manson represented the dark side of sex, drugs, and rock and roll, and the cult's shocking actions helped bring an end to the era's carefree counter-culture.

Helter Skelter

When Manson began to form the Family in 1967, he was an unemployed former convict on the fringe of the Los Angeles music scene. A charismatic speaker, Manson attracted a small group of followers while preaching that the Beatles' song "Helter Skelter" predicted an impending race war. In Manson's mind, the murders he ordered would prompt blacks to rise up and slaughter whites, leaving Manson in charge.

Manson began the summer of 1969 by shooting and leaving for dead Bernard Crowe, a drug dealer he had defrauded. Although Crowe survived, other victims would not. Over the next five weeks, the Family would kill eight more people in and around Los Angeles, starting with music teacher Gary Hinman, who they sought to rob, but instead stabbed to death on July 31. Family members used Hinman's blood to scrawl the words "political piggy" on the wall near his body.

On August 9, the Family struck again, taking the life of actress Sharon Tate and four others who were staying at Tate's rented Los Angeles home. Tate, the wife of film director Roman Polanski, was more than eight months pregnant when she was stabbed 16 times. Manson follower Susan Atkins used a towel

Members of Charles Manson's "family." From left: Lynette "Squeaky" Fromme, Sandra Good, Mark Ross, Paul Watkins, and Catherine "Gypsy" Share holding Sandra Good's son Ivan. The two men partially hidden in back are unidentified.

Who joined the Family?

Most of Manson's followers were in their early 20s. Insecure young women seemed particularly susceptible to becoming mesmerized by his charisma.

Susan Atkins. Involved in eight of the Manson Family killings, Atkins is thought to have personally killed Sharon Tate. She was later described as a model prisoner who accepted responsibility for her crime. Denied parole 18 times, Atkins died in prison in 2009, after serving 40 years.

Steve Grogan. A petty criminal before he met Manson, Grogan was involved in the 1969 killing of ranch hand Donald Shea. Declared by the judge to be "too stupid and too hopped up on drugs to decide anything on his own," Grogan was released from prison in 1985.

Mary Brunner. A former library assistant, Brunner was the mother of Manson's son, Valentine Michael, called "Pooh Bear." She served time for credit card theft and armed robbery, and received immunity in the Hinman murder case in exchange for her testimony.

Patricia Krenwinkel. Krenwinkel was convicted for her role in the Tate and LaBianca murders. She was loyal to Manson during her trial, but has grown critical of Manson in the years since. Denied parole 13 times, she is now the longest-incarcerated female inmate in the California penal system.

Lynette "Squeaky" Fromme. Though not involved in the Family murders, Fromme attended the trials to show her support of Manson. In 1975, Fromme failed in her attempt to kill U.S. President Gerald Ford. She was sentenced to life imprisonment but was released on parole in 2009 after serving 34 years.

Charles "Tex" Watson. An honor student as a younger man, Watson had dropped out of college by the time he met Manson. He participated in the murders of both Sharon Tate and Leno and Rosemary LaBianca. He has been in prison since 1971.

dipped in Tate's blood to write "PIG" on the front door. Three others at the Tate home were also knifed to death, including Polish actor Wojciech Frykowski, who sustained 51 wounds. The fifth victim was shot dead. Manson was said to have criticized the killers—Atkins, Tex Watson, and Patricia Krenwinkel—for doing an unnecessarily messy job.

The following night, the Family targeted supermarket executive Leno LaBianca and his wife, Rosemary, in their home, slashing them dozens of times with various weapons. The killers carved into the bodies

words such as "WAR," "Helter Skelter," and "Death to Pigs," and smeared similar slogans onto the walls and various surfaces.

In December 1969, Manson and several of his followers were arrested for the crimes. Manson was convicted under the joint-responsibility rule that makes each member of a conspiracy guilty of the crimes committed by fellow conspirators. Manson and four other members of the family received the death penalty, but their sentences were later commuted to life imprisonment. Today, Manson is an inmate in Corcoran State Prison.

ANATOMY OF A CULT LEADER

CHARISMATIC LEADERS AND THEIR FOLLOWERS HAVE A SYMBIOTIC, AND FATEFUL, RELATIONSHIP.

JIM JONES
(1931–1978)
Peoples Temple
Led a mass suicide

DAVID KORESH
(1959–1993)
Branch Davidians
Led members to die in FBI siege

Cult leaders Jim Jones of the Peoples Temple, David Koresh of the Branch Davidians, and Marshall Applewhite of Heaven's Gate all had different sets of beliefs, but they shared a number of predictable personality traits. They each tended to over-inflate their own importance, were arrogant, did not consider other people's needs, and demanded to be obeyed without question, experts have observed. In clinical terms, these men were pathological narcissists. And while there are plenty of charismatic people who don't use their charms to control murderous cults, experts warn the public to be wary of leaders who exhibit these self-aggrandizing behaviors.

There are some classic red flags. A group leader may not allow members to leave if they want to. He may sever the group's contact with the outside world by relocating it to a remote place. In some cases, cult leaders have been known to employ mind-control techniques on their followers.

Jim Jones, for example, successfully used many forms of brainwashing on his flock: At his Jonestown, Guyana camp, Jones broadcast propaganda constantly over loudspeakers. He asked followers to tell him their deepest fears and then used those fears against them in front of others. He fostered an us-against-the-world mentality, even holding "suicide drills" in preparation for an invasion from outsiders. The end was mass tragedy when more than 900 of Jones's followers committed suicide in 1978, many by swallowing cyanide-laced fruit punch.

The Followers

But how do cult leaders attract followers in the first place? There is no profile of a typical cult recruit; although the average age is about 25, older people do join up, according to researchers. And being intelligent is not a guaranteed defense against a cult's tactics. Those most vulnerable to cults tend to be people going through changes. Perhaps they've just ended a relationship or moved to a new town.

Existing members reel in newcomers with the promise of friendship, security, or even sex. Often, a recruit is invited to a special event or a seminar where existing members shower him or her with attention and affection. As described by a Harvard University Medical School psychiatry professor to *the New York Times*, "The mark is placed in a panicky, disoriented state, and an emotional crisis is manufactured by the recruiters." The cult then offers a solution to this crisis, and the conversion is complete.

Marshall Applewhite (1931–1997) founder of Heaven's Gate and later organized a group suicide

WHO KNEW?

Early Judaism and early Christianity were both originally maligned as cults.

Some of the tactics used to recover and "reprogram" cult members are as radical as those of the groups themselves.

On June 24, 1980, two men wrestled a screaming Susan Wirth into a van and drove away. A 35-year-old teacher at a San Francisco community college, Wirth was taken out of state by her captors. She later reported that they had starved her and handcuffed her to a bed for two weeks. But the men weren't seeking ransom money. They were deprogrammers, hired by Wirth's mother for a fee of $27,000.

One of Wirth's abductors was Ted Patrick, a self-taught expert in extracting and "un-brainwashing" cult members. Wirth wasn't in a cult at all; her family just wanted to rid her of her liberal political views. In the end, Wirth did not press charges, but in October 1980, a San Diego court convicted Patrick of kidnapping another woman. He was sentenced to a year in local custody and required to remain in the city.

THE PITCH

How do cults and cult-like groups attract new members, and what do the critics say?

Group	Founder	Claims	What the Critics Say
NXIVM (pronounced "nexium")	Keith Raniere	Followers can improve the world by becoming fully empowered through intense life-coaching programs.	Dissenters are called "suppressives"; women members are said to provide sexual favors.
The Family International (formerly Children of God)	David Berg	Members enter into a "sexual relationship" with Jesus.	The group is secretive about its finances and the names of its senior leaders.

ASSASSINS T

UGS THIEVES

The darkest corners of the criminal mind conceal the sickening deviance of cannibals, the insatiable compulsions of arsonists and stalkers, and the cold-blooded intent of snipers and assassins. Whether driven by psychological disturbances or just unconstrained by the kind of morality we take for granted, these monsters prey on their victims in the most troubling ways, and for some of the highest stakes.

Money is at the root of at least some of their evil. Mobster and gangsters—whether the mafia, the Russian mob, Mexican drug cartels, or Asian gangs—have made big business out of intimidation of the masses, preying on our weaknesses for drug, drink, gambling, and illicit sex.

A less aggressive but no less insidious evil hides behind the curtain of correspondence, phone calls, the Internet, and the façade of legitimate business. White-collar thieves hit the jackpot by duping those who trust them, while Internet scammers and con artists beg and steal from gullible strangers. The most daring criminal acrobats manage to pull off huge scores in spectacular robberies and heists, sometimes becoming folk heroes in the process.

Shattered minds and broken lives: The reasons for some of the most horrific crimes still escape our understanding.

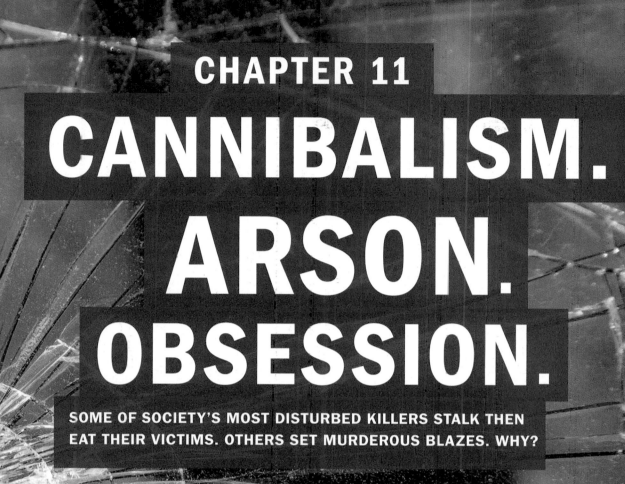

CHAPTER 11

CANNIBALISM. ARSON. OBSESSION.

SOME OF SOCIETY'S MOST DISTURBED KILLERS STALK THEN EAT THEIR VICTIMS. OTHERS SET MURDEROUS BLAZES. WHY?

KILLING TO CONSUME

IT'S HARD TO FATHOM WHAT WOULD DRIVE ONE PERSON TO EAT ANOTHER, BUT IT HAS HAPPENED MORE OFTEN THAN YOU'D LIKE TO IMAGINE.

H. Albert Fish, 1935

JAIL-HOUSE INTERVIEW

"Meek, gentle" Albert Fish

Psychiatrist Fredric Wertham met and interviewed the serial cannibal Albert Fish in his jail cell in 1935 and later said he was shocked that Fish seemed "meek, gentle, benevolent and polite." Wertham added, "If you wanted someone to entrust your children to, he would be the one you would choose."

Wertham said that Fish explained his motives this way: "I always had a desire to inflict pain on others and to have others inflict pain on me. I always seemed to enjoy everything that hurt. The desire to inflict pain, that is all that is uppermost."

Stories of serial cannibalism have been the stuff of folklore since medieval times, when legendary characters such as the Scotsmen Christie Cleek, a butcher, and clan head Sawney Bean were said to have devoured the flesh of their human victims. But there have also been cannibals who were all too real. Here are some of the more horrifying examples from the last 100 years.

→ **IN GERMANY, KARL DENKE WAS ARRESTED IN 1924** after attacking a man with an ax. Police searching Denke's home found human flesh in huge jars of curing salts, along with a ledger containing records of more than 40 people he had murdered and cannibalized between 1914 and 1918.

→ **BETWEEN 1918 AND 1924, FRITZ HAARMANN,** a con man and petty thief, committed at least 24 murders near the city of Hanover, Germany. Haarmann was known to tear out young men's throats to drink their blood before dismembering their bodies and selling their flesh for meat.

→ **HAMILTON ALBERT FISH, AKA "THE GRAY MAN,"** used a meat cleaver, butcher knife, and saw to torture and kill children. After his victims died, Fish mutilated and cannibalized their remains. In one case, he sent a letter to the parents of a ten-year-old victim, describing which parts tasted the best. He was caught and executed in 1935.

→ **JOACHIM KROLL BEGAN RAPING AND MURDERING PEOPLE IN 1955,** when he was 22, and continued his spree over two decades in the Duisberg area of Germany. Kroll told officials that he often cooked body parts in order to save money on groceries; he confessed to a total of 14 murders and died of a heart attack in prison in 1991.

→ **NIKOLAI DZHUMAGALIEV RAPED AND HACKED TO DEATH** seven women in Almaty, Kazakhstan in 1979–80 and ate their remains.

Serial murderer Fritz Haarmann (second from left) after his arrest in 1924

The legendary Sawney Bean, depicted outside his cave in South Ayrshire, Scotland, circa 1500

CANNIBAL PSYCHOLOGY

What goes on in the mind of these murderers?

Freudian psychologists suggest that cannibalism may relate to childhood trauma involving profound feelings of anxiety over separation from the mother. These individuals often become verbally aggressive, and in extreme cases, they might act on an urge to literally "absorb" a person by eating him or her. Other psychologists downplay the importance of childhood trauma and posit that extreme stress at any time of life can trigger deviant behavior.

Many of the individuals found to have committed acts of cannibalism are diagnosed with schizophrenia or some other form of personality disorder. In some of the most horrific cases, the perpetrators confess to deriving sexual satisfaction from fantasizing about and consuming humans. For many cannibal killers, who are almost always men, the act of cutting up the meat itself is sexually exciting, making them feel powerful and in control.

For an isolated and resentful loner, cannibalism fills a void. Killing and eating a victim may make an offender feel as if he is no longer alone, that he will always "have" his victims with him. And, having committed the act, it can become addictive; the killer craves a repetition of the feeling. Whatever the cause, this particularly heinous crime remains a subject of horrified fascination.

→ **IN ANKARA, TURKEY, IN 2007, ÖZGÜR DENGIZ** admitted killing one man. He reportedly skinned the victim's corpse with a cleaver; he ate some of it raw and put the remaining flesh in the refrigerator. After he was caught, Dengiz told the police, "I love to eat human flesh. It makes me ecstatic."

→ **STEPHEN GRIFFITHS BUTCHERED THREE WOMEN** and claimed to have consumed two of them in Bradford, England, in 2010.

→ **MATEJ CURKO, THE "SLOVAK CANNIBAL,"** was killed in a shootout with police in 2011. Investigators found body parts of two missing Slovakian women in his refrigerator.

THE MILWAUKEE CANNIBAL

AFTER JEFFREY DAHMER KILLED HIS VICTIMS, HE SOMETIMES ATE THEM, OR STORED THEIR PARTS IN FILING CABINETS.

A KILLER'S INVENTORY

When police officers stormed Jeffrey Dahmer's apartment, they uncovered:

→ A human head and three bags of organs in a refrigerator

→ Three heads, a torso, and various internal organs inside a free-standing freezer

→ Chemicals, formaldehyde, ether, and chloroform in a closet

→ Three painted skulls, a skeleton, various body parts, and photographs of victims in a filing cabinet

→ Two skulls in a box

→ Acid and three torsos in a 57-gallon vat

→ Driver's licenses and other identification from the victims

→ A King James bible

When investigators first searched the Milwaukee apartment of Jeffrey Dahmer, what they found made them gasp. Severed heads and limbs, skeletons, skulls, and other grisly artifacts filled Apartment 213 at 924 North 25th Street. They were Dahmer's "souvenirs," remnants of the 17 men and boys Dahmer murdered, dismembered, and sometimes ate between 1978 and 1991.

The Making of a Monster

Born in Milwaukee in 1960, Dahmer was the child of a troubled marriage. His father was a workaholic chemist and his mother was an unhappy teletype instructor. The two quarreled constantly and eventually divorced in 1978. Although Dahmer initially seemed unscathed by his parents' relationship, when he reached puberty, he became withdrawn and began drinking heavily.

Dahmer committed his first murder in 1978. Unlike the killings that would follow, it was unplanned. Three weeks after graduating from high school, Dahmer invited an 18-year-old hitchhiker to his house for some drinks. When the young man tried to leave, Dahmer impulsively hit him in the head with a 10-pound dumbbell. He then cut up the body, placed the parts in garbage bags, and buried them in the woods.

Not long after, Dahmer enlisted in the Army for a six-year stretch at his father's urging. Two years into his service, Dahmer was discharged for excessive drinking, which interfered with his performance. He eventually moved in with his grandmother in West Allis, Wisconsin, and found a job working the night shift at Milwaukee Ambrosia Chocolate.

Starting in September 1987, Dahmer began to entice young men to his grandmother's residence, where he murdered and dismembered them. In 1990, he moved into the apartment on North 25th Street in Milwaukee, accelerating his murderous pace. Of his 17 known victims, 12 were killed there.

Gruesome Pattern

Like most serial killers, Dahmer tended to follow a pattern. He would hone in on his victims at bus stops, bars, malls, and adult bookstores and lure them to his home with

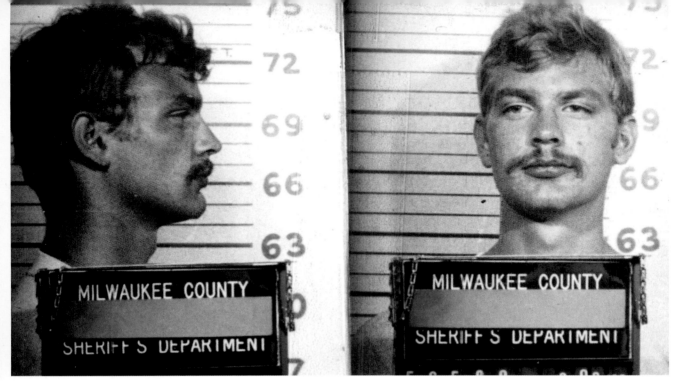

Jeffrey Dahmer in a police mug shot, 1982. He was murdered in prison in 1994.

promises of alcohol and money if they agreed to pose for photographs. In his apartment, Dahmer would drug his prey and then kill them, usually by strangulation. He liked to collect body parts and sometimes engaged in cannibalism. He also took photos that he could later use for his own pleasure.

Dahmer was finally caught and arrested in 1991, when a prospective victim broke free and ran into the street with a handcuff dangling from his wrist. During his trial, Dahmer pleaded guilty by virtue of insanity, with his lawyers arguing that only an insane person could have committed such atrocious acts. The jury found him guilty on all counts, and the judge sentenced him to 15 consecutive life terms in prison. When asked about his motives, Dahmer said that his compulsion to kill became "an incessant and never-ending desire to be with someone at whatever cost....It just filled my thoughts all day long."

Less than three years after he was convicted, Dahmer was beaten to death in prison by Christopher Scarver, a 25-year-old fellow inmate with schizophrenia-like delusions.

CONNING THE LAW

One of Dahmer's victims escaped, only to be returned to to the killer by the police.

In 1991, Konerak Sinthasomphone was found wandering the streets of Milwaukee, drugged, confused, and bleeding. When the 14-year-old Laotian was questioned by two police officers, he named Dahmer as the perpetrator. Dahmer told the officers that the boy was his 19-year-old lover and that the two had had a fight.

Though the women who had found Sinthasomphone insisted that he was in trouble, the police chose not to run a background check on Dahmer and did not verify the boy's age. Instead, they allowed Dahmer to take the 14-year-old back to his apartment, where he promptly killed and dismembered the victim. Following news of Sinthasomphone's murder, there were protests accusing the police of racism and homophobia.

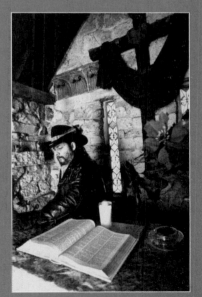

Self-described street minister Jean-Paul Ranieri was one of the few to warn gay men against serial killer Jeffrey Dahmer.

ALARMING FIRES

A DRUNKEN ARGUMENT IGNITED ONE OF THE DEADLIEST BLAZES ON RECORD IN NEW YORK CITY.

Julio Gonzalez, who set the Happy Land fire, during an appearance at the Bronx County Courthouse in New York, 1990

On the evening of March 25, 1990, a 36-year-old Cuban refugee named Julio Gonzalez got into an argument with his ex-girlfriend, Lydia Feliciano. She was working as a coat check clerk at Happy Land, an unlicensed social club in the Bronx, and Gonzalez, newly unemployed, had been drinking. When the club's bouncer ejected Gonzalez, the immigrant threatened, "I'll be back!"

Around 3:30 AM, Gonzalez did return, carrying a plastic jug containing about $1 worth of gasoline. He doused the stairway leading up to the club—the only way into or out of the second-floor space—and lit it. Black smoke quickly filled the room upstairs, which was packed with Honduran immigrants celebrating Carnival. The alarm sounded at 3:41, but when firefighters arrived only three minutes later, it was already too late—87 people were dead.

First Deputy Mayor Norman Steisel described the scene as "shocking," noting that there were almost no burns on the victims—they had all died of smoke inhalation, many in a tangled mass on the dance floor. Some seated victims were still holding their drinks; Richard Harden of Ladder Company 58 said it looked "like they were sleeping."

Multiple Counts of Murder

Gonzalez's ex-girlfriend, Feliciano, miraculously escaped the fire, along with two or three others. Acting on her testimony, the police arrested Gonzalez. A psychiatrist declared him not responsible "due to mental illness or defect," but he was tried on 174 counts of murder—two for each victim.

On August 19, 1991, Gonzalez was convicted of 87 counts of murder and 87 counts of felony murder and given the maximum sentence of 25 years to life for each count—a total of 4,350 years. Since the charges resulted from a single crime, the sentences are being served concurrently; Gonzalez will be eligible for parole in March 2015.

Failure of Regulation

The Happy Land tragedy was one of the deadliest arson cases in U.S. history, resulting in the worst loss of life due to fire since the infamous Triangle Shirtwaist

John Orr not only set fires and investigated them, he also wrote a novel about arson.

The charred facade of the Happy Land social club in the Bronx, New York City, 1990

Factory fire, which coincidentally happened on the same day in 1911.

Though not caused by arson, the Triangle fire, which ended the lives of 146 workers, resulted in the establishment of safer building code regulations. Ironically, the city had ordered Happy Land to close in November 1988 based on those very regulations.

For their role in the 1990 fire, the landlord and lease-owner pleaded guilty to not having an adequate sprinkler system. In a plea bargain, they agreed to perform community service and help pay for a community center.

THE TIME FACTOR

Years can pass before police can collect enough evidence to arrest serial arsonists.

→ **John Orr.** Nicknamed the Pillow Pyro for his signature incendiary device—a lit cigarette strapped to a pack of matches wrapped in paper—Orr was an arson investigator for the Glendale, California, fire department. Over time, he set about 2,000 fires, including one that killed four in a hardware store. When Orr was caught in 1991, he got 20 years for arson and murder.

→ **Thomas Sweatt.** Responsible for at least 350 arsons and two fatalities, Sweat set fires in Washington, D.C., for some 30 years before he was caught. One of the few clues that led police to Sweat was that he often used a plastic jug of gasoline to set his blazes. In 2005, he was sentenced to life in prison.

→ **Raymond Lee Oyler.** A mechanic who had trained to become a volunteer firefighter, Oyler set the disastrous Esperanza fire in Cabazon, California, in 2006. The blaze ran wild for four days, spread by the Santa Ana winds, and killed five firefighters. Prosecutors alleged that Oyler had set 25 fires in the summer of 2006 alone. He was sentenced to death.

CRIME VS. DIAGNOSIS

Contrary to popular belief, most arsonists are not pyromaniacs.

The term *pyromania* is often used in reference to arson, but it's rarely an accurate description of the crime. Both acts involve fire-setting, but arson is an intentional, malicious act done to satisfy a motive such as revenge or financial gain; fire is just the means. Pyromania, on the other hand, is an impulse disorder, like gambling or substance abuse.

Most arsonists don't meet the criteria for a diagnosis of pyromania, but compared to homicide offenders, they are more likely to have a history of other psychiatric disorders and treatment, as well as suicidal tendencies and alcohol problems. Studies have also found arsonists to be more socially isolated, less educated, and even less physically attractive than murderers.

DEADLY, UNWANTED ATTENTION

STALKERS OBSESSED WITH CELEBRITIES MAKE HEADLINES, BUT MOST TARGETED VICTIMS ARE EVERYDAY PEOPLE.

In 1988, Margaret Mary Ray was arrested for joyriding with her three-year-old son in a stolen Porsche owned by talk-show host David Letterman.

Margaret Mary Ray, who stalked David Letterman, struggles before a competency hearing.

Ray had stalked Letterman for almost ten years, sometimes claiming that he was her husband. On several occasions, she had broken into his home and left him strange gifts. Ray was arrested eight times for trespassing and similar charges; once, Letterman found her asleep on the tennis court at his home in Connecticut. The entertainer made jokes about Ray on his television show, but it was no laughing matter. In 1998, Margaret Mary Ray committed suicide by kneeling in front of an oncoming train.

Ray suffered from erotomania, a type of delusion associated with schizophrenia in which a person believes that someone, usually a stranger or celebrity, is in love with him or her. When you hear about a stalker, it is possible that person is an erotomaniac.

While celebrity stalkers tend to make news, the typical stalker does not harass a famous person. The U.S. Department of Justice estimates that more than 1.5 million people, two-thirds of them women, are the victims of stalkers every year.

Lead-in to Violence

About 60 percent of stalkers have had a prior relationship with the victim and want to continue it, according to government statistics. Their form of passive aggression often leads to violence. Nine out of every ten women killed by husbands or boyfriends were the victims of stalking before they were murdered. According to one estimate, one out of every 12 U.S. women—and one out of every 45 U.S. men—has been or will be stalked.

Stalking is difficult to define precisely, but if a person repeatedly watches, follows, or harasses you, making you feel unsafe or afraid, you can consider yourself stalked. Stalkers often use threats and violence to frighten their victims, and may engage in vandalism. The results of this harassment are predictable; victims of stalking suffer from anxiety, insomnia, and severe depression at a much higher rate than the general population.

Motivations for stalking vary, ranging from an attempt to reassert power over a rejecting partner to an obsessive search for a loving relationship. Most stalkers are older and better educated than the average

Two-thirds of stalking victims are women, according to government figures.

Jack Jordan leaving criminal court during his trial for stalking Uma Thurman

RICH, FAMOUS, AND HOUNDED

When stalkers target a big-name television or film star

It's easy to envy celebrities, but their fame can also attract dangerous fans.

→ **Uma Thurman** was stalked by Jack Jordan from about 2004 to 2011. Jordan sent Thurman bizarre letters, called her family, tried to enter her trailer on a movie set, and showed up at her home late at night. He was issued a restraining order and given three years probation.

→ **Gwyneth Paltrow** was stalked by Dante Soiu for a year. He sent Paltrow hundreds of letters and emails, as well as gifts of flowers and candy. He even located and visited the home of Paltrow's parents. Soiu was declared legally insane and hospitalized in 2000.

→ **Rebecca Schaeffer**, a former model and star of the television sitcom *My Sister Sam*, was stalked for three years, then murdered in front of her home by Robert John Bardo in 1989. Bardo was given life in prison without parole.

→ **Jodie Foster** was the unwitting fixation of John Hinckley Jr., who was obsessed with the movie *Taxi Driver*, in which she'd starred. In 1981, Hinckley unsuccessfully attempted to assassinate President Ronald Reagan to capture Foster's attention. Hinckley was found not guilty by reason of insanity and remains institutionalized.

criminal, but also tend to be unemployed or underemployed, according to government statistics. Most do not experience hallucinations or delusions, although many suffer from depression, substance abuse, and personality disorders. Stalkers are quite adept at rationalizing their behavior. Many see no reason to get help.

Unfortunately, advances in technology have made stalking easier. Computer spyware can send a stalker a copy of every keystroke and password entered on a victim's laptop, the websites he or she has visited, even personal documents and emails. Stalkers can also use the internet to harass the victim or post things about him or her on message boards and discussion forums.

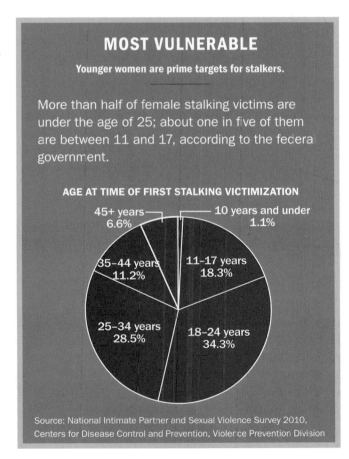

MOST VULNERABLE

Younger women are prime targets for stalkers.

More than half of female stalking victims are under the age of 25; about one in five of them are between 11 and 17, according to the federal government.

AGE AT TIME OF FIRST STALKING VICTIMIZATION

- 45+ years 6.6%
- 10 years and under 1.1%
- 11–17 years 18.3%
- 35–44 years 11.2%
- 18–24 years 34.3%
- 25–34 years 28.5%

Source: National Intimate Partner and Sexual Violence Survey 2010, Centers for Disease Control and Prevention, Violence Prevention Division

IN THE
LIMELIGHT

THE LINE BETWEEN AN OBSESSED FAN AND A DELUDED KILLER CAN BE A FINE ONE, AS ASSAULTS ON HIGH-PROFILE CELEBRITIES HAVE PROVED.

THE MURDER OF THEO VAN GOGH

This controversial director was slain for a film that criticized radical Islam.

In November 2004, Dutch film director and producer Theo van Gogh was assassinated while bicycling to work in Amsterdam. It is believed that his killer, a Muslim fundamentalist named Mohammed Bouyeri, targeted van Gogh for directing a ten-minute short film that criticized violence against women in Islam. The movie, called *Submission*, aired on Dutch public television and included scenes of an actress clad in a see-through chador, her naked body painted with texts from the Quran. Bouyeri shot van Gogh eight times. At his trial, Bouyeri expressed no remorse. He told van Gogh's mother, "I don't have any sympathy for you. I can't feel for you because I think you're a nonbeliever."

Today's musicians, writers, and artists can be huge media personalities, idolized and scrutinized by millions around the world. But sometimes a fan's attention can take a wrong turn, swerving from enthusiasm to disillusionment to violence. Stalkers have harassed performing artists like Beyoncé and Miley Cyrus, and a few deluded individuals have gone as far as attempting to harm or even kill their famous targets.

An Attempt on Warhol's Life

No one understood society's obsession with celebrity better than the Pop artist Andy Warhol, who presciently observed in 1968 that in the future, everyone would be famous for 15 minutes. What Warhol may not have expected was that he would become a victim of the phenomenon and that his own life would be jeopardized.

On June 3, 1968, radical feminist writer Valerie Solanas entered Warhol's studio and, as he talked on the phone, shot at him three times, missing twice. Solanas's third bullet penetrated both of Warhol's lungs, as well as his spleen, stomach, liver, and esophagus. She also fired at art critic Mario Amaya,

hitting him in the hip, and attempted to shoot Warhol's manager, Fred Hughes, but her gun jammed. Warhol and Amaya both survived the attacks, though Warhol's friends said the event changed him.

Solanas, who had written that women should "overthrow the government, eliminate the money system, institute complete automation, and eliminate the male sex," claimed Warhol was trying to control her. She was diagnosed as paranoid schizophrenic and served a three-year prison sentence, including psychiatric hospital time. She drifted into obscurity.

Andy Warhol

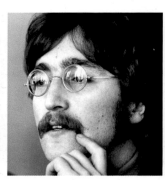
John Lennon

Selena

Silencing Lennon

Mark David Chapman, a 25-year-old born-again Christian from Fort Worth, Texas, was obsessed with two things: J.D. Salinger's coming-of-age novel *The Catcher in the Rye*, and the former Beatle John Lennon. Chapman had been introduced to the book by a school friend and was said to have wanted to model himself after its protagonist, Holden Caulfield. He likewise idolized Lennon, but turned on him after the singer commented that the Beatles were "more popular than Jesus." Chapman later said he objected to the fact that Lennon preached love and peace but was very wealthy.

On December 8, 1980, Chapman spent the day in front of The Dakota, the New York City apartment building where Lennon lived. That evening, as Lennon returned home from a recording session, Chapman shot him four times in the back. In the aftermath of the murder, Chapman stayed put, calmly reading *The Catcher in the Rye* until police arrived. Chapman pleaded guilty to murder and was sentenced to 20 years to life; he has been denied parole seven times since 2000.

A Fan Turns on Selena

The murder of Selena Quintanilla-Pérez, known as Selena, became all the more shocking when it was established that her killer had been president of her fan club. Between 1990 and 1995, the Latina star had 14 top-ten singles on the Latin chart, including seven number-one hits. Her fan club was headed by Yolanda Saldívar, a nurse, who was accused by Selena's family of embezzling money from the club. Saldívar was fired in early 1995 and arranged to meet Selena at a motel in Corpus Christi to return some financial records. When Selena arrived, Saldívar shot her once in the right shoulder, severing an artery. Selena died at a hospital from loss of blood, two weeks before her 24th birthday.

Saldívar argued that the shooting was accidental, but the prosecution noted that she did not call 911 or use her medical skills to help Selena in any way. Saldívar remains in prison, eligible for parole in 2025.

Mark David Chapman shot Beatle John Lennon in 1980.

THE DARK SIDE OF ARTISTIC FAME

Singers, musicians, fashion designers, and talk-show hosts have been targeted by assassins. Here are some well-known examples.

	 Alan Berg	Tupac Shakur	The Notorious B.I.G.	Gianni Versace
TARGET	American radio talk-show host (1934–1984)	American rap artist (1971–1996)	American rap artist (1972–1997)	Italian fashion designer (1946–1997)
THE ASSASSIN	Members of a white nationalist group	Unknown assailant	Unknown assailant	Andrew Cunanan
LOCATION AND DATE	Denver, Colorado June 18, 1984	Las Vegas, Nevada September 7, 1996	Los Angeles March 9, 1997	Miami Beach, Florida July 15, 1997
THE MURDER	Members of The Order shot Berg in his driveway for being Jewish and liberal.	Shakur was hit multiple times in a drive-by shooting. He died six days later.	The rapper was killed in a drive-by shooting.	Versace was killed on the steps of his lavish Miami mansion.
THE AFTERMATH	Two group members received life sentences for their roles in the killing.	The case remains unsolved.	The case remains unsolved.	Cunanan's motive was unknown. He committed suicide days later.

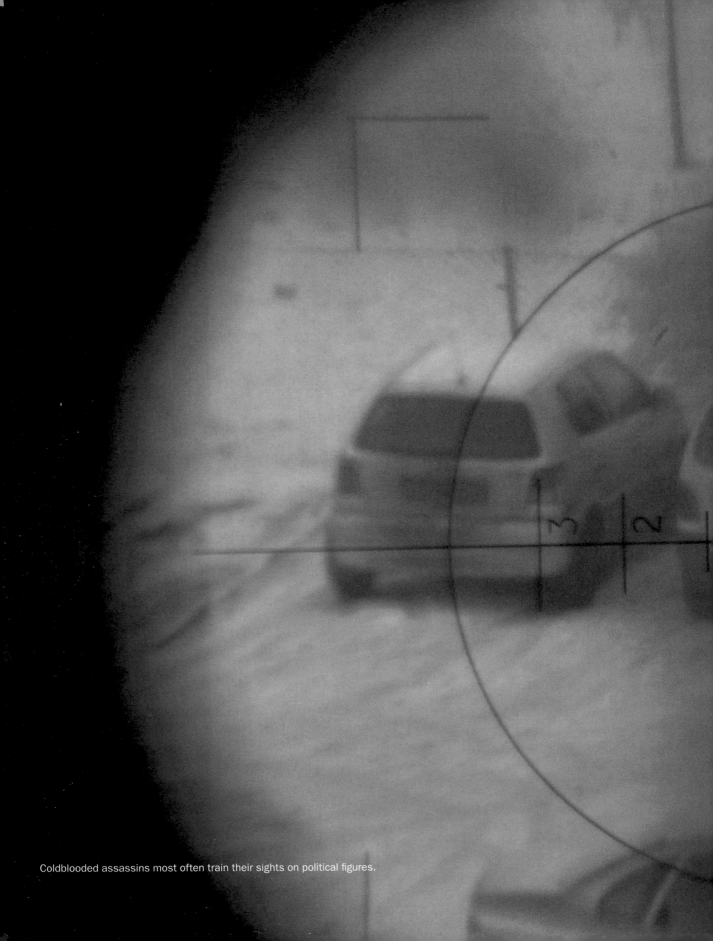

Coldblooded assassins most often train their sights on political figures.

CHAPTER 12

IN THE CROSSHAIRS

WHEN PSYCHOPATHY AND POLITICS MIX, THE RESULT CAN BE TRAGIC AND DEADLY.

The Killing of Booth, the Assassin. A wood engraving from 1865 shows the dying Booth being dragged from the barn where he had taken refuge.

THE MAN WHO SHOT LINCOLN

THE STAGE ACTOR JOHN WILKES BOOTH HAD ALWAYS DREAMED OF IMMORTALITY. WITH ONE CALCULATED ACT OF VIOLENCE, HE ACHIEVED IT.

John Wilkes Booth was born in 1838 near Bel Air, Maryland, into a family of famous stage actors. His father was Junius Brutus Booth, renowned in Great Britain and the U.S., and his brother was Edwin Booth, famous for his portrayal of Hamlet. John joined the family business too, making his stage debut at 17. He toured widely, often playing in Shakespearean productions, and once commented that his favorite role was Brutus, slayer of the tyrannical Julius Caesar.

As the national debate over slavery and secession heated up in the late 1850s, most of the Booth family declared their support for the Union, but John made clear he sympathized with the Confederate cause. He joined the Virginia militia in 1859, but once the Civil War broke out he did not see battle and instead continued his lucrative theatrical career in the North. Eventually, Booth grew depressed at what he referred to as his four-year "idleness," especially when it became apparent that the South was going to lose the war.

Plot Against the President

For six months in 1864–1865, Booth concocted various schemes to abduct President Abraham Lincoln and carry him off to Richmond, Virginia. On March 17, 1865, Booth and six conspirators went as far as lying in wait to seize Lincoln on the outskirts of Washington, D.C., but the president changed his plans and never appeared. Within weeks, after the Union Army captured Richmond on April 3, Booth concluded that his kidnapping scheme was no longer feasible. He began to formulate plans to assassinate the 16th president instead.

On April 11, Lincoln gave a speech supporting limited suffrage for African Americans. Booth, who was strongly opposed to emancipation, told a friend, "Now, by God, I'll put him through. This is the last speech he will ever make." He put into motion his plan to kill Lincoln as well as Vice President Andrew Johnson, Secretary of State William Seward, and possibly Secretary of War Edwin Stanton and General Ulysses Grant.

After learning that Lincoln intended to attend a performance of *Our American Cousin* at Ford's Theatre in Washington, D.C., on Friday, April 14, Booth and his conspirators took action. That night, two of Booth's accomplices, Lewis Thornton Powell and David Herold, worked together to attack Seward and three others at Seward's house. Another accomplice, George Atzerodt, was assigned to Andrew Johnson, but lost his nerve. The potential assassins of Stanton and Grant, if they existed, have never been uncovered.

Shortly after 10 PM, Booth entered the presidential box in Ford's Theatre unobserved. Using a .44 caliber Derringer pistol, a small and easily concealed handgun, Booth fired a single shot into Lincoln's brain at point-blank range before jumping to the stage. Booth shouted, *"Sic temper tyrannis!"*—"Thus always to tyrants," the motto of the state of Virginia—then ran down the back stairs to a waiting horse and escaped into the Maryland countryside. Lincoln died at 7:22 AM the next morning. His body was brought to Springfield, Illinois, for burial, as more than seven million somber spectators lined the railroad tracks to view the funeral train. Two weeks later, Union soldiers tracked down and shot Booth, who was hiding out on a Virginia farm.

The Derringer pistol used by John Wilkes Booth to assassinate President Abraham Lincoln.

Poster of the hunt for Booth

JOHN WILKES BOOTH'S FLIGHT

After leaving Ford's Theatre, Lincoln's killer made a daring escape to a farm in Maryland.

In the wake of President Lincoln's assassination, panic and anguish swept the nation. After a two-week search, John Wilkes Booth was discovered in a barn on a farm near Bowling Green, Virginia, on April 26. The barn was set on fire, and Booth was shot by his pursuers when he refused to surrender. Although his body was identified by numerous witnesses, the myth that Booth escaped has persisted. Booth's route and the spot where he was felled remain a source of fascination for many Civil War buffs, some of whom enjoy tracing it by car or tour bus.

A studio portrait of John Wilkes Booth, circa 1860–1865

Assassin John Wilkes Booth relied on the help of many operatives including:

George Atzerodt, carriage repairman assigned by Booth to kill Vice President Andrew Johnson. He failed to follow through.

David Herold, pharmacist's assistant involved in the attack on Secretary of State William Seward. Helped tend Booth's injuries.

Lewis Payne, Confederate soldier who attacked Secretary Seward.

Mary Elizabeth Jenkins Surratt, boardinghouse owner who held guns and supplies for Booth and his accomplices.

PRESIDENTIAL
TARGETS

DEATH THREATS AND ASSASSINATION PLOTS ARE A HAZARD OF THE JOB FOR OCCUPANTS OF THE OVAL OFFICE.

Charles Guiteau, assassin of President James A. Garfield in 1881.

John F. Schrank, who attempted to assassinate Theodore Roosevelt in 1912.

John W. Hinckley Jr., who attempted to assassinate President Ronald Reagan in 1981.

The Leader of the Free World lives dangerously. Since the nation's founding, there have been more than 20 documented assassination plots to kill sitting and former U.S. presidents as well as the president-elect. Mental illness, the desire for notoriety, and political beliefs have all played roles in the planning and execution of the various attacks.

"I Am a Man of Destiny…"

In 1881, just 16 years after President Lincoln's assassination, lawyer and preacher Charles Guiteau shot President James Garfield in a Washington, D.C., railroad station. Garfield died less than four months after he had been sworn in.

Guiteau displayed obvious mental instability during his two-month trial, constantly insulting his defense team, reciting long poems to the jury, and claiming that his act wasn't murder at all, but the will of God. "I claim that I am a man of destiny as much as the Savior, or Paul, or Martin Luther, or any of those religious men of the kind I was," he proclaimed. Guiteau was found guilty and hanged on June 30, 1882.

A Radical Anarchist

Leon Czolgosz, who killed President William McKinley in 1901, was a former steelworker who had lost his job during the economic panic of 1893. He turned to radical anarchy, a philosophy based on the abolition of all government, and fixated on McKinley as a symbol of imperialism. He shot the 25th president twice as McKinley shook hands in a reception line at the World's Fair in Buffalo, New York. One bullet grazed McKinley; the other entered his abdomen and was never found. In the days between McKinley's death on September 14 and Czolgosz's trial on the 23rd, Czolgosz refused to speak to his lawyers, making it impossible for them to prepare a defense. After only a half hour of deliberation, the jury convicted Czolgosz. He died in the electric chair less than seven weeks after the assassination.

Bulletproof

In 1912, John Schrank, a saloon-keeper from New York, attempted to assassinate former president Theodore Roosevelt, who was seeking to return to the oval office after a few years as a private citizen. Schrank, who stalked Roosevelt for weeks before the incident, approached the candidate after a campaign speech in Milwaukee, pulled out a gun, and fired.

Among his acquaintances, Schrank was known as a fluent Bible scholar and debater, but had not been considered unstable. Eventually Schrank would claim the ghost of William McKinley advised him in a dream to avenge his death by killing Roosevelt. Although he shot Roosevelt directly in the chest, the bullet was slowed by a metal eyeglasses case and the 50-page campaign speech text Roosevelt had tucked into his pocket.

James Brady and a police officer lying on the ground after being shot, while the suspect John Hinckley Jr. is apprehended, moments after the attempted assassination of President Ronald Reagan in 1981.

Roosevelt decided he was not dying and held forth for nearly an hour with blood oozing through his shirt.

Schrank was found legally insane and committed to the Central State Mental Hospital in Wisconsin in 1914, where he died in 1943 from natural causes.

Desperate for Attention

John Hinckley Jr., the man who attempted to assassinate President Ronald Reagan in 1981, was obsessed with the 1976 movie *Taxi Driver*, in which a disturbed character plotted to kill a presidential candidate. He also was infatuated with Jodie Foster, the actor who played a child prostitute in the film.

Hinckley concocted various plots, including an aircraft hijacking and suicide, to impress Foster. Eventually he decided to take Reagan's life on March 30, after a speaking engagement in Washington, D.C. Four men were shot and wounded in the attack; Reagan was struck by a single bullet, which broke a rib, punctured a lung, and caused serious internal bleeding. He was rushed to a nearby hospital for emergency surgery and hospitalized for two weeks. Hinckley was found not guilty by reason of insanity and remains under institutional psychiatric care.

WHO KNEW?

Leon Czolgosz, McKinley's killer, was beaten viciously by a crowd as he was transported to prison. Rioters seemed determined to lynch him.

Train commuters read about the assassination of John F. Kennedy.

THE PRESIDENT HAS BEEN SHOT

JFK'S ACCUSED ASSASSIN LEE HARVEY OSWALD TOLD REPORTERS, "I DIDN'T SHOOT ANYBODY...I'M JUST A PATSY!"

On November 22, 1963, facing reelection the following year, President John F. Kennedy traveled to Dallas, where he hoped to heal divisions in the Texas Democratic Party. As his motorcade entered the city, he encountered friendly crowds. At about 12:30 PM, the open car carrying Kennedy, his wife, Jacqueline, Texas Governor John Connally and his wife, and several Secret Service agents traveled through Dealey Plaza and passed in front of the Texas School Book Depository.

Suddenly, shots rang out. As bullets ripped through Kennedy's head and throat, the president slumped forward. Connally, who would eventually recover, was wounded in the back, chest, wrist, and thigh. Half an hour later at Dallas's Parkland Memorial Hospital, the 35th president of the United States was pronounced dead. Within a short time, Dallas police had arrested Lee Harvey Oswald, a 24-year-old ex-Marine, and accused him of the assassination, as well as the murder of J.D. Tippit, a Dallas police officer who was killed about 45 minutes after Kennedy.

Senseless Shooting or Conspiracy?

But what was the motive? Oswald would never be able to explain. On November 24, as he was being moved from his cell in the basement of Dallas police headquarters, the sniper was shot dead. This time, there was no doubt about the identity of the gunman. Jack Ruby, a nightclub operator with connections to crime figures, committed his crime on live television in front of an audience of millions. Ruby claimed he had been distraught over Kennedy's death and that he wanted to save Mrs. Kennedy from "the discomfiture of coming back to trial."

The events unleashed a storm of conspiracy theories that reverberate to this day. An investigating commission headed by Supreme Court Chief Justice Earl Warren was appointed to put the public and world at ease. Almost a year later, the panel, which met primarily in closed sessions, concluded that both Lee Harvey Oswald and Jack Ruby acted alone. Commission members could find no motive for Oswald's actions.

The Warren Commission report, issued just before the election of 1964, was loudly criticized, with the media and public at

First Lady Jacqueline Kennedy and President John F. Kennedy, before he was shot in Dallas, November 22, 1963.

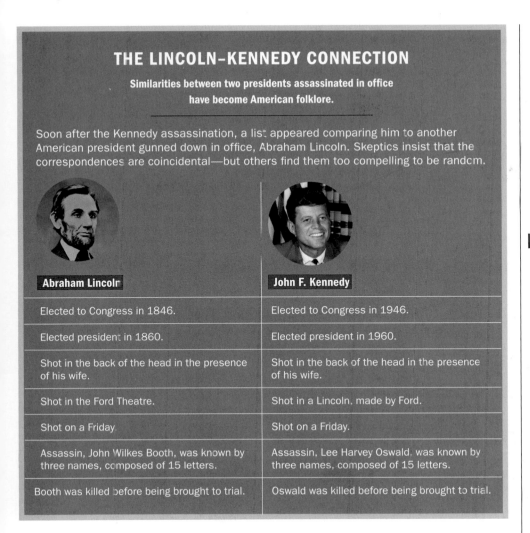

THE LINCOLN–KENNEDY CONNECTION

Similarities between two presidents assassinated in office have become American folklore.

Soon after the Kennedy assassination, a list appeared comparing him to another American president gunned down in office, Abraham Lincoln. Skeptics insist that the correspondences are coincidental—but others find them too compelling to be random.

Abraham Lincoln	John F. Kennedy
Elected to Congress in 1846.	Elected to Congress in 1946.
Elected president in 1860.	Elected president in 1960.
Shot in the back of the head in the presence of his wife.	Shot in the back of the head in the presence of his wife.
Shot in the Ford Theatre.	Shot in a Lincoln, made by Ford.
Shot on a Friday.	Shot on a Friday.
Assassin, John Wilkes Booth, was known by three names, composed of 15 letters.	Assassin, Lee Harvey Oswald, was known by three names, composed of 15 letters.
Booth was killed before being brought to trial.	Oswald was killed before being brought to trial.

Police mug shot of Lee Harvey Oswald

POWER PLAYER OR PAWN?

Oswald was a Communist with ties to the Soviets and possibly Cuba, raising questions about his motives for killing Kennedy.

After dropping out of high school in 1956, Lee Harvey Oswald joined the U.S. Marines, where he learned marksmanship. But military life did not suit him, and by October 1959 he had become a Communist and moved to the Soviet Union. He was refused Russian citizenship, and in 1962 he returned to the United States with a Russian wife and an infant daughter.

By 1963, Oswald is thought to have been involved with a number of fringe political groups, and may have tried to assassinate right-wing U.S. General Edwin Walker. He is believed to have visited the Soviet and Cuban embassies in Mexico City in an unsuccessful attempt to get a job. In October 1963, Oswald was hired at the Texas School Book Depository in Dallas, where, from the sixth floor, he supposedly fired three shots in five seconds, two of which hit the intended target.

Was Oswald the sole gunman? He denied killing Kennedy and police officer J.D. Tippit, denied owning a rifle, and claimed that photographs of him holding a rifle and a pistol were fakes.

large speculating that the investigation was neither thorough nor impartial. In the following decades, hundreds of articles and books claiming to reveal the "real" assassin(s) and motive have been written. Competing theories about the number of shots, the trajectory of the bullets, and the nature of the president's wounds still attract attention.

Secrets and Lies

Polls consistently reveal that more than 60 percent of American adults still do not accept the official account of the Kennedy assassination

Some conspiracy theorists implicate the Mafia, which was angry at U.S. Attorney General Robert F. Kennedy—JFK's brother—for launching his massive crackdown on

organized crime. Still another enduring theory, supported by a number of books written since the assassination, holds that Lyndon B. Johnson, who succeeded President Kennedy, orchestrated the murder plot to ensure his own path to the Oval Office. One of the most persistent theories maintains that the Cuban government was involved, following revelations that the CIA had attempted to murder political leader Fidel Castro.

Finally, several conspiracy theorists point the finger at the CIA itself, which had a strained relationship with the President after the disastrous Bay of Pigs invasion of Cuba. (Agency leaders blamed Kennedy for their failed attempt to overthrow Castro, claiming it was his lack of military support that doomed the commando operation.)

217

THE BLOODY 1960s

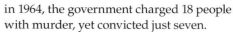

"VIOLENCE IS A PART OF AMERICA'S CULTURE. IT IS AS AMERICAN AS CHERRY PIE."

—**H. Rap Brown,** chairman of the
Student Nonviolent Coordinating Committee, 1967

Dr. Martin Luther King displays pictures of three civil rights workers slain in Mississippi, from left, Michael Schwerner, James Chaney, and Andrew Goodman. Dec. 4, 1964.

The assassination of President John F. Kennedy in 1963 ushered in a tumultuous ten years in the United States in which several major political figures and civil rights leaders were killed in cold blood. The killings played out against a backdrop of social upheaval and racial unrest as well as protests against one of the most unpopular wars in the nation's history. With many of the murders captured live and broadcast to viewers across the nation, Americans experienced the violence in a personal way in their own living rooms.

Much of the era's violence was racially motivated, executed by Southern whites struggling to maintain the status quo of segregation. But with few witnesses willing to come forward and some evidence in the cases destroyed, prosecutors at the time had difficulty identifying perpetrators and obtaining convictions. When four young girls were killed in the 1963 bombing of a Baptist church in Birmingham, Alabama, only one of four alleged perpetrators was arrested initially. The same year, white supremacist Byron de la Beckwith killed NAACP leader Medgar Evers, but he wasn't convicted of the crime until 1994. Following the slaying of three civil rights workers in Mississippi

in 1964, the government charged 18 people with murder, yet convicted just seven.

In some cases, the murderers were thought to be working alone or with a small group of collaborators. As time passed, however, the public began to suspect that larger organizations were involved. Conspiracy theories have swirled around the murders of both President Kennedy and his brother, U.S. Senator Robert F. Kennedy, who was assassinated in 1968. When the charismatic civil rights leader Malcolm X was gunned down in 1965, one man admitted his role and served time for the killing; another served time but denied guilt. Over the years, theories involving the Nation of Islam and others have circulated, but the Nation has repeatedly denied involvement.

In a similar vein, James Earl Ray, who had a record of armed burglary, theft, and prison escape, quickly pleaded guilty to the 1968 assassination of civil rights leader Dr. Martin Luther King. He later recanted and claimed he was just a pawn in a larger conspiracy. In 1997, King's family met with Ray in prison and came away convinced that he had been manipulated. His role in King's murder is still in dispute.

The funeral for victims of the 16th Street Baptist Church bombing.

FREEDOM SUMMER

In 1964, the murder of three civil rights workers in Mississippi enraged the nation. Who were they?

James Chaney: 21-year-old Chaney, an African-American, was born in Mississippi and began his civil rights activism in high school. He participated in a Freedom Ride and voter education.

Andrew Goodman: Goodman, 20, was a white New Yorker working to register black voters in Mississippi. He was killed at the end of his first full day volunteering in the state.

Michael Schwerner: A 24-year-old white New Yorker, Schwerner was a volunteer for the civil rights group the Congress of Racial Equality. He was on assignment in Mississippi with his wife when he was killed.

CONSPIRACY THEORIES

The government obtained convictions for some of the high-profile political murders committed in the 1960s and 1970s, but many people continue to believe a wide range of groups, including law enforcement and the Mafia, were involved.

NAME	DATE ATTACKED AND OUTCOME	LOCATION	SUPPOSED ASSASSIN	COMMONLY HELD REASON	CONSPIRACY THEORY BEHIND IT...
John F. Kennedy U.S. President	November 22, 1963. Died that day.	Dallas, Texas	Lee Harvey Oswald. Assassinated by Jack Ruby.	Unknown	CIA, Mafia, Anti-Castro Cuban exile groups, Fidel Castro, J. Edgar Hoover, the Soviet Union, others
Malcolm X Civil rights leader	February 21, 1965. Killed immediately.	New York City, New York	Thomas Hagan, paroled in 2010; Thomas Johnson, paroled in 1986, died in 2009; Norman Butler, paroled in 1985.	Break with the Nation of Islam	FBI and/or the New York City Police Department
Martin Luther King Jr. Civil rights leader	April 4, 1968. Died that day.	Memphis, Tennessee	James Earl Ray. Died in prison in 1998.	Anti-black racism, opposition to civil rights	U.S. government, FBI
Robert Kennedy U.S. Senator from NY. Presidential candidate	June 6, 1968. Died that day.	Los Angeles, California	Sirhan Sirhan. Still in prison.	Opposed to RFK's support for Israel	CIA
George Wallace Governor of Alabama. Presidential candidate	May 15, 1972. Paralyzed from the waist down.	Laurel, Maryland	Arthur Bremer. Paroled in 2007.	Desire for fame	Questions have arisen about who funded Bremer's travel.

IS THIS AN ASSASSIN?

JAMES EARL RAY WAS EITHER A RACIST WHO MURDERED ONE OF AMERICA'S GREATEST CIVIL RIGHTS LEADERS, OR A RACIST WHO DIDN'T.

The family of Martin Luther King Jr. asked for a new investigation into his murder after the death of convicted shooter James Earl Ray.

For 30 years, James Earl Ray insisted he was a patsy. He pled guilty in March, 1969, to murdering the Reverend Dr. Martin Luther King Jr. on a balcony in Memphis, Tennessee. By doing so, Ray escaped a trial and the death penalty. But just days later, he recanted, and for the rest of his life, as he served his 99-year prison sentence, Ray would insist that he had been set up by a man he'd known only as Raoul. The military and government intelligence agencies, he maintained, were the puppetmasters.

Ray's arguments were persuasive enough that in 1978, after a two-year inquiry, a Congressional committee concluded that even though he had fired the fatal shot, there had likely been a conspiracy behind the assassination. And when Ray died in 1998 of complications from hepatitis C, King's family asked for an investigation of "all new and unexamined evidence."

It's hard to know what to believe. Reputable investigative journalists have failed to find plausible evidence that Ray was set up. A comprehensive book published in 1998, entitled *Killing the Dream: James Earl Ray and the Assassination of Martin Luther King, Jr.*, concluded that Ray acted alone.

A Highly Orchestrated Plot?

Whether you believe that Ray was solely responsible for King's tragic murder or a pawn in a larger plot, certain facts are undisputed.

Ray was an avowed racial separatist with a long history of getting in trouble. Born in Illinois in 1928, he was the oldest of eight children in a poor and unstable family. He dropped out of school at age 15 and eventually joined the army, where he was cited for drinking and was discharged for incompetence. In 1949, he moved to Los Angeles and embarked on a career in petty crime, distinguishing himself mostly by his ineptitude and propensity for getting caught. He did several stints in jail—and that's when it gets complicated.

Ray escaped from the Missouri State Penitentiary in 1967, and ultimately fled to Canada. It was there that he met the mysterious figure called Raoul who Ray later said enlisted him in what he believed was a gun-smuggling venture but turned out to be an elaborate plot to frame Ray for King's murder.

On April 4, 1968, after months of performing covert errands for Raoul, Ray ended up in Memphis. Under an alias, he checked into a rooming house across the street from the motel where King would be slain later that day. The deadly shot was found to have been fired from Ray's room, and, using fingerprints from a gun and other evidence abandoned near the scene, the FBI identified Ray as the shooter. After a two-month, $2 million manhunt, Ray was apprehended in London. He was extradited

James Earl Ray after his capture, 1977

WANTED BY THE FBI

CIVIL RIGHTS - CONSPIRACY
INTERSTATE FLIGHT - ROBBERY
JAMES EARL RAY

FBI No. 405,942 G

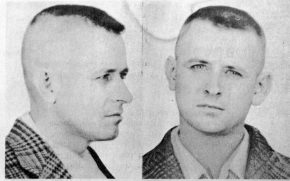

Photographs taken 1960   Photograph taken 1968
(eyes drawn by artist)

Aliases: Eric Starvo Galt, W. C. Herron, Harvey Lowmyer, James McBride, James O'Conner, James Walton, James Walyon, John Willard, "Jim,"

DESCRIPTION

Age: 40, born March 10, 1928, at Quincy or Alton, Illinois (not supported by birth records)
Height: 5' 10"   **Eyes:** Blue
Weight: 163 to 174 pounds   **Complexion:** Medium

James Earl Ray on an FBI Wanted poster for the slaying of Dr. Martin Luther King Jr., 1968.

Ray made a lot of mistakes, but he was clever enough to break out of jail not once but twice.

Had James Earl Ray not managed to escape from prison the first time, he might not have been able to assassinate Martin Luther King Jr. in 1968.

In 1967, Ray was several years into a 20-year sentence in the Missouri State Penitentiary for robbing a Kroger store in St. Louis. He had made two failed escape attempts but finally succeeding by stowing away in a large breadbox from the prison bakery that was loaded onto a delivery truck. Ray slipped out as the truck made its rounds.

A decade later, while he was serving time for King's killing, Ray made his second escape, this time from the Brushy Mountain maximum-security prison in Petros, Tennessee. On June 10, 1977, while some inmates staged a fight to distract the guards, Ray and six other prisoners scrambled up and over a 14-foot wall using a ladder they'd made in the prison machine shop. Guards shot one of the escapees and the FBI eventually captured the rest—including Ray, whom a bloodhound sniffed out three days later, about 8 miles from the prison.

to the United States, where the case was closed—for everyone except Ray.

"I assumed if I did enter a plea of guilty, and I could have had an investigation after the plea, with newly discovered evidence, there's a possibility that the case could have been reversed," Ray said in a television interview from prison in 1977. "I think a lot of people have a sort of a Pollyanna view of the legal system.... That's not the way it is."

DID HE OR DIDN'T HE?

The conspiracy theories surrounding Ray are based on his behavior and intellect. But so are the theories that Ray acted alone.

RAY WAS A PAWN	VS.	RAY ACTED ALONE
Ray was too dumb to have pulled off the assassination by himself.		He was clever enough to engineer a complicated prison break from Brushy Mountain.
It seems awfully convenient that Ray left his fingerprint-covered gun for the police to find.		He had a history of bungling crimes and getting caught.
Ray was a nonviolent petty criminal with no real reason to kill King.		He was demonstrably racist and pro-segregation.

DEADLY TARGET PRACTICE

SOME SNIPERS HONE THEIR SKILLS IN THE MILITARY. THEN THEY TURN ON INNOCENT CIVILIANS AND MENACE THE PUBLIC.

Lee Boyd Malvo stands in court.

Michael Andrew Clark was a seemingly normal 16-year-old living in Long Beach, California. He was known as a good saxophone player, an A student, and "a real fine boy."

Early on Sunday morning, April 25, 1965, Clark mounted a hill near his home, overlooking Highway 101, with a military rifle equipped with a telescopic sight. Hiding in the tall grass, Clark began firing at cars traveling along the road. He killed three people and wounded ten more before committing suicide as police rushed the hill. No motive was ever established.

It's the randomness and unpredictability of sniper attacks that make them so terrifying. Snipers' targets are usually just ordinary strangers going about their daily routines. With a marksman at large, areas that once felt safe become potential danger zones.

The Beltway Sniper

No sharpshooter in recent years has caused more alarm than the so-called Beltway sniper who paralyzed Washington, D.C., and its suburbs for three weeks in October 2002. Ten people were killed and three others critically injured in random attacks on the streets of the capital, Maryland, and Virginia. A landscaper was shot dead while mowing the lawn of an auto dealership; a man was murdered while refueling his car. Others were shot while sitting on a bench waiting for a bus, vacuuming a car at a gas station, walking down the street, and loading shopping bags into a vehicle. The victims were wide-ranging: men as well as women, African American and white, a 72-year-old and a 13-year-old child.

Metropolitan Washington was shadowed by fear. When the killer began planting messages at his crime scenes, the anxiety was magnified. He left tarot cards with chilling imagery, and dropped death threats. One note read, "Your children are not safe, anywhere, at any time." Parents panicked and schools closed.

Experts presumed the Beltway sniper was a single white male with military experience, but he surprised his profilers. Although it turned out that the sharpshooter had indeed served in the Persian Gulf, he was not white and he was not working alone. He was John Allen Muhammad, an African American, with a teenaged accomplice named Lee Boyd Malvo. The two had met in the Caribbean, and after Muhammad had taught Malvo how to shoot, they had embarked on a robbery-and-killing spree across the U.S. in February 2002.

John Allen Muhammad, center, stands with his attorney Jonathan Shapiro (right) as he is sentenced to death.

Charles Joseph Whitman, right, with his wife, Kathleen, and a friend just a few months before his killing spree began.

INSIDE CHARLES WHITMAN'S HEAD

The University of Austin sniper had a tumor pressing against a part of the brain that regulates emotions and drives.

Charles Joseph Whitman was a 25-year-old engineering student and former American Marine sniper. On August 1, 1966, he climbed to the 28th-floor observation deck of the University of Texas Tower in Austin with an array of guns, and proceeded to kill 13 people and wound 32 others. Whitman fired almost unimpeded for 96 minutes before he was killed by Austin police.

→ A doctor Whitman visited before the shooting reported that Whitman had said something seemed to be happening to him and that he didn't seem to be himself.

→ In his suicide note, Whitman wrote that he had been "a victim of many unusual and irrational thoughts."

→ On the morning of the shooting, Whitman murdered his mother and wife. He left a note reading, "I love [my wife] dearly. I cannot rationally pinpoint any...reason for doing this."

→ During Whitman's autopsy, doctors discovered a tumor pressing against regions of the brain responsible for regulating emotions and drives, including fighting and fleeing.

No real motive for the bloody escapade was ever determined. Investigators suggested that Muhammad had intended to kill his ex-wife, who was keeping him from his children, and that the other murders were meant to camouflage the crime. This theory, however, was never presented in court due to lack of evidence. While he was in jail, Muhammad wrote rambling screeds against the United States, illustrated with images of Osama bin Laden and characters from the film *The Matrix*. He was executed by lethal injection in 2009. Malvo was convicted of three counts including capital murder and terrorism. He received multiple life sentences without parole.

GUN CRIMES IN AMERICA

According to a report issued by the U.S. Bureau of Alcohol, Tobacco, and Firearms in 2000, the most recent broad government study available, commonly used guns used in U.S. crimes include two different revolvers, a shotgun, and seven semiautomatic weapons. The list is dominated by models that are either available at low cost or have been produced for decades. In 2012, the ATF issued a more general report. Semiautomatic pistols remained by far the most commonly used gun in crimes.

THE TOP 5 GUNS USED IN CRIMES IN 2012

42,560 **9mm semiautomatics**

34,130 **.22 caliber handguns**

20,674 **.40 caliber handguns**

20,606 **12-gauge shotguns**

19,425 **.38 caliber handguns**

GUNS SEIZED BY POLICE AT CRIME SCENES

119,273 **pistols**

46,037 **revolvers**

Semiautomatics reload automatically, but the trigger must be pulled for each shot. They generate a lot of shots quickly; 16 bullets in 4 seconds and 20 rounds in 5.3 seconds are typical.

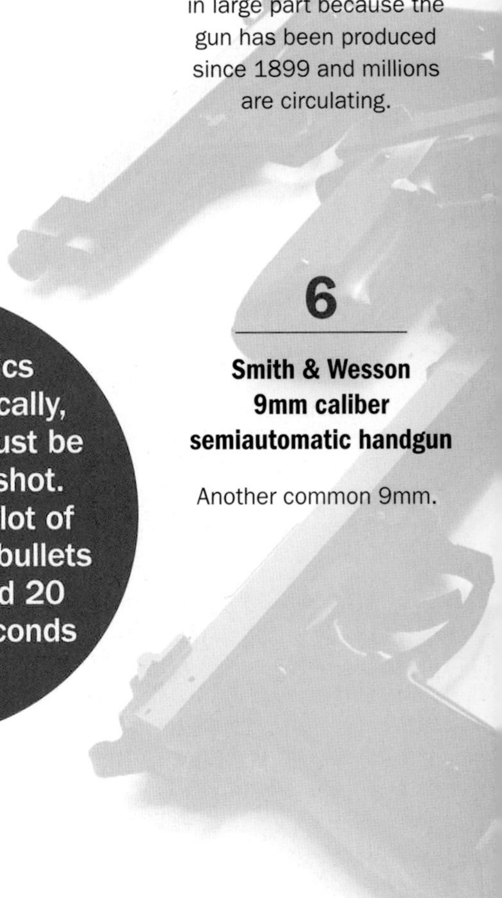

1

Smith & Wesson–style .38 caliber revolver

A Smith & Wesson–style .38 revolver is the most commonly used weapon, in large part because the gun has been produced since 1899 and millions are circulating.

6

Smith & Wesson 9mm caliber semiautomatic handgun

Another common 9mm.

THE TEN MOST COMMON GUNS USED IN CRIMES IN 2000

2

Ruger 9mm caliber semiautomatic handgun

In 2000, a new Ruger 9mm semi cost about $500. The gun was made by Connecticut-based Sturm, Ruger & Company, one of the larger producers of handguns in the United States.

3

Lorcin Engineering .380 caliber semiautomatic handgun

Lorcin Engineering, which produced this gun, is now out of business. It specialized in small caliber pistols, many of which retailed for less than $100.

4

Raven Arms .25 caliber semiautomatic handgun

Like Lorcin Engineering, the firearms manufacturer Raven Arms was known for producing inexpensive handguns. The company went out of business in 1991.

5

Mossberg 12-gauge shotgun

The Mossberg is the most common shotgun used in crimes. Different models of the Mossberg have been on sale since 1961.

7

Smith & Wesson .357 caliber revolver

Like the .38, the larger .357 has been around a long time; the first model was introduced in 1935.

8

Bryco Arms 9mm caliber semiautomatic handgun

Bryco semiautomatics retailed for less than $100 new and around $55 used in 2000. The company was founded by the son of the creator of Raven Arms.

9

Bryco Arms .380 caliber semiautomatic handgun

Bryco Arms was one of the manufacturers of the inexpensive handguns referred to as Saturday Night Specials. The company declared bankruptcy in 2003 and was later sold to another gun maker.

10

Davis Industries .380 caliber semiautomatic handgun

Davis Industries, founded by the son-in-law of the founder of Raven Arms, also specialized in producing Saturday Night Specials.

Law enforcement has been battling organized crime in the United States since the 1930s.

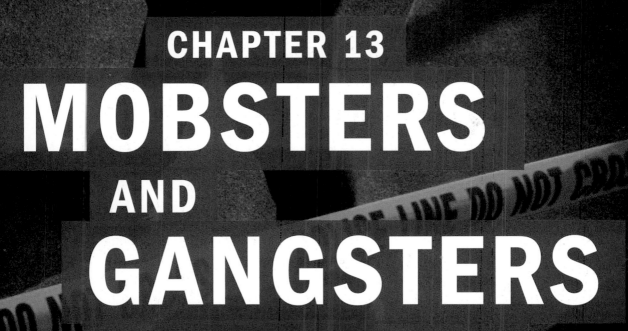

CHAPTER 13
MOBSTERS
AND
GANGSTERS

**ORGANIZED CRIMINALS ARE BOUND BY A STRICT
VOW OF SILENCE. IT IS THE FBI'S JOB TO BREAK IT.**

ALL IN THE FAMILY

ITALIAN-AMERICAN ORGANIZED CRIME IS KNOWN FOR ITS RUTHLESSNESS AND IRONCLAD CODE OF SILENCE.

As far back as 1869, a newspaper in New Orleans was reporting on criminal acts perpetrated by Sicilian immigrants passing through on their way to South America. Three decades later, the loosely organized Italian and Sicilian criminal body that we now call the Mafia had coalesced in a notorious New York City slum known as Five Points. The Five Points Gang was soon involved in racketeering, robbery, prostitution, and local politics. Many of its members went on to become powerful crime figures, including Lucky Luciano, the original leader of the Genovese crime family, who by 1930 had become the boss of bosses.

Prohibition and Profits

The sale of liquor had been illegal in the U.S. since 1920, but plenty of people still wanted to drink. Organized crime stepped in to fill the void, figuring out ways to

An investigator's bulletin board with photos of bosses, underbosses, capos, and soldiers in five New York organized crime families: Bonanno, Colombo, Gambino, Genovese, and Lucchese (misspelled in photo).

procure booze and sneak it to thirsty Americans.

Competing Italian crime families often cooperated with one another to control everything from hidden distilleries to storage and distribution to speakeasies and nightclubs. Mobsters from different parts of the country—including not only Italian-American Mafia families (Cosa Nostra) but also Jewish and Irish organized crime rings—started to communicate, resulting in the formation of a national crime syndicate. In May 1929, some of the underworld's most pivotal figures, including Lucky Luciano, Al Capone, Meyer Lansky, and Albert Anas-

tasia, met for a summit in Atlantic City, New Jersey, to solidify the loose networks formed during the bootlegging operations. It is believed by historians to have been the first organized crime conference in the United States.

But as the Mafia insinuated itself into the black market economy, it spawned a wave of turf wars and violence—perhaps culminating in 1929's bloody Saint Valentine's Day Massacre, in which men disguised as policemen (thought to be affiliated with Al Capone) slaughtered a group of unarmed bootleggers in Chicago--that continued even after Prohibition was repealed in 1933.

Mobster Charles "Lucky" Luciano (right)with three of his criminal associates.

The 1970 RICO Act paved the way for Rudolph Giuliani, U.S. Attorney for the Southern District of New York in the 1980s, to lead a major crusade against organized crime in New York City. In 1985, after a lengthy investigation by law enforcement, Giuliani indicted the reputed bosses and other members of New York's Five Families on charges of extortion, racketeering, and murder for hire. The subsequent trial, known as the Mafia Commission Trial, was one of the most significant in U.S. Mob history. "The Mafia will be crushed," Giuliani vowed.

Eight of the 11 defendants were found guilty on all counts. G. Robert Blakey, a Notre Dame Law School professor who drafted the 1970 RICO law, called the verdicts "the twilight of the Mob. It's not dark yet for them, but the sun is going down."

Among those the Mafia Commission Trial put behind bars:

Anthony Salerno
"Fat Tony"

The reputed head of the Genovese crime family was sentenced to 70 years. He died in prison of a stroke in July 1992.

Carmine Persico
"Junior"

Persico, the alleged boss of the Columbo family, and, at 53, by far the youngest of the bosses at the time of the trial, is serving a 139-year sentence at a medium-security prison in North Carolina.

Anthony Corallo
"Tony Ducks"

Corallo, the purported leader of the Lucchese family, was sentenced to 100 years in federal prison. He died in prison of natural causes in August 2000.

Bathrobe-clad Vincent (The Chin) Gigante under arrest.

HONOR AMONG THIEVES

A single guiding principle, with harsh consequences for those who violate it, keeps organized crime in business.

We keep our mouths shut. We take care of our own problems. And we never, ever cooperate with the cops. This ironclad code of conduct, *omertà* in Italian, meaning "code of silence," is central to the smooth operation of any criminal group, from the Mafia to street gangs. Violators are punished swiftly and severely.

Those who do decide to testify against their own, usually in exchange for personal immunity from prosecution, are often enticed by the promise of protection by the government. Once informants have testified, they are spirited into a witness protection program, given new identities, and instructed to cut all ties with their past.

In order to thrive, the Mob continually branched out into new areas. Besides gambling and prostitution, it gained a foothold in a variety of legal businesses, such as garbage collecting and garment manufacture, profiting from kickbacks and shakedowns. Historians estimate that by the 1950s and 60s, there were about 5,000 Mafiosi nationwide, making up 24 Mafia families, plus many more loosely affiliated associates.

Organizing Against Crime

Mafia activity might have continued unabated had Congress not passed tough laws against organized crime in 1970, known as RICO (Racketeer Influenced and Corrupt Organizations Act). Federal authorities are now able to prosecute and imprison the leaders of criminal organizations even if it can't be proved that they personally have

committed any specific crime. Since the inception of RICO, the American Mafia has diminished in power: The FBI estimates that there are now 3,000 members and affiliates in the United States. But the worldwide Mafia still reaps $100 billion in profits every year from activities such as money laundering, the heroin trade, illegal gambling, extortion, fraud, counterfeiting, and weapons trafficking.

Italian organized crime is not the only game in town these days. The Vory V Zakone, a network of former Soviet criminals, is involved in financial fraud, illegal drugs, and human trafficking. There are organized Nigerian heroin traffickers and identity thieves, plus criminal enterprises from Asia, the Middle East, and the Balkans.

Overall, according to the FBI, organized crime groups as a whole profit illegally to the tune of $1 trillion every year.

CRIME FIGHTER NUMBER ONE

UNDER THE IRON RULE OF DIRECTOR J. EDGAR HOOVER, THE FBI CRACKED DOWN ON BAD GUYS BUT ALSO SPIED ON EVERYDAY CITIZENS.

At the turn of the 20th century, American law enforcement was in disarray. As corruption boomed, state and federal agencies struggled to track criminals who moved easily from one locale to the next to evade capture. A hapless Bureau of Investigation (BOI), formed in 1908 to coordinate national efforts to contain crime, quickly became more depraved than the factions it was designed to combat.

President Calvin Coolidge recognized change was needed. To muscle national law enforcement efforts into

J. Edgar Hoover, 1936

shape, Coolidge in 1924 appointed a rising star in the Department of Justice as the BOI's new chief: 29-year-old J. Edgar Hoover, a man who would become the most famous, or infamous, director the agency would ever have.

Hoover at the Helm

Recognized for his work during World War I arresting and jailing disloyal foreigners, Hoover's first action at the BOI was to oust political cronies and dirty agents. He introduced rigorous hiring criteria, including background checks for all applicants. In 1928, he launched the first formal program for recruits, and when the agency's name changed in 1935 to the Federal Bureau of Investigation, Hoover became its first director.

Hoover also worked to centralize crime-fighting efforts nationwide. He ordered the creation of a federal identification system, nicknamed Ident, which

compiled all fingerprints from police agencies across the country. He unified criminal files and created the FBI Technical Laboratory to provide forensic-analysis support for the FBI and other agencies. These innovations would prove critical in the 1930s War on Crime and efforts to destroy regional gangsters such as Chicago's Al Capone.

Enter the Mafia

But even as the FBI succeeded in bringing down some notorious bootleggers and bank robbers, a more subversive influence was taking root in American communities: a syndicate of criminal gangs with ties to the Sicilian Mafia. Dedicated to a smorgasbord of illegal enterprises, the American Mafia grew rapidly by bribing corrupt officials and corporate leaders. It succeeded in infiltrating dozens of legitimate businesses but was difficult to combat, in part because of a rigorous code of silence that prevent-

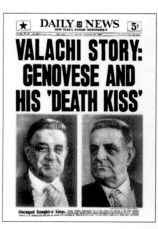

New York Daily News front page on September 28, 1963, reporting the testimony of Mafia informer Joseph Valachi.

ed members from cooperating with law enforcement. Many Americans were skeptical that there even was a national crime network and believed instead that the groups were operating locally. Finally, when police in the town of Apalachin, New York, raided a gathering of more than 60 mobsters in 1957, the public began to grasp the power of the American Mafia.

In the 1960s, U.S. Attorney General Robert F. Ken-

WHO KNEW?
Prohibition gangster George "Machine Gun" Kelly allegedly shouted, "Don't shoot, G-Men!" when surrounded by federal forces. The nickname stuck and is still used today for FBI agents.

George Kelly Barnes, aka Machine Gun Kelly, is led away by FBI agents after his arrest, September 1933.

nedy stepped up pressure on Hoover and the FBI to prosecute members of the Mafia. In 1963, convicted New York mobster Joseph Valachi became a government informant and acknowledged the existence of what he called "La Cosa Nostra," or "our thing." This was the first time a crime-family member had revealed specific details about the organization's structure and customs.

Hoover continued to serve as the FBI's director until his death in 1972—a total of 48 years. After his tenure, Congress passed legislation limiting FBI directors to ten-year terms.

CAPONE VS. THE UNTOUCHABLES

The FBI and Al Capone rose to fame together as the Federal government struggled against bootlegging prohibition.

The 1920s were a banner era for crime gangs that thrived on bootlegging and illicit activities tied to Prohibition. Few were more successful than the flashy leader of the Chicago syndicate, Al Capone, known for his large appetite, bespoke suits, and female companions.

In 1929, Eliot Ness, an agent for the Bureau of Prohibition in Chicago, was chosen to head operations targeting Capone's illegal breweries and supply routes. Aware that Capone had paid off many members of local law enforcement, Ness combed through agency files to find colleagues who were known for incorruptibility. The media dubbed the team of nine agents "The Untouchables."

Each time the team conducted a raid of a Capone business, Ness made sure the press was there to see them ripping open crates and smashing bottles. The raids infuriated Capone and led to multiple assassination attempts on Ness and his men.

Capone and his syndicate continued to thrive, however, until the government investigated the gangster's income taxes. In 1931, Capone was charged with 22 counts of tax evasion and convicted on five of the charges, enough to sentence him to 11 years in prison.

Ness went on to become the Safety Director of Cleveland, Ohio, and was instrumental in implementing the use of patrol cars rather than walking "beat" cops. Ironically, he declined into alcoholism and died of a heart attack in 1957, at the age of 54.

Elliot Ness, circa 1930

KISSING AND KILLING

BONNIE AND CLYDE WERE YOUNG, BEAUTIFUL, AND IN LOVE. THEY WERE ALSO ARMED AND DANGEROUS.

WHO KNEW?
The famous photo showing Bonnie chomping on a cigar was a shot she posed for as a joke. She didn't really smoke cigars.

It was love at first sight when Bonnie Elizabeth Parker, 19, and Clyde Chestnut Barrow, 20, met in Dallas in 1930, at the home of a mutual friend. Bonnie, a pretty, petite strawberry blonde, was estranged from the man she'd married at 15. Clyde, compact and dark-eyed, was a burglar and car thief who would soon do a stint in a Texas prison. While he was behind bars the two pined for each other, and when Clyde was released in 1932 they reunited. Shortly afterward, the couple embarked on their now-infamous string of armed robberies, hitting banks and small stores with a rotating gang of accomplices. They were adept at eluding authorities, often shooting their way free of capture. Soon they were a media sensation.

Romance of the Outlaw
During the Great Depression, with so many Americans out of work and suffering, Bonnie and Clyde were seen as folk heroes, the oppressed striking back against their oppressors. The fact that they were an extremely attractive unmarried couple and clearly attracted to each other only added to their illicit appeal. But no matter how glamorous they seemed, Bonnie and Clyde were killers. Their band of compatriots, known as the Barrow Gang, was responsible for about a dozen murders in several states between 1932 and 1934.

Bonnie and Clyde committed their crimes for a simple reason: They needed the money. Both grew up poor, and they regularly returned to Texas to share their ill-gotten wealth with their families. In addition, Clyde had grown to loathe authority during his time in Eastham Prison, a maximum-security hellhole in Texas where guards beat, abused, and even murdered inmates. Once on the outside, Clyde plotted his revenge. In early 1934, he and Bonnie helped a group of Eastham prisoners escape from a work detail.

From Glamorized to Despised
The public rooted for the outlaw couple until they went too far.

On Easter Sunday, 1934, the Barrow Gang killed two Texas highway patrolmen. Local newspapers repeated the account of an eyewitness, a local farmer who said he had seen Bonnie shoot one of the officers and laugh when his head "bounced like a rubber ball" on the road. The story ultimately proved to be false, but the public had had enough.

Although the two were crafty, they were also predictable, often traveling the same routes in order to visit their families. A Texas police officer began tracking their whereabouts, and on May 23, 1934, law enforcement was ready for Bonnie and Clyde. Setting up an ambush alongside a remote Louisiana highway, the officers waited for

Bonnie Parker points a shotgun at boyfriend Clyde Barrow, circa 1932.

A long line of gun-wielding lovers have wreaked havoc in the name of greed or protest.

→ **Charlie Starkweather and Caril Fugate**
Spree: 1958

Charles Raymond Starkweather was 19. Caril Ann Fugate was 14. After Caril's mother and stepfather told Charlie to stay away, he shot them—and the two Nebraska teens fled, embarking on a two-month murder spree. The final body count: ten people and two dogs. He was executed; she served time and was paroled in 1976. Their story would inspire numerous movies, including *Badlands* and *Natural Born Killers*.

→ **Jerad Miller and Amanda Miller**
Spree: 2014

Wed in 2012, Jerad and Amanda Miller, "two wacko idiots," as one federal law enforcement official called them, loved comic-book characters but hated the government. They ambushed and murdered two Las Vegas police officers eating lunch in June 2014. Amanda also killed a good Samaritan who tried to intervene. Shortly after, police shot and killed Jerad; Amanda shot and killed herself.

the couple to drive past. When they did, in a stolen Ford V-8, all six members of the police posse opened fire.

By the time the officers had finished unloading their weapons, they had shot the Ford more than 100 times. Bonnie and Clyde's corpses were so full of holes that when it was time to embalm them, the fluid leaked out as fast as it went in.

The two wanted to be buried together, but their families balked. Although they are eternally linked in American popular culture, they rest in two different Texas cemeteries.

The bullet-riddled automobile in which Clyde Barrow and Bonnie Parker were trapped, shot, and killed.

DO I INTIMIDATE YOU?

GANGBANGERS AND OTHER MEMBERS OF ORGANIZED CRIME OFTEN RELY ON SCARE TACTICS TO KEEP PEOPLE IN LINE.

Judge Nicholas Garaufis was fed up. It was the 2014 murder trial of Brooklyn crack dealer Ronald "Ra Diggs" Herron, and Garaufis thought the gang leader's supporters were trying to rattle a witness by "making faces and gesturing and talking." Garaufis threatened to clear the room if the behavior continued and yelled from the bench, "No one's going to eyeball my witnesses!"

The judge had good reason to be tough. Herron had eluded a previous murder conviction by allegedly threatening two witnesses, who then refused to testify against him. Following that trial, Herron had posted videos on the internet in which he fired weapons and warned against "snitching."

Don't Mess with Us

Whether wielding a knife, a gun, or just a threatening stare, members of criminal organizations use intimidation to keep victims, rivals, witnesses, and even their own members in line. The Italian-American Mafia, for example, has made it clear that any member who violates its rules will be dealt with brutally. In 1979, when Brooklyn mobster and drug trafficker Carmine Galante was suspected of skimming profits, he and his bodyguards were assassinated in a restaurant. Similarly, the Mob has "taken care of" associates who have cooperated with law enforcement.

Authority Figures

Gangs, cartels, and other criminal groups act as neighborhood terrorists, assuring that even residents who aren't involved in the gang bow to the group's authority. The goal is to develop an ongoing, community-wide sense of fear and to keep bystanders from going to the police. A U.S. Department of Justice report called it "The wholesale intimidation of neighborhoods."

In 1984, Boston mobster Whitey Bulger reportedly coerced Stephen Rakes, a liquor store owner, into selling his business by holding a gun to his head as his daughters looked on. Nearly 30 years later, after Bulger was finally apprehended (see pages 232–233), Rakes hoped to testify at Bulger's racketeering trial. He was murdered before he got the chance, although authorities found no connection.

Even law-enforcement officials aren't immune. In 2014, gang thugs kidnapped and threatened to torture the father of Colleen Janssen, a North Carolina assistant district attorney who had prosecuted one of their members. The FBI successfully rescued the father after several days, but Janssen's boss later told CNN, "I've never seen our office as anxious."

The bloodied body of mafia chieftain Carmine Galante lies in the backyard garden of a New York restaurant, 1979.

236

Alleged organized crime members Nicholas Marangello (left) and Salvatore Palmieri are escorted from the Manhattan District Attorney's office in 1980 after refusing to answer questions about the murder of Mafia boss Carmine Galante.

Gold-plated and diamond-encrusted weapons confiscated from a ranch in Mexico

THE MAN WITH THE GOLDEN GUNS

What does the drug lord who has everything spend his money on?

In 2010, Mexican soldiers discovered a trove of gold- and diamond-encrusted pistols and assault rifles in the Jalisco home of alleged drug lord Oscar Orlando Nava Valencia. One pistol had a Ferrari logo on the handle; another spelled out the powerful drug lord's nickname, "Lobo" (wolf) in diamonds. Valencia, who is reportedly linked to the deadly Sinaloa Cartel, was already in custody when the cache was unearthed.

The bedazzled firearms may or may not have been used to threaten people, but they certainly sent a clear message: *I am one bad dude, with more money than I know what to do with.*

OTHER LETHAL WEAPONS

Guns send a message quickly, but criminals have many other menacing tools at their disposal.

Tool	Organization	Use
MACHETE	MS-13 Long Island, New York	In 2010, members of this Central American gang allegedly murdered a fellow member they deemed not tough enough by lodging a machete in his skull.
GROUP BEATDOWN	Latin Kings Chicago	In 2006, a hidden camera allegedly caught more than two dozen gang members simultaneously pummeling one of their own for failing to obey an order.
CHAINSAW	Los Zetas Mexico	In 2013, a video posted on Facebook supposedly showed the gruesome beheading of a snitch. The perpetrator claimed membership in the crime syndicate Los Zetas.
PIGS	Calabrian Mafia Italy	In a 2012 revenge killing, gang assassins allegedly beat a rival, then tossed him into a sty of starving pigs, who gobbled him alive.
BASEBALL BAT	Russian Mafia Russia	In 2013, 40 thugs allegedly descended on a popular pizza restaurant whose owner had not paid "protection money," terrorizing customers, demolishing the place, and beating employees.

MOB MENTALITY

THESE THREE CRIME KINGPINS AMASSED THEIR FORTUNES BY CATERING TO SOCIETY'S DARKEST DESIRES.

Beer barrels being destroyed by prohibition agents, 1920

WHAT WAS PROHIBITION?

It was supposed to stop crime, but America's ill-fated ban on alcohol backfired in a big way.

In the late 19th century, drunkenness was seen as a nasty vice and the root of numerous evils. Men did most of the drinking back then, and many who did exhibited the worst kinds of alcoholic behavior. Booze was also seen as fueling crime. In 1919, anti-drinking activists—the Temperance Movement—persuaded the U.S. Congress to pass the 18th Amendment to the Constitution, which outlawed the sale, manufacture, and transportation of intoxicating beverages. Among the many unintended consequences of Prohibition was the rise of organized crime. The amendment was repealed in 1933.

Americans have a seemingly insatiable appetite for illicit substances and activities, and the best mobster minds have capitalized on it.

Organized crime in the United States took root during Prohibition, when a new Constitutional amendment banned the sale and consumption of alcohol beginning in 1920. The law was a boon to mobsters like Lucky Luciano, who realized there was big money to be made by bootlegging. Luciano, who got his start as a teenage gang member in New York, was already considered the era's most powerful American mobster and he quickly marshaled his partners to assemble a booze-smuggling operation. By 1925 Luciano's gang was sitting on top of an empire, raking in the equivalent in today's dollars of more than $50 million a year. After Prohibition ended, he cashed in on other vices, including prostitution, gambling, and—beginning in the late 1950s—narcotics.

Mob Accountant

Meanwhile, Luciano's longtime associate Meyer Lansky was busy cornering the gambling market. Born in what is now Belarus, Lansky immigrated with his family to New York as a boy and settled in the same impoverished neighborhood as Luciano, with whom he eventually went into business. Lansky was Jewish, so he was never a true member of the Italian Mafia, but that didn't stop him from becoming the financial wizard of organized crime, nicknamed the "Mob's Accountant."

Like Luciano, Lansky profited from Prohibition, and in the early 1930s he used some of those to invest in illegal gambling casinos in New York State, Florida, and New Orleans. Later, he played an active role in the legal casino business in Cuba and Las Vegas, most notably investing in the Flamingo Hotel & Casino, which was run by his childhood friend and associate Bugsy Siegel. Though the two men were close as brothers, Lansky turned on Siegel when it was discovered he was skimming profits from the Flamingo and backed his 1947 assassination.

King of the Midwest

Meanwhile, in Chicago, Al Capone controlled a vast criminal underworld catering to a variety of Roaring Twenties vices. Gambling, brothels, illegal liquor, drugs—Capone handled it all. Born and raised in Brooklyn,

WHO KNEW?
Although the Church of Jesus Christ of Latter-Day Saints officially condemns gambling and drinking, Mormon bankers helped the Mob finance the early casinos in Las Vegas.

Mafia boss Charles "Lucky" Luciano (right) walks handcuffed into the New York Supreme Court in 1936.

HOW IT ALL ENDED

Health problems, not law enforcement, did in three of America's top tough guys.

➜ **Al Capone.** Income tax evasion landed the gangster in Alcatraz for 11 years. By the time he got out, Capone was sick from complications of un-

treated syphilis. He died of the disease in 1947, at age 48.

➜ **Lucky Luciano.** After living large in New York for years, Luciano was sentenced to prison on extortion and prostitution charges in 1936. He was

paroled and settled in Cuba before being deported to Italy. In 1962 he died of a heart attack in Naples at age 64.

➜ **Meyer Lansky.** As hard as they tried, the Federal authorities could never pin any crime worse than illegal gambling on Lansky, and for that he spent

a mere two months in prison. He retired to Miami Beach, where he died of lung cancer in 1983, at the age of 80.

New York, Capone cut his teeth in the same gang as Luciano before heading out to the Midwest around 1920 to help run a prostitution ring in Chicago. Five years later, when his boss and mentor Johnny Torrio retired, Capone took over, cementing his status as the king of crime in the Windy City.

Today, alcohol and casino gambling have lost their illicit status, leaving organized crime to focus on everything from murder to extortion, gun smuggling, human and drug trafficking, and more.

THE CRIME BOSS WAS A RAT

BOSTON CRIME KINGPIN WHITEY BULGER WAS ALSO AN FBI INFORMANT, UNTIL HE BECAME ONE OF AMERICA'S MOST WANTED.

He was clever, vicious, and the reigning boss of Boston's Irish-American organized-crime underworld. So it seemed like a coup in 1975 when the Federal Bureau of Investigation turned James Joseph "Whitey" Bulger Jr. into an informant. He was recruited by Special Agent John Connolly, who had grown up in the same South Boston housing project as the Bulger family and convinced Whitey to provide information about his rivals in the local Italian-American Mafia.

In exchange for this cooperation, Connolly and his fellow agents agreed to turn a blind eye to Bulger's own criminal activity, including drug trafficking and racketeering. Over time, the relationship between Connolly and Bulger grew so cozy that the two exchanged Christmas gifts. But holiday presents seemed to be the least of it.

In one instance, Connolly supplied information that led to the 1982 murder of a gambling executive. In De-cember 1994, the agent, then retired from the FBI, alerted Bulger that he was about to be indicted by the feds.

Whitey on the Run

Even before Connolly's warning, Bulger was prepared for a life on the lam. He had already set up safe-deposit boxes full of cash, jewelry, and phony passports in cities all over North America and Europe. From Boston, he fled to a succession of locations, including New York, New Orleans, Los Angeles, Chicago, San Francisco, and London, always eluding the authorities.

But the FBI didn't give up, and in 1999 added him to its Ten Most Wanted Fugitives list, putting him in the company of Osama bin Laden. Bulger was described as armed and dangerous, and the reward for his capture was ultimately raised to $2 million. His former link to the FBI, Connolly, was convicted on federal racketeering charges stemming from his relationship with Bulger. In 2008, Connolly was convicted again, this time for his role in the 1982 murder of the gambling executive.

Finally, in 2011, after almost 16 years of chasing the former crime boss, the FBI tracked him down to an apartment in Santa Monica, California, that he shared with his longtime girlfriend. Two years later, the octogenarian was found guilty of participating in 11 of the 19 murders with which he was charged. A Boston judge handed down two consecutive terms of life in prison. "Moments later, in his orange jump-suit," the *Boston Globe* reported, "Bulger gave his lawyer an awkward embrace and shuffled silently out of the public eye, possibly for good." In a 2014 development in the case, a Florida court overturned the murder conviction of Connolly, the former FBI agent, raising the possibility that he could be freed. Prosecutors are challenging the ruling.

FBI TEN MOST WANTED FUGITIVE

RACKETEERING INFLUENCED AND CORRUPT ORGANIZATIONS (RICO) - MURDER (18 COUNTS), CONSPIRACY TO COMMIT MURDER, CONSPIRACY TO COMMIT EXTORTION, NARCOTICS DISTRIBUTION, CONSPIRACY TO COMMIT MONEY LAUNDERING; EXTORTION; MONEY LAUNDERING

JAMES J. BULGER

Photograph taken in 1994   Photograph taken in 1994   Photograph altered in 2000

An FBI Ten Most Wanted Fugitive poster shows Boston mobster James "Whitey" Bulger.

WHO KNEW?
Bulger's nickname is a reference to the prominent streak of blond in his hair. He was given the moniker as a kid and reportedly hates it.

James "Whitey" Bulger in a prisoner transfer photo from the U.S. penitentiary at Alcatraz, in San Francisco.

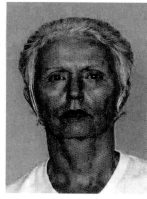

Catherine Greig, the longtime girlfriend of Whitey Bulger.

"HAVE YOU SEEN THIS WOMAN?"

Stymied for years in their attempts to find Whitey Bulger, the FBI finally found his Achilles heel: his ladylove.

The FBI couldn't find Whitey Bulger, but the agency did know a few things about the crime boss's longtime girlfriend, the 60-year-old Catherine Greig. A pretty, green-eyed blonde, Greig liked to go to the beauty salon. She also got her teeth cleaned frequently and had regular plastic surgery. Figuring that someone out there in America—a doctor, manicurist, hairdresser, or neighbor—had to have encountered Greig, the Bureau got creative. In June 2011, it produced a television public service announcement and bought airtime in 14 cities during shows that were popular with Greig's female contemporaries.

"Have you seen this woman?" the spot began. It went on to describe Greig's appearance and habits and offered up to $100,000 for her capture. Tips began to pour in so quickly that the FBI arrested the couple in Santa Monica, California, within a day. Greig was sentenced to federal prison for harboring a fugitive. She is scheduled for release in 2018.

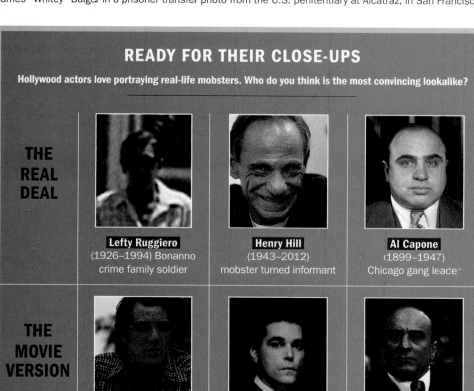

READY FOR THEIR CLOSE-UPS

Hollywood actors love portraying real-life mobsters. Who do you think is the most convincing lookalike?

THE REAL DEAL	**Lefty Ruggiero** (1926–1994) Bonanno crime family soldier	**Henry Hill** (1943–2012) mobster turned informant	**Al Capone** (1899–1947) Chicago gang leader
THE MOVIE VERSION	**Al Pacino** *Donnie Brasco*, 1997	**Ray Liotta** *Goodfellas*, 1990	**Robert De Niro** *The Untouchables*, 1987

THE
SQUEALERS

COOPERATIVE INFORMANTS HAVE HELPED PUT AWAY SOME SEEMINGLY INDESTRUCTIBLE CRIMINALS, BUT AT WHAT PRICE?

Government witness Salvatore "Sammy the Bull" Gravano appears in court.

THE INFORMER IS INFORMED UPON

He put 36 behind bars, then wound up behind bars himself.

The testimony of Salvatore "Sammy the Bull" Gravano helped jail 36 of his former mafia associates. After being given a new identity in the federal witness protection program, in September 2002 Gravano was sentenced to 20 years in prison on federal and state charges of drug trafficking. Informants within his own organization helped the government convict him.

"Joe Cargo" was the first turncoat. In 1963, the mob henchman, whose real name was Joseph Valachi, appeared before a Senate subcommittee and revealed something shocking to the American public: Yes, the Mafia really did exist. He named names, detailed the organization's history, and cleared up some unsolved murders. In doing so, Valachi changed history. By the time he was done talking, the Cosa Nostra—"our thing"—was no longer a secret operation.

At the time that Valachi began cooperating with the government, the mobster was in prison for heroin trafficking and had heard that his boss, Vito Genovese, wanted him killed. His next move? Valachi whacked a fellow inmate whom he believed was a hitman coming to get him. When the FBI questioned Valachi in connection with that killing, he began explaining the inner

REPEAT OFFENDERS

What happens when bad guys blow their own cover.

Almost all witnesses in the protection program were criminals themselves, and a number of them commit new crimes after relocation—about 17 percent, according to the U.S. Department of Justice. On the upside, that's still considerably lower than the 40 percent recidivism rate of regular paroled offenders.

Real Identity	How He Helped	New Identity	Then...	Result
Herman Goldfarb New York	Informant in a 1973 investigation of organized crime in New York's garment industry	Herman G. Martin, Solana Beach, California	Had a lawyer who owed him money pistol-whipped	Sentenced to prison, verdict later overturned; died in 1990
Marion Pruett Atlanta, Georgia	Testified in a 1979 case regarding the murder of a fellow prisoner	Sonny Pearson, Rio Rancho, New Mexico	Went on a murder spree and killed five people	Executed in 1999
Salvatore "Sammy the Bull" Gravano New York	In 1991, became a government witness against Mafia boss John Gotti	Jimmy Moran, Tempe, Arizona	Started a major ecstasy-trafficking business	Sentenced to prison; eligible for release in 2019

Joseph Valachi, convicted murderer and former Cosa Nostra mobster, testifies before the Senate Permanent Investigation Committee in Washington, D.C., 1963.

Mobster Jimmy Burke is led handcuffed by police in New York.

workings of the Mafia. Valachi maintained that he'd decided to talk because it was his civic duty. Whatever his motivation, he benefited somewhat from his service. He avoided the death penalty for the prison murder and was given solitary confinement as a form of protection. Valachi safely outlived Genovese and died of a heart attack in prison in 1971.

Safe Harbor

By 1970, the government had set up more formal protection for prized informants: The Witness Security Program. Known officially as WITSEC, the federal witness protection program helps ensure the safety of those who provide information against certain particularly dangerous criminals. WITSEC is overseen by the U.S. Marshals Service, which protects, relocates, and gives new identities to those who meet the program's guidelines.

The media tends to portray witness protection as a cushy gig. In one case, a protected witness was reportedly allowed to bring along 16 family members, all paid for by the government. But that is not the standard. Participants don't get to choose where they want to go, and though they can get job training and cash for expenses such as medical care, they aren't paid millions. Typically, only two or three loved ones are relocated along with the informant. As for the witnesses' former identities, they are completely expunged from all records. Those people simply cease to exist.

According to the government, none of the more than 18,500 witnesses and family members in the program have been killed—at least, none who followed the rules.

Dangerous Game

The fate of those who don't toe the line is not so secure. In 2008, Justin Lee, a San Francisco witness under a local version of WITSEC was shot to death. Lee had testified against a man suspected of murdering Lee's brother. He was relocated to another part of the state and repeatedly instructed not to return to San Francisco. Ignoring the warnings, Lee went back and was shot multiple times on the street. As a city official later put it, "The cardinal rule of witness relocation is: Stay…where you've been relocated."

THE LUFTHANSA HEIST

A brazen robbery at New York's John F. Kennedy International Airport reaped a cash bonanza, but left behind too many potential rats.

It was a daring plot, even for the mob. On December 11, 1978, a team of Lucchese crime family associates headed for JFK International airport, where workers had just transferred a load of American currency from a Lufthansa plane to a vault. The gangsters rounded up Lufthansa employees, held them at gunpoint in a break room, and made off with the goods—about $6 million in cash and jewelry, or more than $21 million today. It was the largest cash robbery on U.S. soil at the time.

But the job wasn't quite done. To ensure details didn't leak to the police, mobster Jimmy Burke, who organized the robbery, had most the participants assassinated. His plan worked, sort of. Some of the gangsters became informants and the crime was solved, but the cash and jewelry were never recovered. The caper became the basis for the popular film *Goodfellas*.

243

ASIAN ORGANIZED CRIME

CHINESE AND JAPANESE GROUPS EXPLOIT THEIR COUNTRIES' TRADITIONS FOR THEIR OWN PROFIT.

It's a tough time to be in a Japanese gang. For generations—even centuries—the country's citizens coexisted with the organized crime groups collectively called *yakuza*. These groups operated publicly and billed themselves as "chivalrous organizations" that extended protection to local businesses. After Japan's devastating 2011 earthquake and tsunami, yakuza groups even trucked in supplies to devastated areas.

But much of the yakuza's "protection" has come at a price—often a percentage of a business's profits, which has varied depending on how much the yakuza could take.

Sick of the gangs' extortion rackets, Japanese society has begun turning against them. Police now refer to yakuza as *bōryokudan*, or "violence groups," and are using newly-passed anti-gang laws to crack down on the gang's activities. Some businesses have begun hanging signs that forbid entry to yakuza members or anyone with tattoos, often a sign of gang membership. Even the American government has taken a stand, announcing in 2012 that the Department of the Treasury would freeze yakuza groups' American bank accounts.

The strategies may be helping. In 2010, the number of known yakuza members fell to about 79,000, the lowest number since the 1960s.

Chinese Organized Crime

In China, criminal gangs called *triads* engage in typical yakuza activity like gambling, prostitution, and arms smuggling, but they also specialize in counterfeit-ing. Historically, the groups focused on minting phony money, but these days have moved on to copying products produced legitimately in China, including DVDs, electronics, and designer handbags.

Chinese organized crime has been active in the U.S. since the late 19th century. Back then, American society was particularly unfriendly to Chinese immigrants, who were treated as job stealers willing to work for lower wages. For protection, these immigrants banded together in big cities such as San Francisco and New York and formed *tongs*—voluntary organizations meant to support their members. To keep themselves afloat financially, some of the tongs began operating illegal businesses, such as gambling dens and brothels.

In San Francisco in the late 1880s, rivalries between these organizations erupted into the Tong Wars, bloody clashes a lot like the Italian-American Mafia violence of later years. The Tong Wars raged for decades, but a key contributor to their demise was the San Francisco earthquake of 1906. The quake sparked fires that destroyed Chinatown, and with it the tongs' illegal businesses.

Officers from Hong Kong Police's organized crime bureau display cash seized in an operation with China to smash an illegal cross-border gambling syndicate, 2014.

The late Yoshinori Watanabe, leader of the Yamaguchi-gumi yakuza group

THE HEIST

A record-breaking Tokyo robbery is said to be linked to a yakuza group.

The May 2011 robbery of a security firm on the outskirts of Tokyo was the biggest heist in Japan's history. Two masked thieves broke into the building through a window whose lock they knew had been broken for months. They beat the dozing watchman, stabbed him for good measure, and forced him to give up the security code to the room in which the money was kept. Then they bound him with adhesive tape and made off with the equivalent of $7.4 million.

A member of the largest yakuza group, the Yamaguchi-gumi, is suspected of masterminding the crime. But neither of the burglars who actually carried out the job was yakuza. Both appeared inept. A store security camera near the crime scene caught the duo buying the adhesive tape they used on the guard. After their arrest, the two returned some of the money, but most of it is assumed to have ended up in the hands of the Yamaguchi-gumi.

NOT SO INNOCENTS ABROAD

Organized crime is as popular a film topic in Japan, China, and Korea as it is in America. Here are some favorite *Godfather* equivalents.

Country	Original Title	English Title	Date	Plot
Japan	*Auto eiji*	*Outrage*	2010	A yakuza leader ignites a gang war.
China	*Mou gaan dou*	*Infernal Affairs*	2002	A police officer infiltrates a triad, while a triad member infiltrates the police.
Korea	*Sinsegye*	*New World*	2013	An undercover cop is caught in a succession struggle for leadership of Korea's largest crime syndicate

LAWLESS AND FEARLESS

MEXICO'S BRUTAL DRUG CARTELS USE MURDER, TORTURE, AND EXTORTION TO MAINTAIN POWER.

In the fall of 2013, Harry Devert, a seasoned traveler in his 20s, set off by motorcycle from New York. His plan was to bike through Mexico, Central America, and South America and blog about his experience. In January 2014, Devert went missing in Mexico. In June, police in the violence-plagued southwestern state of Guerrero discovered a motorcycle—and, next to it, Devert's dismembered corpse. He was another victim of the country's dangerous organized-crime syndicates.

MEXICAN MOB MONIKERS

You're probably familiar with the colorful nicknames of Italian gangsters—Sammy the Bull, Vinny the Chin, and the like. But how about Barbie and Winnie the Pooh?

GANGSTER/POSITION	NICKNAME	EXPLANATION
Osiel Cardenás Guillen Ex–Los Zetas leader	El Mata Amigos ("Friend Killer")	Known for vicious violence against his enemies.
Óscar Guerrero Silva Ex–Los Zetas leader	El Winnie Pooh	Unknown
Joaquín Guzmán Sinaloá Cartel head	El Chapo ("Shorty")	He is 5'6" tall.
Edgar Valdez Villarreal Beltrán-Leyva enforcer	El Barbie ("Barbie")	He has light eyes and fair skin.

Federal police guard the armored vehicle where suspected member of the Gulf Cartel Gregorio Sauceda Gamboa was held during his transfer at federal police headquarters in Mexico City, 2009.

Joaquín "El Chapo" Guzman is escorted in handcuffs by Mexican navy marines.

THE OSAMA BIN LADEN OF COCAINE

Joaquín Guzman Loera, the most powerful drug lord in the world, is now in prison—again.

The Drug Enforcement Administration calls him "the Godfather of the Drug World." His net worth of $1 billion makes him one of the richest people on the planet. Until his capture in February 2014 in the Sinaloá resort city of Mazatlán, he was the world's most wanted criminal—a spot formerly reserved for Osama Bin Laden.

As the alleged head of the Sinaloá Cartel, Joaquín Guzman Loera is responsible for getting more drugs into the United States than any other kingpin. He is married to a beauty queen more than 35 years his junior and has twin daughters. He is also a local folk hero, inspiring songs about the dirt-poor boy who made it big.

In reality, Guzman is a ruthless criminal who isn't above hanging the bodies of his enemies from meat hooks to prove a point. Captured once in 1993, he escaped from a Mexican prison in 2001 (legend has it he hid in a laundry cart) and remained on the run until Mexican and American authorities finally caught up with him in Mazatlán.

Officially they're called TCOs, Transnational Criminal Organizations, but most people know Mexico's infamous drug cartels by their fearsome names and deeds. There is the technologically sophisticated Los Zetas, based across the border from Laredo, Texas, and known for decapitating enemies with chainsaws and posting videos of the carnage on the internet. Kidnapping and extortion are two specialties of the Mexico City–based Knights Templar, named after the medieval Christian military order. And the omnipotent Sinaloá cartel, which operates in the coastal state of the same name along the Gulf of California, dissolves bodies in vats of chemicals.

The cartels are responsible for transporting narcotics produced in South America into the United States, and it's big business: Estimates of the size of the wholesale drug trade vary widely from about $14 billion to almost $50 billion a year. The fortunes at stake lead to bloody clashes between rival groups, and the government in Mexico has been engaged in an ongoing war against the gangs since 2006.

Systemic Problems

As a result, many areas of the country, particularly near the U.S. border, are plagued by drug-related brutality. Mexican police are often underpaid and subject to bribes by the cartels. The country's poor and poorly educated citizens, desperate for jobs, are ripe for the picking by crime syndicates looking for new recruits.

Nor are Americans immune; the cartels have operatives in cities such as Chicago and Atlanta. In Mexico, 81 American citizens were murdered and 90 or more kidnapped in 2013. Other visitors have found themselves in the middle of gun battles between rival gangs, or between the cartels and Mexican authorities or citizen vigilante groups. These battles often take place in broad daylight or at busy restaurants and clubs.

The gangs even use unsuspecting travelers to transport illegal cargo into America. In some cases, they target Americans who cross the border frequently for work, attaching drugs to the undersides of their cars while they're parked in Mexico.

русская мафия*

THE RUSSIANS

A LOOSELY KNIT ORGANIZATION OF ELITE "THIEVES IN LAW" RUNS RAMPANT THROUGH THE FORMER SOVIET UNION AND IN THE U.S.

Illya Trincher of Beverly Hills is the son of a champion professional poker player, and Helly Nahmad of New York City is the son of an international art dealer. And according to the Federal Bureau of Investigation, both men are part of the network of organized criminals known as the Russian mafia.

In 2013, the U.S. Attorney for the Southern District of New York slapped Trincher, then 27, and Nahmad, then 34, with a long list of charges. They included money laundering, extortion, and unlawful internet gambling—for running a sports betting ring that targeted billionaires and multi-millionaires. According to the indictment, the duo laundered $100 million in illegal profits.

The Brotherhood

While other criminal enterprises dirty their hands with the drug trade and blue-collar endeavors, the Bratva, or Brotherhood, stands out. Make no mistake—the Russian mob has its tentacles in the seamier stuff, too: prostitution and sex slavery, the prescription-drug black market, narcotics, murder. But these sophisticated criminals are especially genius at white-collar swindles that involve vast amounts of money and entangle businesses viewed as legitimate. In a scandal uncovered in the late 1990s, the Russian mafia used accounts at the Bank of New York, an American financial institution founded by Alexander Hamilton, to launder $7 billion worth of illicit money.

The culture of lawlessness, many say, reaches all the way to the top of Russia's political food chain. Many U.S. officials view Russia as a kleptocracy—a government ruled by thieves—and

EVERY PICTURE TELLS A STORY

The fine art of deciphering Russian tattoos.

Russia's original gangsters were known for their symbolic tattoos, and the practice continues to some extent today.

Although the images can vary depending on the individual, some markings are said to have standard meanings.

Tattoo	What It Means
Skull	The wearer murdered someone significant.
Barbed wire on face	The wearer is serving a life sentence without parole.
Stars on knees	"I will kneel before no one."
Dots on knuckles	Number of years in prison.
Insect trapped in spider web	Wearer is an addict.

*Russian Mafia

Helly Nahmad (left) leaving Manhattan federal court with his attorney Benjamin Braffman.

Russian president Vladimir Putin is alleged by some experts to have engaged in illegal financial dealings himself. The country is viewed as so corrupt that notorious Russian mobster Vyachesla Ivankov, who emigrated to the U.S. in 1992 to ply his trade, once described his homeland as "one uninterrupted criminal swamp."

As for Trincher and Nahmad, in the spring of 2014 a federal judge handed down their prison sentences, rejecting Nahmad's request to serve his confinement at home in exchange for donating $100,000 to start a program to introduce inner-city kids to the arts. Instead, Nahmad made a plea deal to forfeit more than $6.4 million in cash and a painting worth several hundred thousand dollars. He was sentenced to a year and a day in prison, and Trincher got six months.

WHO KNEW?
Brighton Beach, a Brooklyn neighborhood with a high Russian émigré population, is ground zero for the Russian mafia in the United States.

Beware of a new email scam where the sender claims to have access to phased out U.S. $100 bills.

CHAPTER 14
CON ARTISTS
AND
THIEVES

"YOU HAVE TO FIGURE OUT SOMEONE'S WANTS AND NEEDS AND CONVINCE THEM THAT WHAT YOU HAVE WILL FILL THEIR EMOTIONAL VOID" —A FORMER CON ARTIST

KIND SIR, PLEASE HELP

HAVE YOU BEEN CORRESPONDING WITH A TROUBLED NIGERIAN PRINCE? STOP RIGHT NOW.

In 2003, 72-year-old Jiří Pasovský of the Czech Republic lost some $600,000—his life savings—to a Nigerian letter scam. Distraught, he shot two employees at the Nigerian embassy in Prague, killing one of them.

It's one of the definitive memes of the internet age. An email arrives from a supposed member of the Nigerian royal family or other high-ranking African official. It requests assistance in transferring a large fortune out of his troubled country in exchange for a monetary reward. A gullible recipient takes the bait, hoping to cash in, but instead is conned out of hundreds, thousands, or even millions of dollars. In some cases, victims have lost their lives.

The ploy goes by several names: the Nigerian bank scam, Fifo's fraud, advanced-fee fraud, and the 419 scam, after its designation in the Nigerian criminal code. Typically, the missive sent out is written "as fairly well-educated foreigners speak English, with a word misspelled here and there, and an occasional foreign idiom." At least that's how the *New York Times* described it—in 1898. And the scam wasn't a new idea, even then.

"Kind Sir, I Request Your Help..."

One of the earliest swindles to fit the pattern dates to the French Revolution of the late 1700s. The crooked correspondent would pose as an aristocrat displaced by the war; he would say that he had sent a servant back into unsafe territory to retrieve his valuables and that the aide had been captured. If the recipient of the letter would provide some financial assistance in freeing the servant—and thus the waiting treasure—he would reap a substantial share of the loot in return. Eugène François Vidocq, the legendary French criminal investigator, called this "the letter from Jerusalem," as it often referred to a party to the scheme who was supposedly located there.

The scam came back into fashion at the turn of the 20th century in the form of the "Spanish prisoner letter." In this version, the action was moved to Spain or Cuba and the recipient was promised a large payout if he would assist in retrieving a hidden trunk full of riches. Needless to say, the "assistance" involved an up-front investment.

Nothing for Something

Throughout the 20th century, the Nigerian con thrived via "snail mail" and faxes, its details altered as necessary to fit current events. In the 1990s, political upheaval in Zaire and Nigeria, along with the development of the internet, made it even more widespread and profitable. The average 419 scam victim in the U.S. loses an estimated $5,000, but one American businessman was

419

The Nigerian criminal code designates advanced fee fraud as a "419," giving the scam one of several names by which it's known.

fleeced of $5.6 million. In 1999, Norwegian millionaire Kjetil Moe fell so hard for a 419 scam that he traveled to South Africa, where he was kidnapped and murdered.

In 2013, a new iteration of the 419 scam emerged, involving a sender who claimed to be an American soldier stationed in Iraq with access to millions in phased-out U.S. $100 bills. As such letters have ended for hundreds of years, it concluded with a request for "your discreet assistance in dealing with the matter."

ANATOMY OF A SWINDLE

A good scam artist knows how to follow the rules.

While the details differ, the advance-fee con follows a distinct pattern. It starts with a message from someone claiming to be in the midst of a crisis. The sender offers the recipient a sizable share of a large fortune, while emphasizing the need for discretion, since they might be treading the line of legality. Once the scammer has established trust, he sets up the transaction, but then something goes wrong: A middle man disappears, a friend in customs loses his job—and money is needed to take care of bribes, processing fees, or some such complication.

The charade continues, the payout never materializes, and the recipient eventually breaks off contact.

You might be surprised at how far along these arrangements can go before the target gives up. Once someone has invested even a small amount in such a scheme, what economists call the "sunk cost fallacy" keeps them in the game, desperate for a payoff that never comes. The more they have spent, the longer they hang in—and when it finally falls apart, shame often keeps victims from reporting the incident to authorities.

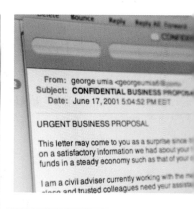

VARIATIONS ON A SCHEME

Thanks to email, scammers can send out thousands of messages without paying a cent of postage. Even a small percentage of responses can net a tidy fortune. Here are some favorites.

→ **Advance-fee scams.** The variations are myriad. Imagine meeting the man of your dreams online, only to have him ask for a little money for a ticket to visit you, then for help with a parent's hospital bill, then something else...until you walk away broken-hearted, or just plain broke.

→ **Overpayment scams.** The tactic here is to dupe sellers on eBay, Craigslist, or similar sites. After committing to a purchase, the scammer sends a check or money order for more than the selling price, supposedly in error, then asks for the difference back. The seller complies, only to find that the original check was counterfeit or has bounced.

→ **The begging letter.** One of the oldest mail cons, named by Charles Dickens in 1850, this works by appealing to the victim's sympathies. It requests a donation to a person or organization in need, such as a disaster relief fund.

THE CYBERCRIME BREAKDOWN

The two most common types of cybercrime involve viruses, which can copy themselves and infect a computer, and malware, a type of software that disrupts a computer and can spy on users. Malware cannot copy itself.

GLOBAL TARGETS

The adult residents of five countries account for more than three-quarters of the world's cybercrime victims, according to the antivirus software maker Norton. The countries with the highest percentage of victims are:

RUSSIA
92%

CHINA
83%

BRAZIL
76%

INDIA
76%

USA
73%

WHERE THE CRIMES ORIGINATE

China 30.6%

USA 19.2%

Russia 13.4%

India 9.5%

Germany 7.3%

France 4.7%

North and South Korea 4.5%

Ukraine 3.9%

UK 3.6%

Brazil 3.3%

TYPES OF CYBERCRIME AROUND THE WORLD

computer viruses and malware 51%

social network profile hacking 7%

online scams 10%

online credit card fraud 7%

phishing 9%

sexual predation 7%

other 9%

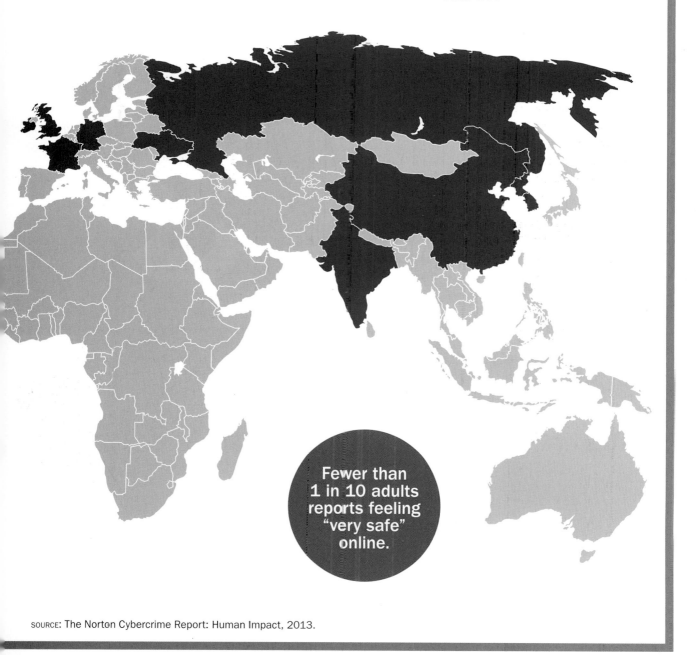

Fewer than 1 in 10 adults reports feeling "very safe" online.

SOURCE: The Norton Cybercrime Report: Human Impact, 2013.

TRUST ME

IF IT SOUNDS TOO GOOD TO BE TRUE, IT PROBABLY IS— SO WHY WE DO WE FALL FOR SCAMS?

Con artists are masters of deception, cheating, lying, and doing anything they need to do to gain your trust, usually for the purpose of getting your money. In fact, the term *con artist* is a shortened version of "confidence artist," because what these criminals need first is for their victims to have faith in what they say. Most succeed because they are emotionally intelligent, astute observers of human behavior. But all the best con artists share another trait: the ability to remain emotionally detached from their marks.

"The key to a conman is not that you trust the conman, but that he shows he trusts you," neuro-economist Paul Zak has written. "Social interactions engage a powerful brain circuit that releases the neurochemical oxytocin when we are trusted and induces a desire to reciprocate the trust we have been shown—even with strangers."

Four Famous Con Artists

"BIG BERTHA" HEYMAN (C. 1851– UNKNOWN)

Known as the Confidence Queen, Prussian-born Heyman masqueraded as a wealthy woman temporarily unable to access her riches, swindling many well-

to-do men out of thousands of dollars while living large in high-class hotels. In an interview with the *New York Times* in 1883, she said the scams mostly interested her for the intellectual challenge of duping men, and she claimed she gave most of the money to the poor.

Heyman was arrested a number of times and finally went to prison, where she still managed to con a man out of his life savings.

GEORGE PARKER (1870–1936)

Using forged documents, Parker sold the Brooklyn Bridge several times on the premise that the buyer could put up barriers to collect tolls—which some even tried to do. He also sold the Statue of Liberty, the Metropolitan Museum of Art, Madison Square Garden, and Grant's Tomb—in the last case presenting himself as Ulysses S. Grant's grandson.

In 1928, after his third conviction for fraud, Parker was sentenced to life and sent to Sing Sing prison in Ossining, New

Crowds watch as ships sail beneath New York's newly completed Brooklyn Bridge (Currier & Ives, c. 1883). George Parker conned several gullible investors into buying the bridge from him.

Magician Simon Lovell, a reformed con artist, has revealed tricks of the trade to the public.

For most con men, identifying a mark is a matter of observation.

Like the best salesmen and card sharks, con artists pick up cues through body language and facial expressions, then tailor their game to the particular victim. "I can spot someone's weakness a mile away. In any room I can pick out the best target," reformed con artist Simon Lovell, now a magician, said. "You have to figure out someone's wants and needs and convince them that what you have will fill their emotional void."

York, where his colorful stories reportedly were popular with inmates and guards alike.

VICTOR LUSTIG (1890–1947)

This Austrian-Hungarian trickster was fluent in seven languages and was thought to have 45 aliases.

Among other scams, he peddled a contraption he claimed would perfectly replicate $100 bills. He also sold Eiffel Tower parts to scrap metal dealers, and persuaded Al Capone to invest $50,000 in a phony stock deal (Lustig returned the money to the gangster).

In 1934, Lustig pleaded guilty to counterfeiting and served 11 years before dying in jail in Missouri.

JAMES HOGUE (B. 1959)

Hogue got his start as imposter in his 20s when he posed as a 16-year-old to enroll in a high school in Palo Alto, California; he was exposed by a reporter. His next gig was gaining admittance to Princeton University in 1988 at age 28, posing as a self-taught orphan. This time around, he was outed by a high school classmate who recognized him at a university track meet.

Hogue was sentenced to 270 days in jail for the college scam. In 1992, he was hired as a guard in one of Harvard's museums, and was arrested after just a few months and charged with grand larceny for stealing gemstones worth $50,000. In 2007, he pleaded guilty to felony theft after valuables worth more than $100,000 were found in his home.

Charles Ponzi, the namesake for the infamous pyramid scheme, was deported from the U.S. in 1935.

HOW A PONZI SCHEME WORKS

The investment fraud is named for a con artist who ran an international postage scam in the 1920s.

→ Step 1: Convince a few naive investors to get in early on an amazing opportunity.

→ Step 2: Use some of the early investment funds to rent office space and acquire other trappings that may persuade more investors to get onboard.

→ Step 3: Pay old investors using capital from the new investors.

→ Step 4: Continue the cycle, while enriching oneself.

When early investors see healthy returns, few complain. But the ruse can only be kept up by continually attracting new investors. When the stream of investment slows or stops, earlier investors stop seeing returns and the scheme collapses.

POWER, CORRUPTION, AND LIES

FINANCIAL ADVISOR BERNARD MADOFF WAS RESPECTED ON WALL STREET. HE WAS ALSO ROBBING HIS CLIENTS BLIND.

On December 11, 2008, as the global economic crisis was unfolding, Wall Street fixture and noted investment advisor Bernard Madoff made a confession to his two sons: He had been operating "a giant Ponzi scheme" for decades and the asset management division of the family business was "all just one big lie." It soon became clear that Madoff had masterminded the largest financial fraud in history, with some $65 billion in fabricated gains and investments missing from clients' accounts.

Victims of Madoff's scam included such celebrities as actor Kevin Bacon and director and producer Steven Spielberg; charities including a foundation that funded diabetes research and the New York Public Library; and his own employees, some of whom lost their life savings. In March 2009, Madoff pleaded guilty to 11 felony counts, including money laundering, fraud, and perjury. He was sentenced to 150 years in prison.

How He Pulled It Off

Many people who knew Madoff socially or through business dealings were shocked by the revelations. His firm, Bernard Madoff In-vestment Securities, had been around since 1960 and had a sterling reputation, managing billions of dollars for clients. He even served as president of the board of directors of the NASDAQ stock exchange in the 1990s.

The key to Madoff's success as a con artist, it seemed, was his ability to ingratiate himself with members of Palm Beach society and New York power brokers. He then parlayed those connections to attract additional elite investors, wrapping "himself in an Oz-like aura, making him even more desirable to those seeking access," wrote the *New York Times*. Just as important, Madoff developed cozy relationships with regulators. "He was smart in understanding very early on that the more involved you were with regulators, the more you could shape regulation," an associate told the *Times*.

Had the economy not tanked in 2008, Madoff might have continued on unabated. "The only reason that this ended was because, at one given point in time, the economy did so badly that people wanted—needed—to get money out of Madoff's investments," said one of his former clients, Burt Ross, after the scam was revealed.

Bernard Madoff leaves U.S. district court in Manhattan after a bail hearing in New York, 2009.

WHO KNEW?

Many who lost their savings to Madoff did so through special pooled funds and had no idea their money was flowing through his hands.

Narcissistic and Entitled

Madoff himself may have expected to be caught sooner. As far back as 2001, articles in the media cast doubt on his credibility. Financial analyst Harry Markopolos spent nine years trying to persuade the Securities and Exchange Commission to investigate the legendary advisor, at one point presenting them with a 19-page memo titled "The World's Largest Hedge Fund Is a Fraud." But when the agency finally did investigate, it found no evidence of wrongdoing.

Following Madoff's arrest, forensic psychologist J. Reid Meloy commented that his behavior reminded him of criminal psychopaths he'd studied: "Typically, people with psychopathic personalities don't fear getting caught. They tend to be very narcissistic with a strong sense of entitlement."

THE WHITE COLLARS

In recent years, a number of high-profile business-world stars have been convicted of fraud and other rogue activities.

Michael Milken Former executive at investment bank Drexel Burnham Lambert, dubbed the "junk bond king" for his work on the dodgy securities vehicles.
Crime and punishment: Convicted of six counts of securities and tax fraud in 1990, Milken was fined $200 million, banned from the securities industry, and sentenced to ten years in prison. He was released after serving just two.
Where he is now: Milken spearheads a number of philanthropic efforts.

Dennis Kozlowski Former CEO of the global conglomerate Tyco International. Kozlowski was known for his aggressive acquisition strategy and extravagant lifestyle. One oft-cited example: his $6,000 shower curtain.
Crime and punishment: Kozlowski was convicted in June 2005 of grand larceny, conspiracy, and fraud.
Where he is now: After eight years in prison, Kozlowski was granted parole in 2014.

Kenneth Lay Chairman of Enron, the energy-trading giant that famously collapsed in 2001, wreaking havoc on the savings of shareholders and employees.
Crime and punishment: Convicted in 2006 of fraud, conspiracy, and insider trading.
Where he is now: Lay died of heart failure two months after the trial.

Ivan Boesky Founder of Ivan F. Boesky & Company. Nicknamed "Ivan the Terrible," he traded stocks in companies targeted for takeover and bet on corporate takeovers using inside information.
Crime and punishment: Convicted of securities fraud; fined $100 million, sentenced to 3.5 years in prison, and permanently barred from working in securities.
Where he is now: Boesky is reportedly living in La Jolla, California.

SPECTACULAR HEISTS

IN SOME CASES, ALL IT TAKES TO PULL OFF A GRAND ROBBERY IS A GOOD COSTUME, SOME SHARP BOX CUTTERS, AND A LOT OF NERVE.

On February 16, 2003, notorious jewel thief Leonardo Notarbartolo and a four-man crew pulled off what looked like the perfect crime. Penetrating ten layers of security at Belgium's Antwerp Diamond

Safety boxes, jewelry, money, and diamonds, which Notarbartolo and his crew left behind on the floor of a safe within the vaults of Antwerp's Diamond Center

Center, the thieves made their way into a subterranean vault, eluding infrared heat detectors, a seismic sensor, and an army of private security guards. After breaking open more than 100 safe-deposit boxes, they walked away with a haul of gems estimated at $100 million, making it the most valuable jewel heist in history.

Years in the Making

The robbery had been years in the planning. In 2000, after spending time studying jewelry salesmen, Notarbartolo posed as a gem importer and rented a space in the Diamond Center. He began to assemble a crack team of collaborators, including a lock specialist and a master forger. On the appointed day, the crew arrived equipped with a hidden pen camera to photograph the area while casing it, hairspray to disable motion sensors, homemade polyester shields to prevent body heat detection, and a makeshift aluminum slab to redirect a magnetic field away from the vault door.

There was just one hitch: One of the robbers carelessly tossed out trash linking

FBI agents flank mobster Vincent Asaro, who was indicted in the Lufthansa heist dramatized in the movie *Goodfellas*.

Thieves cut 13 masterpieces from their mounts at the Isabella Stewart Gardner Museum in Boston. They left the empty frames behind.

them to the crime, and all five soon found themselves under arrest.

Stop, Thief!

The hallmark of some of history's most successful robberies has been their sheer audacity. On March 18, 1990, two men dressed as cops conned their way into Boson's Isabella Stewart Gardner Museum to "investigate a disturbance." After tying up the security guards, the thieves used box cutters to remove 13 masterpieces worth a total of $500 million from their frames.

"How they went about removing the paintings…is indicative of a rank amateur," said FBI agent Geoff Kelly, who noted that the thieves probably had no idea of the magnitude of their crime. The works still have not been recovered.

A few years later, in Cannes, France, masked gunmen forced their way into the Carlton Hotel jewelry store, fired shots into the air, and made off with $60 million in goods. Though their guns had been loaded with blanks, the shooters got away clean; the jewels have never been recovered.

WEB OF INTRIGUE

FROM ONLINE SCAMMERS TO HACKERS INFILTRATING SITES, THE INTERNET ATTRACTS PLENTY OF SHADY TYPES.

John Draper used a whistle from a box of cereal to hack phone lines.

CEREAL CRIME

Before the internet was commonly available, even before personal computers, there was a hacker called Captain Crunch.

In the pre-internet era of the 1970s, John Draper specialized in hacking telephones. Draper discovered he could re-create the shrill tone used by AT&T's computerized switching system, thereby scoring free long-distance phone service. The high-tech tool Draper used to pull this off: A toy whistle from a box of Cap'n Crunch cereal.

Draper's exploits were detailed in a 1971 magazine article that caught the attention of a University of California, Berkeley, student named Steve Wozniak and his friend Steve Jobs—the duo who went on to found Apple Computers. They recruited Draper, and he ended up developing software for Apple and several other companies, but only after serving prison time for phone fraud.

I f you're computer-savvy, motivated, and extremely bright, you may have what it takes to be the next internet entrepreneur. Then again, you also may have what it takes to be the next internet criminal. Craftier and more intelligent than your average lawbreaker, online crooks represent the crème de la crème of crime. But just because they wield computers instead of guns doesn't make their wrongdoing any less serious.

The possibility of cyberattacks on America's financial markets, government agencies, and infrastructure is of such concern that it topped the U.S. intelligence community's list of global threats in 2013 and 2014. Perpetrators include "state-sponsored hackers, hackers for hire, organized cyber syndicates, and terrorists," according to Joseph Demarest, the Federal Bureau of Investigation's Assistant Director of the Cyber Division, who testified about the phenomenon in front of the U.S. Senate in 2014.

Beware Lucky12345

Because cybercriminals can infiltrate American computers and websites from anywhere, they are extraordinarily difficult to catch. For example, alleged Russian hacker Evgeniy Bogachev, aka Lucky12345, is considered by the FBI to be one of the most dangerous threats in the world to the American banking system. Bogachev is accused of having infected more than a million computers with malicious software that since 2009 has stolen more than one hundred million dollars from victims' bank accounts. He takes his place on the FBI's Most Wanted list of cybercriminals along with scammers from Greece, Sweden, and China.

Virtual Villains?

Authorities are learning that the best way to fight these slippery characters is through informants. In 2011, the FBI arrested Hector Monsegur—aka Sabu—the New York City–based cofounder of a group that claimed responsibility for breaking into websites of the Central Intelligence Agency, Sony Pictures, and other organizations. The day after his capture, Monsegur, then 27, began cooperating with the agency. The information he provided is said to have helped prevent 300 attacks on systems belonging to the U.S. military, NASA, and other entities.

When internet criminals do come to light, the public doesn't always consider them bad guys. Kim Dotcom, a German-born hacker, is famous for starting the website Megaupload. At its peak, the wildly popular service, which let users share pirated movies and music, was said to be the 13th most frequented internet site. But in 2012 the United States shut it down and charged Dotcom with criminal copyright infringement.

Computer hacker Hector Monsegur (center) leaves Manhattan's Federal Court after his sentencing in New York, May 27, 2014.

By then, Dotcom was living large in New Zealand, enjoying fancy cars and a mansion. He is considered by many to be a hero outlaw, unfairly scapegoated for the illegal actions of his site's users. As of late 2014, Dotcom was out on bail in New Zealand and fighting extradition to the United States.

KNOW YOUR HACKS

As long as there are computers, there will be people creating new ways to attack them. Here are three ways.

Attack Type	What it Is	Notable Example	Also Used...
Distributed Denial of Service (DDoS)	Hackers overload a website by flooding it with traffic so it stops working temporarily.	In 2007, hackers believed to be allied with the Russian government shut down financial and other sites in Estonia.	As a grassroots protest against corporations or government entities
SQL Injection	A code hidden in an innocent-seeming file sent to a company employee instructs the company's computer system to reveal customers' private data.	In 2014, a crime ring was found to have stolen 1.2 billion private usernames and passwords and half a billion email addresses from thousands of popular websites.	One hacker covered his car's license plate with an SQL code in an attempt to fool computerized speed traps as he sped through.
Clickjacking	An ad invites you "click here to claim your prize!" When you do, you unwittingly authorize a hacker to do something else (like access your bank account).	In 2012, Facebook sued a clickjacker that ran a $20-million-a-year spam racket sending users to unwanted advertising sites.	To play pranks on Facebook and Twitter users, tricking them into liking random pages or posting cryptic messages

INDEX

Page numbers in *italic* refer to photos or illustrations.

PHOTO CREDITS

IFC & 1, Özgür Donmaz/Getty Images
2, 4X-image/Getty Images
2, © Itani/Alamy
2, arturbo/Getty Images
2, Andrew Cribb/Getty Images
2, © iStock.com/princessdlaf
2, © iStock.com/cmannphoto
2, AP Photo/Ocskay Bence
2, © iStock.com/macsek
2, © William Whitehurst/CORBIS
3, © Chris Collins/Corbis
3, dem10/Getty Images
3, AP Photo/Don Ryan
3, AP Photo
3, Swell Media/Getty Images
3–4, Ugurhan Betin/Getty Images
6–7, Marianne Barcellona/Time Life Pictures/Getty Images
10–11, 4X-image/Getty Images
12, Boyer/Roger Viollet/Getty Images
13, Alessandro Albert/Getty Images
13, Apic/Getty Images
13, AP Photo/Lincoln County Heritage Trust Archive
13, American Stock/Getty Images
13, Popperfoto/Getty Images
14, Art Media/Print Collector/Getty Images
14, Reg Speller/Fox Photos/Getty Images
15, Stock Montage/Getty Images
16, Science Photo Library - TEK IMAGE/Getty Images
16–17, Seth Joel/Getty Images
17, Andrew Brookes/Fuse/Getty Images
18, AP Photo/Martin Meissner
19, AP Photo/University of Pennsylvania
19, Paul Harris/Getty Images
20, Dorling Kindersley/Getty Images
21, MIRA OBERMAN/AFP/Getty Images
21, Burger/Phanie/SuperStock
22, Photonica/Getty Images
22, Photo Researchers/Getty Images
22, Photolibrary/Getty Images
23, The Image Bank/Getty Images
24, Camazine S/Getty Images
25, © iStock.com/Pashalgnatov
25, JAMES FALLON
26, The LIFE Picture Collection/Getty Images
27–28, © ZUMA Press, Inc./Alamy
28, AP Photo/File

29, AP Photo/Pima County Sheriff's Department via The Arizona Republic, File
31, Visuals Unlimited/Getty Images
31, © iStock.com/chrisgramly
31, Getty Images
34, Getty Images
35, AP Photo/Connecticut State Police
35, Mediablitzimages/Alamy
36–37, © Itani/Alamy
38, AP Photo/M. Spencer Green, File
39, Chris Sweda/Chicago Tribune/MCT via Getty Images
39, AP Photo/Sycamore Police Department
40, Art Rickerby/The LIFE Picture Collection/Getty Images
41, Steve Allen/Exactostock/SuperStock
41, AP Photo/Sycamore Police Department, File
42, mikeledray/Shutterstock.com
43, John Moore/Getty Images
43, Tim Boyle/Getty Images
44, AP Photo/Elizabeth Dalziel
45, JAMES NIELSEN/AFP/Getty Images
45, AP Photo
45, AP Photo/Court TV, Pool
48, Hulton Archive/Getty Images
49, Vetta/Getty Images
49, AP Photo
49, Getty Images
50, AP Photo/LM Otero
51, AP Photo/Craig Ruttle
51, AFP/Getty Images
51, AP Photo/Pedro Famous Diaz
52, AP Photo/Lance Murphey
53, Washington Post/Getty Images
53, ZUMA Press, Inc./Alamy
54–55, Courtesy of the Library of Congress, Washington DC
56, Glenn Van Der Knijff/Lonely Planet Images/Getty Images
57, AP Photo/The Kansas City Star, Fred Blocher
57, Time & Life Pictures/Getty Images
57, AP Photo/Victoria Will
57, AP Photo
57, © iStock.com/EdStock
57, Time & Life Pictures/Getty Images
58, Gregg DeGuire/WireImage
59, © Mary Evans Picture Library/Alamy
60, AP Photo/Steve Nesius
61, Nicole Hill/The Christian Science Monitor via Getty Images

61, AP Photo/Frank Franklin II, File
64, AP Photo/Steve Miller
65, Kyodo via AP Images
65, AP Photo/Reed Saxon, File
65, AP Photo/Denis Poroy
65, AP Photo
66–67, arturbo/Getty Images
68, Mary Evans Picture Library/Alamy
69, De Agostini/Getty Images
69, Universal History Archive/Getty Images
71, Kean Collection/Getty Images
71, Universal History Archive/Getty Images
71, Art Media/Print Collector/Getty Images
73, Original Artwork: Painting by Charles Lucy. (Photo by Three Lions/Getty Images)
73, Published in 'A History of the United States' by Gordy, 1904. Photo by Interim Archives/Getty Images
73, North Wind Picture Archives via AP Images
76–77, © Chris Collins/Corbis
78, Hulton Archive/Getty Images
79, NY Daily News Archive via Getty Images
79, AP Photo/Orange County Sheriff's Department
79, SSPL/Getty Images
79, AP Photo/Vera Mosley Buckner via The Decatur Daily
80–81, Bob Mortimer/NY Daily News Archive via Getty Images
82, NY Daily News Archive via Getty Images
83, Tom Howard/NY Daily News Archive via Getty Images
84, AP Photo
85, AP Photo
85, Silver Screen Collection/Getty Images
85, AP Photo/Ben Margot
86, AP Photo/Wally Fong
87, AP Photo/FBI, File
87, © iStock.com/elise_kurenbina
88, AP Photo
89, AP Photo/Dan Goodrich
89, AP Photo
90, AP Photo/Mary Altaffer
90, AP Photo/Mary Altaffer
90, AP Photo/Jim Cole
91, AP Photo/Ron Frehm, File
91, AP Photo
92, AP Photo/ho
93, AP Photo/Jim Cole
94, AP Photo/Tammie Arroyo

95, Dan Farrell/NY Daily News Archive via Getty Images
95, AP Photo/Mike Albans
96, © iStock.com/PeachLoveU
97, AP Photo/Stephen Petegorsky
97, AP Photo
97, AP Photo/Tony Kurdzuk, POOL
98, AP Photo/Damian Dovarganes
98, AP Photo/Stuart Ramson
99, AP Photo/NYPD
99, Sygma/Corbis
99, NYPD via Getty Images
100, Albert L. Ortega/WireImage
101, AP Photo/Kevork Djansezian
101, AP Photo/Damian Dovarganes
101, AP Photo/Nick Ut, Pool
101, Dahlia Jane
102–103, dem10/Getty Images
104, Time Life Pictures/Mansell/Time Life Pictures/Getty Images
104, AP Photo
104, AP Photo
105, AP Photo
105, STF/AFP/Getty Images
106, AP Photo
107, AP Photo
107, AP Photo
108, AP Photo/Paul Sakuma
109, © ZUMA Press, Inc/Alamy
109, AP Photo
109, © Bettmann/CORBIS
110, AP Photo
111, AP Photo
111, AP Photo
112, AP Photo/File
113, AP Photo
113, Donn Dughi/Bride Lane Library/Popperfoto/Getty Images
113, AP Photo/Wisconsin State Journal
113, AP Photo, File
113, AP Photo
114, AP Photo/Kevin Rivoli
114, AP Photo/Kevin Rivoli
115, AP Photo/Police Niederoesterreich
115, AP Photo/Police Niederoesterreich
115, AP Photo/Police Niederoesterreich, File
116, AP Photo/Fort Worth Star-Telegram, R. Jeena Jacob
116, The LIFE Images Collection/Getty Images
117, AP Photo/Nati Harnik
118, Helen H. Richardson/The Denver Post
118, AP Photo/Boulder District Attorney
119, © Globe Photos/ZUMAPRESS.com/Alamy

PHOTO CREDITS

241, AP Photo/U.S. Marshals Service, File
241, Wikipedia
241, AP Photo/Mike Derer
241, AP Photo/File
241, © AF archive/Alamy
241, Dirck Halstead/Time Life Pictures/Getty Images
241, © AF archive/Alamy
242, AP Photo/Michael Ging, POOL
243, AP Photo
243, AP Photo/File
245, AP Photo
245, Kyodo via AP Images
247, AP Photo/Marco Ugarte
247, LatinContent/Getty Images
249, AP Photo/Louis Lanzano
250–251, Swell Media/Getty Images
253, Richard Goerg/Getty Images
253, Just One Film/Getty Images
256, Wikipedia
257, Currier & Ives (Photo by MPI/Getty Images)
257, Ace Starry
257, Gamma-Keystone via Getty Images
257, The LIFE Images Collection/Getty Images
258, AP Photo, File
259, AP Photo/Kathy Willens
259, AP Photo/J. Scott Applewhite
259, AP Photo/Louis Lanzano

259, Bettmann/CORBIS
259, AP Photo/Eric Gay
260, AP Photo/GDA, HO
261, AP Photo/Josh Reynolds, File
261, AP Photo/Newsday, Charles Eckert
262, Peter Fuller/Getty Images
263, EMMANUEL DUNAND/AFP/Getty Images

FRONT COVER, left to right, top to bottom:
Florida DOC/Getty Images
Donald Uhrbrock/Time Life Pictures/Getty Images
AP Photo
Santi Visalli/Getty images
© CORBIS
AP Photo
AP Photo/New York State Department of Corrections
© Bettmann/CORBIS
AP Photo/HO
AP Photo/Wisconsin State Journal
AP Photo/Boston Police via The Boston Globe
AP Photo
AP Photo/Eric Risberg
© Bettmann/CORBIS

BACK COVER, Top to bottom:
Popperfoto/Getty Images; AP Photo/Stuart Ramson; AP Photo

TIME LIFE

TIME HOME ENTERTAINMENT

Publisher Margot Schupf
Vice President, Finance Vandana Patel
Executive Director, Marketing Services Carol Pittard
Executive Director, Business Development Suzanne Albert
Executive Director, Marketing Susan Hettleman
Publishing Director Megan Pearlman
Associate Director of Publicity Courtney Greenhalgh
Assistant General Counsel Simone Procas
Assistant Director, Special Sales Ilene Schreider
Assistant Director, Finance Christine Font
Senior Manager, Sales Marketing Danielle Costa
Associate Production Manager Kimberly Marshall
Associate Prepress Manager Alex Voznesenskiy
Associate Project Manager Stephanie Braga

Editorial Director Stephen Koepp
Art Director Gary Stewart
Senior Editors Roe D'Angelo, Alyssa Smith
Managing Editor Matt DeMazza
Project Editor Eileen Daspin
Copy Chief Rina Bander
Design Manager Anne-Michelle Gallero
Assistant Managing Editor Gina Scauzillo
Editorial Assistant Courtney Mifsud

Special thanks: Allyson Angle, Katherine Barnet, Brad Beatson, Jeremy Biloon, John Champlin, Ian Chin, Susan Chodakiewicz, Rose Cirrincione, Assu Etsubneh, Mariana Evans, Alison Foster, Kristina Jutzi, David Kahn, Jean Kennedy, Hillary Leary, Amanda Lipnick, Samantha Long, Amy Mangus, Robert Martells, Nina Mistry, Melissa Presti, Danielle Prielipp, Kate Roncinske, Babette Ross, Dave Rozzelle, Matthew Ryan, Ricardo Santiago, Divyam Shrivastava

Produced by The Stonesong Press, LLC
Project Director Ellen Scordato
Project Editorial Director Laura Ross
Writers Kerry Acker, Walter Bonner, Bree Burns, Jennifer Foley, Tom Gavin, Constance Jones, Lauren Lipton, Nancy Ellen Shore, Jon Sterngass
Photo Researchers Eric Harvey Brown, Aaron Clendening
Designed by Vertigo Design NYC
Art Director Alison Lew
Designers Gary Philo, Lisa Story